The first time I truly felt a "negative" feeling, it absolutely blew me away. Even after several months of beginning to explore my feelings, I was not prepared for this experience. While *betrayal* was not something I wanted to feel, once I settled into it, it felt just fine! In fact, it felt great! When I just felt it without any fear, judgment, or preconception, it started to flow freely and it felt wonderful!

From here, I knew I could feel ANYTHING and I would be fine. Good, even! I stayed with betrayal for a long time, just because it felt good and there was plenty of flow with it, but after a while I thought I'd explore, so I tried *failure* just to see what would happen. And it also changed inside me, but it still felt great, just different. It wasn't good or bad, it just was. After enjoying failure for a while, I tried *success*. Then I just had such a good time hopping between these different feelings. I laughed every time I switched to failure again, because now it was nothing more than a feeling.

My feelings would change, but I remained the same. I was present and having an experience of failure, success, and betrayal, but the feelings weren't me. I was feeling them, not identifying with them. I was free.

— Sofia Hirsch

Healing: The Path to Freedom

Dr. Michael Winer

BALBOA.
PRESS

A DIVISION OF HAY HOUSE

Balboa Press books may be ordered through booksellers or by contacting:

Balboa Press
A Division of Hay House
1663 Liberty Drive
Bloomington, IN 47403
www.balboapress.com
1 (877) 407-4847

Because of the dynamic nature of the Internet, any web addresses or links contained in this book may have changed since publication and may no longer be valid. The views expressed in this work are solely those of the author and do not necessarily reflect the views of the publisher, and the publisher hereby disclaims any responsibility for them.

This book is not meant to diagnose or treat any illness, disease, or dysfunction. The information in this book does not constitute medical advice. This book is not meant to replace qualified health care for any health concern and the reader is encouraged to seek qualified professional assistance for any health-related problem that they may have.

Any people depicted in stock imagery provided by Thinkstock are models, and such images are being used for illustrative purposes only.
Certain stock imagery © Thinkstock.

Printed in the United States of America.

ISBN: 978-1-4525-1925-8 (sc)
ISBN: 978-1-4525-1927-2 (hc)
ISBN: 978-1-4525-1926-5 (e)

Library of Congress Control Number: 2014914881

Balboa Press rev. date: 08/18/2014

Contents

Introduction

This book was written for those of you who wish to undertake a sincere study and practice of healing. A discussion of the principles of healing and an understanding of those principles are essential. However, a successful practice of healing involves much more than just understanding. Healing is a new way of being that requires a willingness to expand your awareness and to become someone other than who you think you are. It requires bringing up issues and moving through them. Who you really are, your true Self, is on the other side of your issues and you have to embark on a journey of healing to become your true Self.

Because this book is all about healing, and because you must bring up issues and move through them to create healing, you can expect the book material itself to raise issues about the healing process that require attention. When an issue arises, it would be wise to stop reading and heal that issue by applying the process you are learning in this book before continuing. By resolving each issue that arises, you will evolve your healing process along with the specific areas affected by that issue. The more willing you are to have issues arise and to allow changes in your life, the more you will get out of this book.

While I hope this book is entertaining to read, it is not something that can simply be glossed over if you wish to understand and use what it communicates. This book is meant to be read at a relatively slow pace—perhaps out loud with a friend—and only as many paragraphs, pages, or chapters as can be assimilated at one time. By allowing the energy that is present to guide you, you can use this material as a meditation to align your energy with healing.

When you read this book for the first time, I recommend that you read it in the order in which it is presented. Each chapter establishes the desired context for understanding the ensuing material. And the concepts in the later chapters build upon those of the earlier material. It is also important that you actually perform the exercises that accompany many of the chapters. This is to get beyond the mental understanding of the material and to put it to use in your life. These tools and principles will only become practical and real through their usage. And only by challenging them in the real world will you be able to validate their utility.

As you heal, this book will grow with you. With healing, your awareness will expand and subtler levels of energy will become apparent. Each reading will yield greater benefits, facilitating a deeper understanding of, and appreciation for, the path of healing.

Before Words

The more experience I have with my own healing and with that of other people in my practice, the more I realize that something unique is happening with this work. It is not just that people's symptoms are improving or that they feel better emotionally. It is that my clients and I are living and functioning from a different perspective, one that is based on what is *behind* our experience.

Energy is the term that I use to name what is behind our experience. It is not a new term, of course, and it has come into widespread use in the field of healing. However, what is usually included in the terms "energy" and "healing" is only a small portion of the whole.

When we look at the total extent of energy and healing, almost all of the focus and growth is centered in one area. It has the mind as the focal point. And while this area is rich and fertile and has supported diverse and plentiful growth, it is only a tiny part of the whole. The rest of the realms of energy have seen little exploration and their existence is rarely noticed.

Imagine a tract of old-growth forest that has a radius of just a few hundred yards and is surrounded by fields that go far beyond the horizon. The mind, in this metaphor, is like the old-growth forest, which is well-established and has seen tremendous development. The remaining 99+ % of the realms of energy are like the surrounding countryside; they have a different experience of growth and have potential and possibilities that are largely unrealized. This should give you a picture of the scope of what is involved with the whole of energy and with the untapped potential that lies beyond the realm of the mind.

Because energy is such a broad arena, healing requires that we develop ways to work with the full spectrum of energy. Within my healing practice, we are exploring and evolving everything from our cellular potential and physical body function, to our personality and our relationships, to our awareness of subtle energy and our connection with that energy. Our goal is to master every aspect of our experience and to realize the full potential of our true Self.

By using the material presented in this book, we can take our healing to an unprecedented level of fulfillment. From this place of Self-realization, we are then free to be our true Self.

In today's world, it is common for people to have no real engagement with their life. Many participate in work and relationships as if they are just doing time, waiting for their sentence to end. Others operate without any sense of purpose and not knowing what they really want to do when they "grow up." We have become used to living a life that does not have anything to do with us. Our models for work, relationships, economics, politics, health, and psychology—to name a few— are so limiting that they do not leave room for a genuine human being. How did we get so out of touch with our true Self?

Healing is the path of being true to our Self. Through healing, we remember who we are and how we truly want to live. We can create ways of being that we can exult in and that many would love to share with us. And we can reclaim our aliveness and vitality.

Because healing is about being true to our Self, it calls for more than just a one-time effort or a short-term program. **Healing is a life choice**—one that we have to make every moment of every day. However, while being true to our Self is not something that is accomplished overnight, every time we practice our healing process, we will experience immediate positive changes that will move us towards our goals.

For many people, healing is a new approach to life. And even though healing is relatively simple, it is not necessarily easy. Because it is different from what people are used to, it will take determination and perseverance to master the unfamiliar. Yet, in our life, we have learned to walk an unnatural path and to do it well. Therefore, learning a simpler but more comprehensive way of functioning is well within our ability. Mastering a new way of being can be as natural as riding a bicycle or walking—it just takes practice.

When we choose to heal, many beautiful but unexplored possibilities become available to us. We will discover potential and parts of ourselves that we probably did not know existed. There really is something much more fantastic going on in our life in which we can more fully participate. We truly can create whatever we choose if we are willing to heal all of the obstacles to that experience.

Healing will also help us become more aware of something that really makes sense: the energy that underlies everything. Energy is something that we can learn to perceive, utilize, and evolve. Everything in the world can be clearly understood in the context of energy. It is something we can count on and that can support all of the choices and decisions we face on our journey. **Energy is something on which we can stake our life.**

Words

There is great potential in the use of words and their exchange between people. We readily employ them as a means of communication and we are all familiar with them as a way to share concepts, feelings, and energy. Verbal expression is a pervasive and valuable means of interaction between people.

Through books, the media, and the internet, we are accustomed to using words for gathering and distributing information. We use these sources as avenues for the acquisition of facts, ideas, and others' perspectives.

The printed word is a powerful tool in terms of reaching a large number of people and especially as a way to reach people with whom we would not normally have a chance to interact. The possibilities that exist through the magic of circulation dramatically increase our connections with other people.

The greater the number of people practicing a particular discipline, the easier it is for others to participate in that discipline. The greater the number of people involved with a particular idea or concept, the more energy it has behind it and the more likely it is to manifest in the world. And if enough people participate in a new perspective, a critical mass can be achieved that will enable a worldwide shift in possibilities and in our practical reality.

Books and words may inspire people to take steps they would not normally take for their betterment and for the betterment of others. People may be moved to perform great deeds and to act with courage. There is also the possibility of catalyzing a healing revolution in a person, in a community, or even on the planet.

It is my hope that these words will assist you with your personal evolution in healing—that they will communicate the essence of healing and inspire you to take the steps in your life to achieve that healing. Perhaps with words, you will open the door to a new way of being with yourself and on the planet.

At the same time, there are great challenges with the use of words. One problem lies with the fact that many of us are already so mental in our approach to life that we can easily be fooled by words. Many of us identify with our thoughts and, therefore, believe that to change ourselves, we just have to change our mind. Our mind can grasp the words quickly and discard them just as easily. Our mind can talk us in or out of a feeling, thought, or belief in a moment. Nevertheless, we cannot change ourselves by changing our words.

Our mind can trick us into believing that if we understand the words, we have embodied the knowledge. Unfortunately, this is quite far from the truth. Knowledge is the result of *living* the truth of our words—of mind, body, and spirit being in alignment with the actions that we take and the words that we speak and understand. Only when there is such an alignment is there any power behind the words. Otherwise, the words are empty, devoid of meaning, without power, and of limited value.

Just as there is great potential in the use of words to inspire peace, freedom, and harmony, there is also the potential to use words *against* other people. Words can be used to manipulate others by preying on their issues and vulnerabilities. Words can also be used as a means of directing our own issues at others.

A less obvious and more insidious challenge with words is that they become carriers of the energy of their author or source. Consequently, the reader is exposed to the complete energy of the words and what is behind the words that they read and hear. This can have many beneficial effects, but the unwary reader also risks exposure to the subtler manipulations and distortions in the author's energy that have not been healed. For instance, if an author needs to get validation from others, that need will be present in whatever material the author writes and we may absorb the author's invalidation when we read his or her work. If an author feels powerless, that energy will be communicated with the author's writings and, after reading those writings, we may feel powerless. On the other hand, if an author embodies the mastery of peace, that is what we may experience energetically when reading what the author creates.

In school, we are taught to absorb and reiterate the energy of our teachers and the books we read. We are very familiar with opening to the energy of books and their authors. In fact, we are trained to seek the source of our knowledge *outside* ourselves and, therefore, to open to whatever we encounter, whether it is on television, in a book, or from someone with whom we interact.

Some people are so thoroughly indoctrinated with this programming that they cannot validate their own information *unless* it is confirmed by a book or "recognized" authority. Of course, I must ask, how does one become an authority and who is qualified to recognize them as such? Must one be an author to become an authority?

If an author has foreign energy in his or her space—from another person, for instance—it will be communicated through that author's words as well and can very easily enter the reader's space. This is a very common problem in the genres of spirituality and healing. And unfortunately, many unsuspecting readers lack awareness regarding this vulnerability.

Several years ago, I had a client come into my office with a book about emotional healing. In the course of our discussion and evaluation, it became apparent that she had absorbed the author's feelings of invalidation and judgment, along with several foreign energies that were in the author's space. Prior to her office visit, she was not aware of any of these problems.

More recently, I had another client with the same configuration of energy in her space. I recognized the pattern in the second client and inquired as to whether she had read this particular book about emotional healing. Indeed, she had looked at the book in question for the first time just that morning! The interaction with the material from the book was active and had left a dysfunctional residue of energy that my client was now wrestling with, unbeknownst to her.

Thus, while words have their utility, there is no inherent power in them. They are only as functional as the energy behind them, the energy they carry.

Energy

Our views of life and the world are based on a specific point of reference. That point of reference or orientation can be any aspect of our experience. It is often *mental* or *physical,* but occasionally it is *emotional.* There is also a perspective that includes every aspect of our experience and that has an *energetic* orientation.

Our point of reference is in the background of everything that we perceive and do. We are so enmeshed in it that we assume it is objectively real, factual. As a result, while our orientation has a profound influence on our understanding of ourselves and on how we function in the world, it frequently remains hidden.

Often, a great deal of our experience does not fit into the context of our perspective. Still, because we tend to become fixated on our orientation, it is unusual to examine our view in light of information that does not agree with it or perhaps even contradicts it. And we rarely examine our experience in relation to different perspectives because it is difficult to become aware of a different point of reference and even more difficult to perceive from a different one. Instead, we are inclined to distort our experience to fit the framework of our perspective.

We are all familiar with the *physical* view of the world. When we relate to everything from a physical point of reference, we look for the causal elements of our experience in the physical world. We "know" that the physical world really exists and often believe that everything else is a by-product of that world.

From this point of view, disease and dysfunction are the result of germs and physical causes. So we develop drugs to destroy infectious agents. We cut out and destroy "bad" cells to eliminate disease. And we medicate our body to control it.

This perspective supports the idea that poor health is something that happens to us. This establishes the context for trying to control the world to avoid illness and disease. We manipulate our environment, control our lifestyle, and modify our genes. We try to eradicate the "causes" of our problems to protect our species and ourselves.

This view tends to perceive the mental and emotional aspects of our experience as manifestations of the physical world. Thus, we search the brain to locate the origin of our mind and emotions. We devise medications to manipulate our body in order to control our thoughts and emotions. And, in the near future, we will be modifying our DNA to alter behavior.

Furthermore, there are many who believe that consciousness is simply the result of the interactions of matter with itself. Thus, some people hunt amongst the cells of the brain or perhaps the heart to find the source of life. And some people discuss "artificial intelligence" as if it relates in some way to our experience of consciousness and intelligence.

In the same way, we have been overexposed to a *mental* view of the world. If our point of reference is mental, we relate to everything from that perspective and look for the causal elements of our experience on a mental level.

This view describes our experience in purely mental terms, assuming that thoughts are the only things that are real. From a mental point of reference, it appears that the mind *is* consciousness.

Since emotions *appear* to be the result of thoughts, people focus on controlling their emotions through the control of their thoughts. Furthermore, people pretend that they can evolve themselves by thinking better thoughts. And some people have deduced that dreams are the result of associative mental functions.

Everything can be figured out in a logical and often linear manner. From a mental point of reference, matter is just another feature of the mind to be mastered and controlled in the mind's conquest of experience.

An *energetic* point of view offers a more comprehensive perspective than either a physical or a mental point of view. From an energetic perspective, energy is all there is and everything is energy. Every aspect of energy is a part of this perspective, including the physical, emotional, and mental aspects among others.

From an energetic perspective, we can observe almost the exact opposite relationship between matter and energy than the one we are familiar with from a mental or physical perspective: **consciousness is energy and matter is a manifestation of that energy.** Therefore, altering our energy results in physical, physiological, psychological, and spiritual changes.

For many people it is relatively easy to understand that our emotions and thoughts are energy. And that these words are energy as well as being vehicles that carry energy. From there, it is easier to view animal instincts and other programming as energy as well. Furthermore, we can view all of the structures in the world—including our physical body—as pure energy. And the food we eat, the water we drink, and the air we breathe as special forms of energy that nourish our body.

From this point of view, physical atoms and molecules manifest as *expressions* of energy. Their physical form exists on an energy level before they exist in the physical realm. The physical form carries and transmits the energy.

Every facet of our life is a manifestation of energy. Money is a manifestation of the exchange of energy between people. Verbal communication is another form of energy exchange between people. Making art, having children, and evolving technology are expressions of creative energy. The legal system is a manifestation of a concept of justice. And the Social Security Act was created to avoid the feelings of fear and insecurity.

Energy is real. Every aspect of energy is just as real as this book you are reading. Or perhaps even more so, as it is, in fact, the energy of these words that is being communicated, not the words or the book itself. This book and these words are simply the *carriers* of the energy.

With healing, many will find the abstract energy realms, such as emotions, to be just as real and tangible as anything one experiences in the physical world. Someone else's anger might feel like a strong grating wind. It is possible to think so loudly that others cannot hear themselves think. Having other people's energy in our space may feel like a whirlwind. And foreign energy can easily cause the sensations of pressure, pain, nausea, headaches, and changes in visual acuity.

There are many, many aspects of energy to become aware of and to master. Some are familiar to us. Some we may try to avoid. And still others are probably foreign to most people. Nevertheless, every facet of energy requires awareness, exploration, and healing to attain full knowledge and mastery.

Some aspects of energy that we commonly use include instincts, impulses, creativity, intuition, affinity, emotion, thought, and expression. However, while they are commonly used, there is much to learn, heal, and develop before we have actually mastered any of them.

For instance, we are all aware of the mental realm. In fact, we often indulge in the mental aspect because it *is* so familiar and easy to use. Many of us even use our thoughts to attempt to control other levels of our energy. Yet, while wielding concepts and manipulating words to communicate ideas are great achievements in and of themselves, there is a great deal more involved with mental mastery. Mastery of the mental plane includes being able to distinguish our own thoughts from those of others, and to separate from others' thoughts. It also involves being able to still our mind and to align it with the true Self, instead of using it to control other portions of our energy or as a defense.

We may simply try to deny or avoid some aspects of energy, such as the emotional realm. Nonetheless, the emotional aspect is part of our energy and requires healing, understanding, development, and mastery as well. Mastery of the emotional plane includes developing emotional awareness, being able to heal our own emotions, knowing the difference between our own emotions and others' emotions, and being able to separate from other people's emotions.

In addition, many planes of energy exist beyond the normal scope of our awareness. These include very abstract levels that are difficult to describe in words. For instance, there are energy centers outside our physical body that dramatically affect our bodily function and sense of self. And, even within our body, meridians and chakras are non-physical features that are an important part of us. The mastery of our experience requires that we become aware of every aspect of energy and that we learn to function on those levels.

The mastery of one aspect of energy does not have much effect on other aspects of energy. For instance, we can easily learn to control and direct our thoughts. But, unfortunately, this has little or no impact on the energy of emotion. Our emotions are active whether we are aware of them or not and can only be healed with a process that is specific to the emotions. They are completely unaffected by mental manipulations. In spite of this, many therapeutic approaches attempt to use the mind to manage and control the emotional realm. It is not hard to see why they are destined to fail.

Each aspect of energy has its own unique vibrational quality and, at the same time, every aspect interacts with the energy as a whole. Thus, we will not find an emotion in the mental realm, but there will usually be emotions *associated* with thoughts and vice versa.

Even though each aspect of energy has its own unique qualities, mastery of our emotional experience requires the development of skills that are readily applicable to every aspect of energy. On the other hand, the skills required to master other aspects of energy have limited relevance to the emotional realm. For example, thoughts can be turned on or off like a lamp, whereas emotions must be felt to be transformed. Thoughts can, however, be transformed by experiencing them just like emotions. Consequently, in this book, we will focus on the development of the skills required to heal our emotions as an avenue to enhance awareness and to develop a healing process that is valid for every aspect of energy.

Through healing, we also facilitate the alignment of our energy, which allows us to function with greater integrity and congruence. For instance, after healing apathy, self-doubt, and reluctance to take action, we are more apt to assert our true feelings. By healing our fears, we are more likely to do what we really want to do. And if our emotions are aligned with our words, our speech will actually mean something instead of being empty words like we are used to hearing from many of our politicians.

Greater alignment of our energy gives our thoughts and actions greater intensity and power. Thus, while thoughts are real, they lack power unless they are aligned with other aspects of our energy, such as our emotions and assertiveness. Such an alignment gives our thoughts real value and significance. And while emotion provides energy and power all by itself, it benefits from alignment with other parts of ourselves. We may give it expression, focus, form, and direction with our thoughts, wisdom, and sense of purpose.

From an energetic perspective, the physical body itself is energy. While our physical body is quite complex, everything about it—from genes and hormones to nervous system function and perception—can be experienced, defined, and understood within the context of energy.

Furthermore, our physical body is responding to *all* of the various aspects of energy. Thus, resolving physical body issues may require extensive healing involving many aspects of our energy.

Our body obviously responds to emotion. It is often easy to tell what people are feeling just by seeing them and "reading" their energy. Emotions such as anger, joy, and pain are easily distinguishable. More dramatically, we will observe a fight-or-flight reaction when someone feels threatened.

Diseases and physical dysfunction can also be shown to be expressions of energy. Headaches are mostly due to suppressed anger or to foreign energy with which we have engaged. A common cold is most often due to shutting down our energy flow. The common cold and influenza spread to other people when they match that shutdown energy. Heart disease can result from anger and a denial of love and joy. And cancer is the pathological manifestation of a strong emotion that has been internalized and suppressed. This may occur following the death of a loved one in which the grief and loss are not healed. Or it might result from deeply held pain absorbed from another person or caused by abuse.

Dyslexia can result from emotional distress during learning and speaking experiences. Stuttering can develop from similar forms of emotional distress caused by criticism, perfectionism, and performance demands. And being overweight is more the result of stuffing feelings, needing protection, filling an empty space inside, holding onto what is scarce, or absorbing other people's energy than it is the result of the food that is eaten.

Because the physical body is a manifestation of energy and energy is what is real, the healing of disease and dysfunction involves dealing with the underlying energetic issues. While the disappearance of symptoms may give the illusion of healing, without the resolution of the energetic issues, our physical body still has to deal with that energy. We can try to manipulate and control our physical body all we want, but unless we heal and change the energy behind our experience, disease and dysfunction will never truly be resolved.

EXERCISE: Describe Yourself

Before going further, put the book aside and write a description of yourself. How would you best describe yourself?

When you have finished writing, you will be ready to continue reading. It is important that you perform this exercise, as we will be referring to your description in future chapters.

Who Are You?

How did you describe yourself? Often people use characteristics of their body, thoughts, emotions, personality, job, and relationships to describe themselves. You are male or female. Perhaps you are short or tall. You are a wife, husband, sister, brother, father, mother, son, or daughter. You have a nationality, speak a language, and perhaps have a religion. You hold certain beliefs and may identify with some of them. You may be a teacher, student, accountant, business manager, computer programmer, laborer, salesperson, athlete, or artist.

Maybe you are intelligent, friendly, daring, nice, successful, creative, humorous, happy, romantic, peaceful, or ambitious. Alternatively, you may be depressed, lonely, troubled, or insecure. Perhaps you are talkative, sociable, and a good listener. Or quiet and withdrawn.

No matter how you described yourself, if you look at your description carefully, you will observe that you have not really described who you are. You are not your body, job, or relationships. You are not the shifting thoughts and feelings that swirl around and through you. You are not your personality or the beliefs that you hold. You are not your history and you are not the events of your life. Many of the descriptors that you use to portray yourself do not say anything about who you are—they only describe your *experience*.

Yet, somewhere within the broad spectrum of your total experience, there is one immutable aspect, one constant that underlies everything. That one constant is your true Self. **Your**

true Self is the one *having* the experience. The rest is just the experience.

What exactly is your true Self? By definition, it is the part of your energy that is true. Your true Self is the core of your energy that remains when you have shed everything that is false.

Your true Self is a theme that flows through everything in your life, no matter what activities you participate in and no matter what events transpire. It is not your mind, body, or personality, but a companion to all of them. Your true Self is a witness to every experience, while its existence is independent of your circumstances.

The energy that nourishes and sustains you flows through your true Self. Your knowledge, creativity, health, and well-being also derive from this energy. The quality of the energy flowing through your true Self is directly related to your quality of life.

Because your true Self is *having* its experience, it is not involved in the drama of your life in the same way that your personality is. While your personality has its motives, priorities, and ways of engaging with life, your true Self is having its experience and pursuing its own agenda with your life experience.

The true Self is not a completed project, nor is it an ideal that you are simply trying to regain. Instead, it exists behind the scenes in everything that occurs in your life, involved in its process of becoming its potential. Notice, however, that saying the true Self is immutable and constant does not mean that the true Self is unchanging, only that it is the genuine part of your energy and a constant presence in your life. Thus, rather than thinking of your true Self as what existed before various events occurred in your life, it is more accurate to **think of your true Self as who you are at the core of your energy *and* who you will identify with once you have integrated your experiences.**

Your true Self is *not* what existed before any or all of the difficult experiences that you have had and it is *not* necessarily what you experience at times of your greatest joy and pleasure. Your true Self is *not* your strengths, weaknesses, values, or ideals and it is *not* necessarily related to your hopes and goals. These are all just a portion of your experience.

Instead, your true Self finds expression *through* your abilities as well as *through* the challenges in your life. Your true Self learns *through* the experience of your difficulties, values, desires, hopes, strengths, weaknesses, successes, and so-called failures. These are experiences you are *going through* to become your Self.

Furthermore, the true Self has a vast range of unfulfilled potential. And until each aspect of your Self is experienced and evolved, it only exists as a potential. Thus, **you cannot go back to a previous state to become your true Self. You can only move forward to assimilate everything that occurs and become more your true Self.**

Of course, you cannot go back to undo an event anyway. Although it may appear that ignoring an issue makes it disappear, once an event occurs and an issue is activated, you can only move through it and integrate it to inactivate it. Thus, you have no choice except to resolve your issues. And it is important to understand that your true Self does not evolve *unless* those issues are resolved and integrated.

For example, your true Self is truly *secure*. Yet, it must experience and resolve all of its issues of *insecurity* in order to own its security. Once your true Self owns its security, it will never feel insecure again. Thus, even if it appeared that you felt secure before a difficult experience, if you felt insecure after that experience, your sense of security was incomplete. Only through the resolution and integration of that experience will you be able to claim your true Self security. You cannot go back to a previous time to experience your security because until it is evolved and experienced, it only existed as a latent possibility.

Even though the truth of your security has always been present, it is not experienced until you claim it. Once claimed, both your personality and your true Self live this truth.

Some children are closer to their true Self than adults are, while other children are further away. Some people experience their true Self quite frequently, while others never experience it at all. Some people view the world as their true Self, while some only see it in their dreams.

The idea that your true Self might be a stranger to you can be confusing. You would know your Self, wouldn't you? But that is not necessarily true.

Because your true Self is immersed in your experience, it may be difficult to perceive the difference between your true Self and your experience. They may appear to flow seamlessly into one another and, therefore, be indistinguishable. By losing awareness of the distinction between your Self and your experience, you lose touch with your Self. And if you identify with any part of your experience, you claim ownership for something outside your Self. Thus, it is not surprising that very few people identify with their true Self.

Furthermore, to have a "real" experience, the part involved *in* the experience must often disregard the bigger picture. Otherwise, it would interfere with the learning that is required. Regarding the previous example about security, you cannot explore the experience of insecurity and evolve your security if you always remember the truth of your security. Thus, you may purposely forget your true Self and become engrossed in your experience to benefit your development.

And, significantly, having a strong sense of self and a fixed identity do not imply a knowledge of your true Self. In fact, most people identify with their programming and become fixated on their personality at an early age, forgetting all about their true Self. As a result, most people confuse having a strong sense of self with their true Self.

The element that is missing in all of this is how you can integrate your experience and resolve your issues to become your true Self. And that is where *healing* comes in.

Healing is invaluable for distinguishing the true from the false. It is a practical approach to finding your Self and to having your own unique understanding of your Self. Only by *healing* your issues can you resolve them. Only through *healing* your experiences can you evolve your Self to create your desired development.

So, rather than attempt to further define the true Self, let's address its rediscovery through a process.

The Path of Healing

To find your way from wherever you are in the moment to your true Self, all that is necessary is a healing process. A healing process is a great way to discover the difference between your experience and your Self, and it is the *only* way to navigate your experience to become your evolved Self.

Prior to healing, you are simply living out your issues in your life. With healing, you begin to evolve those issues and integrate them so that your true Self matures and develops. "In its more evolved state, your true Self expresses itself *through* your life experience."

Healing involves the resolution of anything that limits or prevents the full, uninhibited, and free-flowing expression of your energy. **Anything that keeps you from being in the flow of your evolved true Self is a *block*.**

Blocks can develop on *any* level of your energy, affecting everything from your intuition and instincts to your perception, understanding, expression, thoughts, and creativity. They develop from anything that impairs the flow of your true Self, including—but not limited to—emotions, thoughts, beliefs, behavioral patterns, and programming. Blocks caused by beliefs include "negative" decisions, such as "I am poor" or "I am a bad person," as well as "positive" decisions, such as "I am a good person" or "I am a nice person." Blocks caused by feelings include anything that *you hold onto*, such as pain, rejection, failure, or judgment, as well as love, success, or wealth. Even your true Self has unresolved issues, which require healing if it is to achieve its fully evolved state and express its energy in its highest and purest form.

In the context of this work, *positive* is defined as something that is generally considered desirable and *negative* as something that is typically undesirable. While most people understand that negative decisions and feelings hinder their energy flow, it is uncommon to think of positive decisions and feelings as being blocks. Nonetheless, holding onto any feeling, including positive feelings such as love, success, or wealth, stops their movement and impedes the flow of your Self through your experience. This causes the loss of your Self along with the loss of your flow through the positive feelings.

Holding onto a positive decision, such as "I am good and nice," impairs your experience of anything that does not conform with your definition of "good" and "nice." This hampers the flow of your true Self and prevents healing. It also distorts your energy in a variety of ways depending on how you define good and nice. In other words, you are *not* good or nice, you simply are, and any redefinition of your Self that is not the result of healing creates a block.

Blockages can develop in the form of obstructions or distortions of your true Self's energy. If you feel prosperous within your Self, but cannot bring prosperity into your daily life, you are experiencing an energy *obstruction*. If your "concern" does not always feel good or if you are doing work that you do not really want to do, you are experiencing an energy *distortion*. If you cannot recognize what you want to do for work, you have an energy *obstruction*.

Your *capabilities, self-trust,* and *fulfillment* naturally result from being in the flow of your true Self and can be obstructed by specific blockages to that flow. *Intuition* and *instincts* are natural abilities of your Self that can be impaired by issues or blocks. And *disease* and *dysfunction* can result from the presence of blocks that obstruct or distort the flow of your evolved true Self through your body.

The dysfunctional emotions, needs, and issues that obstruct or distort your true Self's energy do not exist as obstacles to being your Self as much as they are areas that the true Self seeks to evolve through to become its healed Self. **The blocks *are* the path**. This is why you want to embrace your blocks as steps to show you the way. Whatever issues arise along your path direct you towards your Self. With healing, you are not trying to get away from what does not feel good, as much as you are trying to integrate what you are experiencing on the path to becoming who you really are. **By choosing to heal, you are simply choosing to walk your path.**

Every aspect of your life is an experience through which your true Self seeks to grow. Loneliness, for example, is not something from which to run. It is telling you there is something more within yourself that you are missing. Healing takes you through the feeling of loneliness so that you connect more fully with your Self.

Even disease and physical dysfunction are not conditions to suppress, overpower, or beat into remission. They are manifestations of energetic issues that require healing for your body and Self to evolve and move through their experience.

Healing a block or an issue does not mean that you automatically *become* your true Self. It simply points you in the right direction by assisting in dissolving your false identity and resolving your dysfunctional ways of being.

For example, the energy flows of security, success, and prosperity are normal and natural for your healed Self; however, just because you heal a feeling of insecurity does not mean that the feeling of security flows through you. And by healing the feelings of failure and scarcity, you do not immediately experience success and prosperity. Further healing is required to be able to distinguish your true Self from the rest of the energy that you are experiencing. Then, with practice and additional healing, you will learn to *identify* with the part of your energy that is true and let go of your false identity.

Many people assume that the true Self is fully evolved and that they are simply trying to remember that state; however, if it were fully evolved, you would not be here now doing what you are doing. In fact, your true Self has many issues that require healing. As a result, your true Self seeks to grow, develop, and express its Self, requiring experience to progress.

It is your task to evolve the qualities of your true Self so that it is functioning at its highest energetic level. This is not just a mental concept or a belief about what the true Self should be like. Advancement of your true Self requires the evolution of its qualities based on what is *energetically* functional. Your healing work will assist you in the development of your awareness about what is and what is not functional so you can take an active role in the growth of your true Self. For instance, if your experience of being understanding or caring creates pain for you, your understanding or caring is not truly functional and will require healing to make it so. Any quality may require healing to make it more functional. You can develop the qualities of fulfillment, acceptance, peace, cooperation, security, happiness, and responsibility—to name a tiny fraction of the possibilities. Through healing, your true Self evolves to realize more of its potential and perfection.

In some traditions, once you remember your true Self and identify with it, you have achieved enlightenment; however, there is much more that is possible with healing. Once you identify with your true Self and have evolved your Self, you may become aware of issues that prevent your true Self energy from flowing through your life. To connect with the flow within as the source of your energy, these issues will require healing as well. You have to let go of your old ways of being and assert your true Self more fully in your life.

There may be issues that prevent your true Self energy flow of security, success, and prosperity from entering your life. Perhaps you believe that you are unworthy or undeserving of those experiences. Thus, once you have healed a particular block, such as failure, and have evolved the quality you are looking for, such as success, you may have to heal the reasons you cannot live as your Self.

To summarize, by healing the issues that you become conscious of, you begin to dissolve your false identity and remember your true Self. With further growth, you begin to identify with that part of your energy as your Self. You can further your development by evolving the qualities of your Self. And finally, you can bring those qualities into your life so that you live as your fully evolved true Self.

Anything that facilitates the resolution of obstructions, distortions, and blockages is healing. Anything that takes you towards your true Self is healing. Anything that evolves the energy of your true Self is healing. Anything that assists you in living as your evolved true Self is healing. What is required is a practice that eliminates the obstacles to functionality and health.

Since impediments to the flow of your true Self can occur on any level of your energy, you require skills and tools to address issues on every energy level. Because emotional healing is the *only* effective approach for healing every aspect of your energy and because it is also the *only* effective method for healing your emotions, **emotional healing is the one essential skill for restoring the flow of your energy and evolving your true Self.**

With the awakening of your healing ability, everything in your life becomes an opportunity to heal. You can apply your healing skills to every part of your experience, including relationships, health issues, meditation experiences, and dreams. Every feeling, large and small, can be transformed, and this changes the quality of your life instantly.

By applying your healing skills to every aspect of your life, you eliminate those parts of your identity that are not real and discover who you really are. You dissolve your illusions to discover the truth.

How You Can Heal

Healing is much simpler than it may seem. **All that is involved in healing is *feeling* the block, obstruction, or distortion.** That's it!

Your true Self is the one having the experience; it is not the experience. By feeling each block, you get the energy moving and return to the state of your true Self *having* an experience.

While you are experiencing the feeling, you will practice relaxation. **Relaxation is what actually creates healing.** Your true Self is having an experience and by relaxing, the experience flows through you and does not become stuck; you do not identify with it. Then by continuing to relax through the feeling, you will fully release it and let it go. Sounds simple, yes? And it is, but just like everything, it will take practice to master the process of healing.

The individual steps of the process can be delineated to help your mind understand where you are going with this and what needs to happen to achieve healing. With practice, you will perform many of the steps without thinking about them. However, every step is important and cannot be missed, whether it is consciously taken or not. The steps are **becoming aware, focusing, separating, relaxing,** and **letting go.** Let's take a look at each of these steps.

Becoming Aware

The significance of *awareness* is underappreciated. Without awareness, there is nothing to heal. To gain awareness, you can learn to focus on your experience and discern the subtleties of your emotions, thoughts, and other aspects of your energy. You can notice areas of your life that do not feel good and that you want to change. You can pay attention to areas of your life that you enjoy so you can enhance and develop them. You can also exercise and develop your awareness with specific energy stretching and strengthening exercises.

One easy way to develop your healing process is to simply pay attention to when you have something going on. How do you know you have something going on? You are triggered off and your feelings have a charge on them. There is tension in your body and a feeling of resistance. When you are defending, arguing, trying to figure things out, blaming, feeling agitated, denying, judging, or feeling panicky, you have something to heal. Anything that takes you out of a state of inner peace and stillness is an issue to heal.

You can watch for both positive and negative feelings that require healing. Typically, people do not do any better with positive feelings than they do with negative feelings. As a matter of fact, many people spend their entire life chasing positive feelings all over the world and with a multitude of other chasers! By healing positive feelings, such as love, compassion, belonging, worth, and security, you connect more fully to your Self, your inner source, just like when you heal negative feelings. You are then freed up to be your true Self and to realize the truth behind your feelings.

While healing requires awareness, greater awareness is also a consequence of healing. Healing will enhance and clarify your perception and understanding. Perspectives will change and develop as your healing work progresses. And every issue that you heal will open the door to subtler energy and feelings that you will become aware of.

Even though awareness is only the first step of healing, certain changes begin just with awareness itself. For one thing, once you are aware of an issue, you have more choice about how you engage in the world and how you respond to those around you. Nonetheless, there is more to be done to totally resolve an issue and eliminate it as an element of your energy. Awareness is only the beginning and there is much more that you will want to accomplish. Once you have awareness, you can apply the rest of your healing process.

Focus

Once you have discerned a feeling or an aspect of your energy that you want to heal, you will have to *focus* on it. You must maintain your awareness of the energy in order to explore it and transform it. Without focus, no healing can occur.

As simple as this sounds, the focus required for healing is often a new skill for healers of all ages. Both children and adults may experience a variety of challenges with maintaining a precise focus on a feeling and not wavering from that focus until healing is accomplished.

Developing your ability to focus also enhances your awareness of energy at the level on which you are focusing. The more you refine your focus, the more you will perceive.

Separating

Once you are focused on the feeling, thought, or other energy, the next step is to completely *separate* from whatever triggered you off. The trigger could be within you or it could be outside of you. It could be another person, a circumstance, or your own pattern that triggers you off.

However, the trigger is not the problem. It is your energy that requires healing and the trigger helped to create the awareness that you have an issue to heal. Forget about who did what to whom or whose fault it is. There is no benefit to blaming others or getting upset. All of these activities are defenses that people use to try to get away from a feeling. Instead, seize the opportunity and do some healing!

If you are still thinking about the event or other person, you have not separated successfully. Allow the trigger and triggering event to fade into the background and hone in on your own energy.

Relaxation

You must experience your feelings in order to heal them. Since feelings must be vibrating and flowing to be felt, *relaxation* is required to set blocked feelings in motion. And once in motion, relaxation maintains their movement so you can feel them and move all the way through them.

Proper relaxation often takes practice to develop. **The goal here is to simply allow the feeling—to feel it without judgment, resistance, or attachment.** With relaxation, you let your feelings flow through you without identifying with them and without becoming stuck in them. You are attempting to find your true Self's level of energy and, therefore, the level of your Self having its experience (See Figure 1). When successful, you may notice the movement of each emotion as it releases and as you progress through it. There will also be a release of bodily tension and resistance.

If you are too light in a feeling, you will not feel it and you also will not be experiencing your true Self. This is an avoidance technique for negative feelings and keeps you from truly experiencing and owning your positive feelings. You will want to go deeper to experience these feelings more intensely.

Figure 1: The True Self's Level of Energy

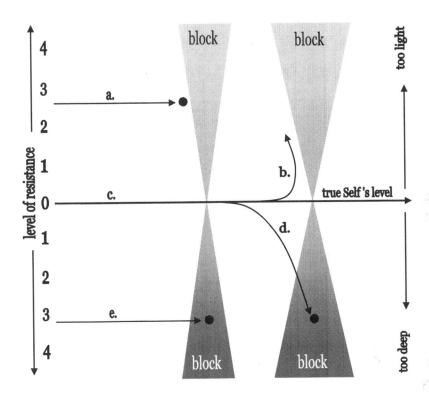

Figure 1: If you are too light in your experience (a & b), you are not feeling your feelings, you are resisting the flow of your true Self, and your blocks are present even though you do not feel them. The further you are from your Self (a & e), the greater the resistance you encounter in your life.

When there is no resistance to the flow of your energy (c), you are in the flow of your true Self. This is the only energy level at which you can heal a feeling and progress along the path of your true Self.

If you are too deep in your experience (d & e), you are resisting the flow of your Self, you will feel stuck, and you may experience pain, tears, or depression. If you are used to being too deep all the time (e), your life will feel heavy and things will be much more difficult than they need to be.

If you are chronically too light in your energy, such as by always avoiding your feelings, relaxation takes you deeper, getting you to feel your feelings and move through them. People who always appear to be upbeat or optimistic are often too light in their energy. However, their blocks are still present just beneath the surface of their awareness. In addition, physical illnesses will tend to develop without their awareness.

If you are too deep in a feeling, there will be a lack of movement and you may wallow around in the feeling forever. This is a common experience among people who are trying to process emotions because it seems that really "getting into" a feeling is the path of healing. However, this is an undesirable indulgence and is both self-abusive and non-productive. When you are too deep, you are identifying with the feeling. You will want to get lighter to relax through the feeling and heal it.

If you are chronically too deep in your energy—which occurs if you are stuck in your feelings or if you identify with your issues—relaxation will lighten you up and help you move through them. People who are always serious, gloomy, overwhelmed, depressed, or pessimistic are often too deep in their energy. Their issues seem larger than they really are and healing is stifled.

Commonly, people try to stop feeling their feelings by clamping down on them or resisting them. This stops the flow of their feelings and temporarily keeps the feelings from vibrating, but it does not heal them. Instead, it prevents them from moving; they are merely suppressed, but still have an adverse effect on the person and remain vulnerable to future activation.

Another way that you can create resistance and impair your healing is by trying too hard to heal a feeling. Effort does not contribute to healing. Your focus and process must be relaxed.

One unusual challenge with relaxation occurs when you attempt to relax through someone else's feelings. Although it is very common to feel other people's feelings, if you try to go through their feelings by relaxing through them, the feelings will not go anywhere. The feelings will actually feel heavier and more stuck with relaxation. In these cases, you are going to want to separate from the other people's feelings and heal how you engaged with them. For more information about separating from other people's energy, you can refer to the chapters titled "Separations" and "Avenues of Engagement."

You must be vigilant as it is easy to confuse being too deep in a feeling with the lack of movement that occurs when you are feeling someone else's feelings. Remember that the true Self level of energy is not usually one with which most people are comfortable and you are trying to find that level again. Since most people have become accustomed to being stuck in many of their feelings and identifying with them, take care to be certain that you are relaxing thoroughly before deciding that you are feeling someone else's feeling. Make sure that you are light enough to flow through your own feelings.

Letting Go

Letting go is the ultimate result of completely relaxing through a feeling. It means that the emotion has been totally resolved and that there is no residual energy remaining. The feeling is gone and there is nothing remaining from the feeling.

By letting go of the feeling, you also free yourself from a dysfunctional way of responding in your life. That is why letting go is such an important aspect of healing—you truly change.

This does not involve pushing a feeling away, ignoring it, dodging the feeling with the mind, or getting away from an emotion. It means that you have gone all the way through the feeling and that it has been transformed.

As simple as it sounds, the ability to let go often requires the development of a new skill. There is a lot involved with this skill and it is common to have to heal your ability to let go.

Some people believe that children are natural at letting go, but that is *not* what I observe. Children are quick to move on to other interests or topics, but that does not mean that they have let go of their issues. Children may also adapt quickly to their experiences, but that is not the same as letting go either as adaptation often just incorporates the blocks into their personalities. The residual feelings of an experience are often still apparent and are not resolved until the person performs these steps to heal them.

Some people start to relax through their feelings but do not let go. This does help to discharge some emotional energy, but it does not take people to their true Self. Instead, it takes them back to their false identity. You really have to be willing to let go of old ways of being to become your true Self.

One reason people hold onto their issues is that they get something out of them. If, for instance, someone gets sympathy and "love" for being a victim, they might not let go of their victim pattern so readily. To be willing to let go of their pattern, they would learn to generate what they want for themselves by relaxing through the feelings of sympathy and love. Or if they get a lot of "validation" for being "caring" and "nice," they may not let go of these aspects of their personality until they can generate their own feeling of validation.

Letting go of an issue is impossible if you do not take responsibility for your part in an interaction. No matter what has transpired, if you are still energetically engaging with the other person, you have something going on that requires healing. Sometimes it is more convenient to blame others without realizing that you have the power to let go of your own issues and the pattern of engagement that is problematic.

Another reason to hold onto an issue is because of what letting go implies. You may think, for instance, that letting go implies that you approve of whatever happened or that by letting go you are allowing someone to circumvent what seems right, just, or fair. However, letting go only means that you are healing yourself. For example, if you perceive that another person inflicted pain, was abusive, or violated your boundaries, then for you to heal, you will relax through all of the associated feelings and let them go. If there are any reasons you cannot let go, you will heal those feelings as well by relaxing through them.

Another potential obstacle involves forgiveness. Many people are taught that they must forgive others, but actually, that is not the appropriate focus. **To heal, you want to forgive yourself; it requires that you truly let go by healing your own feelings of pain, hurt, and loss.** Letting go allows you to experience genuine forgiveness.

Holding onto an issue until "justice is served" does not work. No one can be made to own their issues, and waiting for the other person to accept responsibility delays your healing and extends your suffering unnecessarily. Are you going to wait until the other person takes responsibility before you let go? You may have to wait forever. Holding on simply prolongs your pain and discomfort and maintains a connection with the other person through those uncomfortable feelings. Healing allows you to immediately end your distress and let go of dysfunctional connections with others.

The justice is that everyone has to go through his or her own feelings. Everyone must eventually reclaim their pain, abuse, or violation and heal it themselves. It is up to others to forgive themselves by healing and letting go of their issues. You cannot go through other people's feelings or absolve them of their issues. They will have to go through their feelings themselves.

When you have healed, you will not want others to suffer or pay a price for their actions because that is not healing. You will naturally want everyone to heal their issues, let go of their dysfunctional ways of being and interacting, and remember their true Self. When you are able to accomplish this, you have truly let go. Then you will experience the grace, power, beauty, forgiveness, and freedom of healing.

❋　❋　❋

To create an image of this healing process, you can look at the three states of physical matter—solid, liquid, and gas.

Typically, your experience has a stable structure and "solid" foundation that supports it. You have become accustomed to the patterns, feelings, energy, and issues that are a part of this structure, and often do not notice their presence. As long as the structure of your experience remains solid, you may never detect its existence.

Once you recognize that an issue exists, often through a triggering incident, it may seem weighty and fixed. If you push against it, there is no movement and you experience its inflexibility, apparently confirming its solid state.

Nonetheless, if you focus on it, feel it, and start to relax into it, you will notice that it is not as solid as it seemed at first. It warms slightly and begins to melt. With continued attention and more relaxation, it liquefies and starts to flow, its fluidity increasing the more you relax.

With sufficient relaxation, the liquid warms further and gradually becomes a gas. With complete relaxation, there is a letting go, and the gas disappears into the ethers, the individual molecules never reassembling in the same formation again.

When you let go, the energy associated with an issue dissipates, and you are changed forever.

EXERCISE: Developing Your Awareness

You can enhance your awareness by focusing on different aspects of your experience.

Most people have a steady stream of thoughts flowing through their mind. What thoughts are you having right now? Trace the flow of your thoughts over the last few minutes.

There are also other streams of energy flowing through you, such as emotions, intuition, instincts, physical body sensations, and sensory information. What feelings and emotions are present right now? Trace their flow over the last few minutes.

Focus on the flow of your sensory information, such as your auditory experience, and follow its flow for the next few minutes. Then tune into other aspects of your experience and flow with them.

You can also enhance your awareness by quieting your thoughts. Without thoughts, other energetic aspects of your experience often become more conspicuous. What do you notice when your thoughts diminish?

With practice, you can learn to shift from one aspect of your energy to another as easily as changing stations on a radio.

EXERCISE: Resistance and Relaxation

For this exercise, you will need a partner. Stand facing each other with your right hand grasping the other person's right hand. Then, have your partner attempt to push you around through the clasped hands. Resist your partner's pushes for about 10-15 seconds while both people focus on the feeling of resistance in their body. Then, relax and go into nonresistance to the pushing of your partner for about 10-15 seconds, allowing yourself to be pushed around. You should now focus on the feeling of relaxation in your body. Switch roles with your partner and repeat the sequence of resistance and nonresistance. Both of you will now have a bodily experience of the relaxation that is required to accomplish emotional healing. Repeat this exercise as needed to remind you of the level of relaxation that you are trying to achieve during your emotional healing process.

EXERCISE: Healing Your Past

Pick out any event or person from your past. Notice the feelings—both positive and negative—that remain from that experience. Practice your process by relaxing through every feeling that you are aware of. Continue through the feelings until you have let go of all of them. There will be a pleasant sensation of peace, resolution, and flow when the exercise is complete.

EXERCISE: Healing the Present

Notice the feelings that are present right now. Perhaps a feeling of fatigue after a day of activity. Or perhaps some residual feelings from a recent interaction. Practice your process: awareness, focus, separation, relaxation, and letting go.

This process can be done anytime, anywhere. Develop a new pattern in your life by doing this process every time you have any awareness of an issue or feeling coming up for you. With practice, this can become a part of your daily hygiene and then you will be healing all of the time.

Developing Your Personal Process

When people identify with anything other than their true Self, they tend to resist their issues. Their most uncomfortable experiences occur when something is triggered off and they are actively experiencing their issues. It is even worse when they are just sitting in their feelings without any movement occurring. Thus, many people think they are doing well when nothing is going on or when they are not feeling anything.

One of the most important considerations in developing a healing process is to become relaxed with having active issues—to not be so eager to get away from an issue that you sabotage your healing. Since having an active issue is a requirement in order to have something to heal, you will want to develop your ability to hang out with whatever is going on so you can explore your experience and find your way through your feelings.

Some people have asked what it means to *go through* a feeling. Often, this question stems from the mind seeking understanding. While the motivation may be to truly understand what they are attempting to accomplish, sometimes people are actually trying to figure out how to do this process in their mind without having to feel their feelings.

Going through a feeling is another way to describe the healing process that was just discussed. **Going through your feelings simply means that you have your experience of every feeling without judgment, resistance, or attachment. You feel them and let them go!**

Because healing is an experiential and emotional process, not a mental or verbal process, going through a feeling is difficult to describe in words and may not be clearly understood until after you have experienced it. While emotional healing *does* have a logic that becomes apparent with the development of your process, your mind is not going to get it until after you have *experienced* emotional healing. Allow your Self to have the experience and suspend the need to understand or be in control. Have the experience first and gain your understanding of it afterwards.

Since the process of going through a feeling is new for many people, it may take some work to become familiar and comfortable with it. To develop your emotional healing process, simply *explore* your feelings. Resist them, enjoy them, push them away, touch them, taste them, roll around in them, glide over them, float through them, feel them, and relax into them. Play with your feelings and notice what you experience. Continue to learn about them and discover how to go through them. You must find a way to relax and go through your emotions and feelings.

Remember that you are trying to rediscover your true Self's level of energy. This is the level of relaxation at which your true Self resumes its flow through its experience rather than identifying with its experience. For most people, this involves moving off the level on which they typically function. For some people it will be deeper than what they are used to, while for others it will be lighter than what they are used to.

With successful relaxation, you will feel the immediate release of energy as the feelings flow through you, followed by lightness and a sense of ease. When you attain the proper level of relaxation, you will need only a few seconds to heal mildly charged issues, while it could take several minutes or more to heal those issues that are more highly charged and even hours to resolve those that have multiple layers associated with them.

While some people associate tears and crying with an emotional release, these expressions are *not usually* a necessary part of emotional healing. Even though tears are a perfectly normal and valid companion to a variety of circumstances, they often result from being too deep in a feeling, from defending against a feeling, or from trying to deal with other people's energy. For instance, tears and crying frequently result if you feel someone else's pain or grief, and especially if you feel someone else's pain that was directed at you through abusive behavior. Tears are often present if you have a feeling of loss and are too deep in the feeling. And tears may develop if you feel sorry for yourself or defend against a feeling in other ways.

Tears may also be the result of feeling relief from the release of a block. However, while tears may accompany the healing of a difficult issue, they are usually due to resistance and not finding the optimum level of relaxation. And even if you experience tears of joy, sometimes they are due to your having grown accustomed to being too deep in your energy and having too little joy flowing through you.

Developing your healing process will require the acquisition of new skills, the learning of new procedures, and the broadening of your awareness. It will require practice to master the new ways of dealing with your feelings once you are aware of them: the focus, the separation from others' feelings, the relaxation, and the letting go.

The more you practice these skills, the better you will become at healing. Your skills will not get much better with only the mental understanding of healing. You need to practice going through your emotions to develop your emotional healing skills.

You can make it into a game to see how many feelings you can go through in a day. Start by relaxing through everything you feel: tired, bored, hungry, silly, playful, serious, irritated, rushed, withdrawn, peaceful, angry, and joyful. By exploring your emotions whenever you can, your emotional healing process will become more natural and automatic.

If possible, start with less charged issues so your skills are more developed before you go after bigger challenges. It is, for instance, easier to work on issues that just involve yourself before you get into the more complicated situations that involve other people.

Of course, you may be thrust into difficult interactions without warning and many people seek healing only after troubles arise. In these situations, you may be taking your mid-term examinations without the ideal preparation! Do your best to apply these principles to your "opportunities." And practice your healing process all the time—especially when nothing is going on—to develop your skills and to be more prepared for future chances that come your way.

Enhanced awareness is one result of pursuing a healing process. While this is a goal of healing and a positive development, initially it may seem like you got more than you bargained for because enhanced awareness opens you to all kinds of previously hidden blocks and feelings. It may seem like a never-ending process! However, every issue that you heal is one less issue to deal with and, by continuing with your healing practice, you are creating positive changes. If the process feels overwhelming, relax through that feeling as well. While there are going to be many issues that require healing, you do not have to heal everything today.

Another related phenomenon is that a healing process will increase your sensitivity. What this means is that smaller and smaller blocks will become noticeable as you progress with your process. This can be disconcerting as you may be working on an issue and feel that you are making progress only to experience a greater intensity with the same emotion. It may appear that your healing process is not effective. Often, however, you are simply becoming more sensitive to the same issue *because* of your healing. Again, you must persevere. Once you move completely through a block, the associated feelings will dissipate.

Remember that many of your patterns and issues have been re-enforced over a long period of time with many different people. Therefore, each issue may come up in dozens of situations, requiring the need to work on it many times to resolve it. For instance, if you are used to taking responsibility for other people's feelings and you heal your responsibility in one situation, you would still anticipate needing to do further work on the same issue in other situations and with other people before being completely free of it.

Initially, an important aspect of your healing work will be directed at your healing process itself. You can heal your process! You can pay attention to what, if any, obstacles develop while you are practicing your healing and focus on them as topics for healing. The goal is to make your process as streamlined, as effortless, and as much fun as possible.

You will almost certainly be changing the patterns you have developed around having issues. Often, people have learned patterns to avoid their problems and to pretend that nothing is going on. Nevertheless, as previously stated, **you must have an active issue before you can heal it**. Consequently, you will be redirecting your focus towards your feelings and emotions instead of trying to get away from them.

What feelings arise around having emotional issues? Perhaps there is a feeling of *denial* because you were not allowed to have or acknowledge emotional issues in your family. It may be necessary to heal *judgment* if you were taught to do everything "right" when you were growing up or if you were always being told what you were doing "wrong." You may feel *failure* or *invalidation* for even having problems and issues. *Guilt* could arise if you have previously taken responsibility for others' feelings and now you start to separate from their feelings. A *fear of change* or *insecurity* could crop up around issues involving other people. If you learned that it was *not safe* to have anything going on, you may feel a *resistance* to acknowledging issues. *Depression* can arise when you do not feel that you can change a particular feeling. Feeling *impatient* or *not good enough* might come up when the learning or healing process does not seem to be progressing fast enough. And, of course, you may feel *overwhelmed* by all of the issues that you have to deal with. By healing these feelings, you make it more acceptable to have active emotional issues and your process will become easier.

It is important to remember that **whatever arises in your process is perfect; it is the next step.** Therefore, you do not want to avoid anything that occurs. If frustration and failure come up around your process, those are the next steps that need to be healed. If struggle and resistance arise, those are your next steps. Each step that you take furthers your healing and assists in decreasing the effort involved in your process at the same time.

Another aspect of the perfection of this process is that part of the healing is inherent in the process itself—**by performing this process, you practice and develop the qualities that you are seeking.** For instance, if you feel *failure* around your ability to heal your feelings, by going through the feeling of *failure*, you have just *succeeded* at your process! If you feel *powerless*, you actually use and develop your *power* by going through the feeling of powerlessness; you reclaim your power by doing this process. If you are feeling *lost*, then through this process, you will *find* part of your Self. And if you are feeling *fear*, through healing, you develop your *courage*. You simultaneously practice the feelings you seek, such as success, power, finding your Self, and courage by doing this healing process; they are an integral part of it.

It is useful to notice what makes your healing process difficult and focus on those issues. Whenever you are struggling with a feeling, relax and stop resisting the process. When something is triggered off, the sooner you go through your issues, the sooner you can move on. The longer you remain engaged with the other person or event, the longer you neglect the flow of your true Self. By healing your healing process, you can make it so easy that it does not take a lot of time, effort, or energy.

Enhancing Awareness

While the path of your true Self involves healing and mastering every aspect of energy that is available to you, energy awareness is required before you can exercise the rest of your healing process. Since your awareness may be incomplete, you must always strive to expand it. You must always be looking for those elements of energy that have eluded your observation and contemplation.

Beliefs and programmed patterns, for example, may be so much a part of your experience that it may be difficult to notice them. Issues relating to your physical health may also be outside of your awareness. Only by becoming aware of these features of your energy do you create the possibility of healing and transforming them.

There are many ways to enhance your awareness. My favorite approach is to simply monitor my experience. While paying attention to my experience, I notice any feeling, thought, or other energy that is present. I am especially attentive to what takes me out of my normal peaceful state and heal whatever needs to be healed to reestablish a peaceful state.

Sometimes I rummage around for feelings and am more involved in activating energy to bring it into my awareness. I might seek out experiences, such as studying a new discipline or area of interest, and notice any shifts in my perspective. I might read a book, do some unusual activity, or interact with someone who brings up issues for me. Traveling is one of my favorite ways to create new opportunities for healing and to awaken my awareness. Experiencing other cultures, people, and ways of life can dramatically assist in the development of expanded awareness.

I regularly use specific exercises to stimulate areas of my energy field and pay attention to what pops up. This includes activities like visualizing light in my chakras and various movements to stimulate my energy channels and energy centers. Qi gong, yoga, tai chi, physical exercise, and meditation can be useful practices for developing awareness along with their other benefits. But, truly, any activity in which you participate can bring new awareness if you pay attention to your experience.

When you are working on healing a feeling, it is not necessary to *name* the feeling in order to heal it. You can just relax through it whether you know what it is or not. Sometimes, however, it is easier to heal an issue when you know what you are dealing with. The mind is often more comfortable knowing what you are feeling. You can refer to the lists of positive and negative emotions in the *Appendix* at the end of the book for some assistance in trying to identify your feelings.

Neither do you have to know *where* a particular issue exists in your energy field to heal it. Once you are aware of an issue, you can simply use your healing process to resolve it. Nonetheless, it is valuable to know more about what you perceive to gain greater understanding about what you are dealing with and about how your energy works. For instance, it is very useful to know which chakra or energy center is affected by a particular issue so you can relate this information to your experience. This will enhance your knowledge about energy. It is also helpful to know more about your physical body so that you can relate your energetic and emotional issues to your physical body experience and specific organ function. Thus, as your healing process develops, you will want to explore *where* you experience a feeling in your body and energy to further enhance your awareness.

As your awareness expands, you will discern issues arising in areas of your energy field that were previously unknown to you. It is very exciting to become aware of new aspects of one's energy and to gain experience with them. I have made numerous discoveries of various features of my energy field simply by consciously attending to whatever I noticed within my awareness.

EXERCISE: Enhancing Your Energy Sensing

What are you feeling? Tune into your feelings for a while. There is a constant stream of feelings going on for everyone. Enhance your awareness by tapping into that flow and feeling them.

Consciously draw your attention to the feelings in your body and experience them. Using your emotional process, explore bodily sensations to assist with the resolution of symptoms and to enhance the evolution of your physical expression.

Focus on different people and objects. What do you sense, see, feel, and hear? Focus on a mountain, plant, body of water, star, pet, or other creature, and perceive the different qualities of those experiences.

Focus on a house, office building, city, or sections of a city, and notice what they feel like. What do you notice inside someone's house, in different rooms of their house, and in different office spaces?

The Challenge of Perception

B ecoming aware of energy and issues is only the beginning of the development of perception. A significant aspect of perceptual development entails making sense of what you perceive. You are having an experience, but what does the experience mean?

Obtaining a valid and truthful interpretation of what you perceive is not as simple as it may seem. A number of issues must be considered and addressed to achieve a clear understanding of your experience.

Many factors, such as your point of reference, your current emotional state, and your expectations, affect your experience of reality. You have your own unique perspective and no one else is having exactly the same experience at the same time. What contributes to the differences between people's perspectives? What challenges do you face if you wish to attain an accurate interpretation of what you perceive?

Because you perceive *through* your own energy, your perception is colored by your energy. Your experience is intimately entwined with your energy and it becomes complex to perceive what is going on outside your energy with any certainty. Everything you perceive has the potential of being altered by your issues, beliefs, programming, past experiences, judgments, prejudices, goals, and hopes. It is often more accurate to assume that your experience is just *your own* experience, rather than having much to do with the world around you.

A further complication frequently develops as a result of having other people's energy in your space. When you *engage* with another person's energy, your perception can easily be distorted. Once you engage with other people's energy, you may lose your clarity and perceive through their issues, values, and descriptions of what is going on in the world. It is also easy to *absorb* other people's energy and, once you do, to perceive and live through that energy.

It is common, for example, for students to absorb the beliefs, values, opinions, and viewpoints of their teachers and to perceive through those perspectives without questioning their validity. Children typically do the same thing with their parents. I remember seeing an 8-year-old girl on television speaking vehemently about a political concern that she did not understand. There was no doubt that her parents felt very strongly about the topic and that they had taught their daughter to perceive through their issues. Because perception is easily distorted when there is difficulty separating from another person's issues, trying to raise children to be functional within the family and society while staying true to themselves is a very challenging responsibility.

With everything you perceive, you have the challenge of discerning whether you are noticing your own issues because you are perceiving through them or whether you are aware of something outside yourself. Your perceptual filters affect many of your experiences.

When you perceive through an issue but believe it is coming from outside of you, you project your issue out onto the world. You erroneously experience the issue as if it is in the world, which makes it very difficult to accurately perceive what is going on outside your own energy.

If you feel insecure but do not own your insecurity, you will probably project it onto the world. Then you will experience insecurity with many of the people you meet and in many of the places you visit. You will not feel secure anywhere or with anyone until you heal your insecurity.

If you have a feeling of isolation, it is easy to experience it as if it relates to the world. The truth is that a feeling of isolation is *always* caused by a separation from your true Self and it does not exist in the world outside of your own energy.

Some people see the world as a cold and cruel place, while others trust everyone they meet or see nothing but happy people. Some people see the world as an unfair or lonely place, while others see equality and friendship. Some perceive the world as a place of scarcity where people always need help, while others perceive prosperity and independence. In these instances, people are often perceiving through their own beliefs or issues and projecting them onto the world.

When you project an issue onto the world, you have created more than just a perceptual problem. The energy of your mistaken perception is literally thrown at the object of your misperception. The thought, belief, or feeling is actually directed towards the noun—the person, place, or thing.

Besides the fact that this creates a problem with what you perceive as the truth, the world will do one of two things. It either rejects or accepts your projection. If the world rejects your projection, it is reflected back at you and you will continue to feel it. In this case, you are confronted with your issue and have an opportunity to heal it.

On the other hand, if the world accepts your projection, it absorbs the projection and lives it out. In this case, you have actually assisted in altering the world with your projection! While people may think that this could be desirable with "positive" projections, your projections actually impair the healing of whomever or whatever absorbs them. This problem will be addressed shortly when I discuss the complications involved in dealing with foreign energy.

Recently, one of my clients reported experiencing control issues with her husband and children. Prior to healing, she was feeling controlled by her family and perceived the control issues to be her family's problems. She could not see the issues any other way. An evaluation revealed that she had experienced and internalized many struggles for control with her parents and siblings during her childhood. She had been fighting with others to reclaim control ever since. The healing and resolution of her internalized control issues ended her fight for control with her family, and she no longer experiences her husband or children as controlling.

On a daily basis, people perceive through lots of false beliefs and experience them in the world. I have had numerous clients who firmly believed that they were victims and perceived both themselves and the world through that belief. And guess what? The world agreed, and they got to experience that they were victims.

Some people believe that they can catch a cold because someone sneezes near them, and then they promptly get ill when that occurs. Their experience seems to validate their belief, while there is often no awareness that their belief contributed to their experience to begin with.

People frequently project their feelings of powerlessness out onto the world in the face of various illnesses and diseases that they fall "prey" to and over which they appear to have limited control. Some illnesses are explained in terms of the germ theory, for instance, which is woefully inadequate in accounting for the energetics involved in illness. Yet people perceive through these beliefs, live through their distortion of reality, and experience these beliefs as if they are real, as if they are the only possibility there is. As an alternative, it can easily be argued that since viral and bacterial agents are present all the time and some people do not become ill, other factors are involved in determining people's susceptibility to illness.

Science admits to various influences affecting the outcome of experiments by using a double-blind procedure. The need for a double-blind procedure demonstrates that we influence the results. However, while experimental procedures are devised to eliminate undesirable influences and preserve objectivity, science does not realize that our energy affects the outcome of the experiments anyway. A *procedure* cannot offset the effects of energy, and the results will *always* be affected by our issues, beliefs, hopes, expectations, and programming. Our issues and energy affect the world no matter how we try to control our energy and whether we are conscious of our energy or not.

The placebo effect is another demonstration of the effect of our energy on our experience and perception. When we expect a certain outcome, it is more likely to be experienced. Our expectations affect our perception and experience, and influence our conclusions about cause and effect and about what is real.

Science makes all kinds of observations and turns them into "truths" that we live by, while there is often no recognition that those observations are made through perceptual filters. For example, the deterioration of our body is assumed to be an inevitable consequence of aging. We study the impact of time on our body with the belief that a loss of function is to be expected as a result of "wear and tear." When we have this perspective, it may be difficult to perceive other possibilities; however, other possibilities do exist. From an energetic point of view, we can perceive that the physical body commonly weakens and falls apart because of energetic and emotional issues. These issues can be healed and transformed to create physical enhancement as we mature, rather than letting them contribute to physical degeneration.

Often there are many deeply held beliefs through which we perceive, without awareness of how they affect our perception. For instance, we are used to observing our world through the eyes of Darwin's evolutionary theory, which is only one out of many possible explanations for what we observe. We are so used to looking at our world through this concept that we may not be able to see anything else as a possibility. We just accept the theory of evolution as a fact without understanding that we are making our observations *through* our beliefs in competition, natural selection, and the "survival of the fittest." We are not taking the context of our issues into account, nor does the theory take into account the greater scope of our existence. If we made our observations through eyes of freedom and creativity, we might arrive at completely different conclusions about our world and evolution.

It is common to want to have others agree with our view of reality and, therefore, project our perspectives onto others to get their agreement. Many people just absorb our projections and agree with our view of the world. We see this happen when we get friends to help us blame others for what is happening in our life. Interestingly, the reality we get others to agree with does not usually serve us particularly well.

We have, of course, been the object of numerous projections from other people. Commonly, we have accepted other people's descriptions of who we are, their perceptions of our abilities, and their own issues that are directed at us. We then experience ourselves and the world around us through these filters; we perceive through and live out whatever projections we have absorbed.

One common form of perceptual dysfunction occurs when people think they see what is going on with other people but cannot see their own stuff. These people do not distinguish their issues from other people's issues, and project a lot of their own stuff onto other people and onto the world. People use this defensive maneuver to assist them in not having to deal with their issues. When these people describe their experience of the world or try to tell us about ourselves, they are mostly telling us about themselves.

The other extreme of perceptual dysfunction is when people think everything they experience is their own stuff. They do not distinguish between their issues and other people's issues, but in this case, they incorrectly assume that everything is their issue. These people will be absorbing a lot of other people's energy and projections and will commonly experience depression and a blocking of their energy flow. When these people tell us about themselves, they may be telling us about what is going on around them.

We face a difficult challenge in attaining truthful and meaningful perception. We are having an experience, but what does that experience mean? When we perceive through our issues, beliefs, energy patterns, and other people's energy, it is difficult to perceive in any other way. This severely limits our ability to perceive what is really going on outside our beliefs and energy, and especially to perceive what is going on outside our cultural and species-based patterns.

What is true and real? When we exercise our healing process, we begin to dismantle the fixed structure of our energy. Then we will be able to perceive our own issues as well as what is going on around us. And if we are aware of our own feelings and issues, we can have clearer perception of the world even in the presence of those issues.

With healing, we will achieve greater perceptual clarity and have a more comprehensive context for understanding our perception. For example, rather than simply believing in scarcity or insecurity, clear perception allows us to observe that some people *experience* scarcity or insecurity. We will understand that those experiences are valid and that there are other experiences that are equally valid. We will see that the scarcity and insecurity are *not* in the world. They are in our own energy.

While it is very easy to project our own issues onto other people and onto the world, eventually we have to reclaim our projections and heal them. Furthermore, we have absorbed a great number of projections from others and we will have to separate from them to reclaim our own perception, clarity, and truth. With awareness and healing, we can minimize the problems associated with projections.

Ultimately, with healing, we will be able to determine what is real. Our perception will be free of distortions and we will perceive the truth. Then our actions and responses can be based on clear perception.

EXERCISE: Challenging Your Perception

Regularly spend some time challenging your perception. This is helpful for becoming more aware of your own issues and of the influence your issues have on your experience and on your perception of the world.

When you observe the world around you, ask yourself whether your observations are about the world or whether you are observing something within yourself.

If your observations involve another person, examine whether they relate to the other person or whether they are about you. If they *are* about the other person, are they about his or her programming or are they about the real person, his or her true Self? For instance, if a child appears to be acting immaturely, is that your issue that you are perceiving through, the child's issue, or is it really how the child is?

EXERCISE: Enhancing Perceptual Clarity

Choose an area of your life that you feel strongly about. This could include personal areas of interest, personal concerns, another person, or world events. Then take an honest look at your beliefs and programming around the chosen subject. Do you have any judgment about the person or topic? Are there biases in your beliefs? Are there aspects that you take as factual perceptions that are actually projections, perhaps from past experience?

Make a list of all of your feelings, both positive and negative, about the selected area. Now relax through each of these feelings. You can also just think about the chosen topic and relax through the feeling of the topic itself.

This will heal some of your perceptual distortions and enhance the clarity of your perception. It will also evolve your experience of the chosen topic and allow you to respond differently to it. There may be many layers of feelings associated with the area of your focus, all of which will require healing to completely clarify your perception and ascertain your healthy response to the subject matter. After relaxing through all of the feelings, think about the subject of your process and notice if your response to it is different.

Perhaps you dislike being in high places. Your beliefs may be that they are dangerous and unsafe, and you may have a defensive belief that people should not take risks. Through the exploration of your experience, you may discover feelings of fear, insecurity, distrust, or trauma. By healing these feelings and beliefs, you may begin to perceive that being in high places can be expansive, exciting, and fun! You may enjoy the views and new perspectives.

EXERCISE: *What Does It Mean?*

Spend the day living as though you are a visitor on the planet and that you are trying to discern the *meaning* of everything. What significance do people assign to various behaviors and objects?

What does it mean when people say one thing but do the opposite or act differently? What is really taking place?

Do certain professions or job titles have more validity, importance, or power?

Does having a new car mean prosperity? Does having a big, fancy, expensive car mean status and importance? If someone has money, does that mean he or she is secure?

Does another person's wealth or poverty bring up feelings of insecurity or worthlessness for you? Is it your feeling, the other person's feeling, or your response to the other person?

Does a diamond ring mean love or commitment? Or sometimes ownership?

What "statement" are people making with their clothes and behavior? What do they really mean?

Advertising creates all kinds of associative meanings that do not really exist. Does smoking a cigarette or having a drink mean that you are "cool"? Do the latest styles make you feel better about yourself? Does drinking a particular brand of beer mean that you'll get the guy or girl?

Notice that the meaning attached to everything is often just programming and that the various objects and behaviors may not actually have any inherent meaning.

Intention

When a joke is truly funny, there is no agenda behind it. Then we can laugh at ourselves and at each other and it will be healing. However, if there is an agenda behind the "joke," it ceases to be funny or healing.

We can easily discern when someone is telling a joke with an agenda, even though the person may deny it. We can tell by the way that it *feels*—from the energy *behind* it. When there is an agenda, it will feel like there is a real punch to the "punch line."

The *feeling* behind every activity provides the impetus for that activity and corresponds to our true motivation. The real *intention* of an action or behavior relates to the *feeling* behind it.

While we can be doing any number of things, the *feeling* behind our behavior conveys the real intention or purpose of the thought, words, or activity. Our behavior is only an expression of our intention. Intention is what directs our energy in everything we think, say, and do.

Our true intention is not necessarily related to our façade or conscious intention. In fact, our conscious intention may oppose our true intention. For instance, people may think that they are being helpful when they are actually being selfish. And we may believe that we are being harsh with others when we are actually being supportive of them.

Because our feelings are the impetus for our behavior, they tell us how to be in the world and how to respond to our experiences. Of course, they require healing to align them with our true Self; otherwise, we may simply react out of dysfunction. With healing, our feelings tell us how we truly *want* to respond and be—which is the healed intention of emotion.

Our intention cannot be undone by deeds and cannot be eliminated or counteracted by thoughts. Our intention is always present and can only be transformed through an emotional healing process. Every feeling and emotion that we heal aids in the evolution of our intention, freeing us from having an agenda and acting out dysfunctional feelings.

Although many people are unaware of the feelings behind their actions, those feelings can be brought into consciousness. Then we can use our healing process to evolve our motivation. As we exercise our emotional healing process, awareness of our real intention will expand. With greater awareness, additional healing opportunities will become apparent. By healing everything that we become aware of, we can rectify incongruent aspects of our energy and enhance the alignment of our energy.

Greater alignment allows us to speak and act with increased power and integrity. And when our feelings are aligned with our true Self, we will truly mean what we say and we will do what we truly want to do; we will express the intention of our true Self in our life.

As our awareness expands, we will become more aware of other people's intention. However, we have to be especially wary of our awareness because of the issues just discussed in the previous chapter. In particular, we are used to functioning as our false self, perceiving through our own issues, and projecting those issues onto others. When we have an active issue, it can be very difficult to exercise neutrality and clearly perceive what others are doing. It may take years of healing to gain sufficient clarity to tell the difference between our own issues and other people's issues. Suffice it to say that if we are triggered off, we have an issue going on; and only after we have healed that issue will it be possible to accurately discern other people's issues and intention.

As our perception heals and we gain clarity and neutrality, we will be able to identify other people's intention with greater confidence. However, many people are not aware of their energy and they will not be able to verify our perception. Other people will quickly defend against our awareness and we will have only ourselves to confirm our perception. We face the step in our development of validating our awareness when other people do not want us to perceive what is really going on and when no one else perceives what we perceive.

After we are able to validate our awareness, the next challenge will be to take action based on our perception. This requires a much higher level of validation because we have to be willing to take action on our own. We have to be willing to take action even when other people see things differently or when they disagree with us.

Once we can perceive other people's intention, we will notice when people's words do not match their intention. It will become apparent that people often have a different agenda going on behind their façade. Since intention is the genuine motivation behind everyone's behavior, we will then have a choice about whether to respond to other people's intention or whether to respond to their words and engage with their issues.

Let's say that someone asks for our help but we perceive that their intention is to be a victim and to get someone else to take care of them. If we are "nice" and respond to their façade of wanting help, we validate that their intention of being a victim works to get their needs met. If, instead, we act in response to their intention, we can choose to respond in a manner that does not validate that the person is a victim.

61

It is, of course, quite common for people to ask for assistance and have a healthy intention behind their request. Our perception of other people's intention will allow us to determine the appropriate response to the circumstances.

Several years ago, an acquaintance wanted to sell me a household appliance. He kept going on about the benefits of the product, saying that I would be getting a great deal. However, his energy was screaming at me, "I'm ripping you off! I'm ripping you off!" I confronted him by saying that it felt like a rip-off, which he vociferously denied. However, I listened to his energy and honored my perception of his intent. Later, I found out that he was, in fact, attempting to rip me off.

The mastery of intention requires the development of our awareness and the application of our healing process to our intention. It also involves perceiving the intention of others, validating our perception, and taking action based on that perception. When we have become proficient at these skills, we will finally be living in the *real* world—the world of intention.

On Purpose

While everything *is* energy, intention is what moves and directs our energy in all of our actions and activities. It is the motivation for our behavior and gives meaning to everything we do.

Every component of our energy has its own goals and purposes. Our body, mind, DNA, true Self, and personality each possess and express their own intention. By examining the energy behind our activities, we can perceive the different layers of intention that exist in our energy.

Some physical body intentions are to play, to feel safe, and to obtain nourishment. Our mind might have the intention to understand, to be in charge, to achieve, or to figure everything out. Our personality can have every intention you can imagine, such as being daring, fearful, caring, uncaring, respectful, or abusive. And we can even have contradictory intentions operating at the same time.

Of special importance for our work, if our intention is to get the world to meet our needs, our personality generates goals that take us away from our true Self. In this case, any drive to achieve, to succeed, to validate ourselves, to obtain acceptance, or to find security becomes focused on the world and those around us.

Underneath the motivations of our personality, another level of intention exists that relates to the true Self. The true Self has its own goals that it pursues and seeks to fulfill.

The intention of our true Self requires healing just like every other aspect of our energy. And when healing is accomplished on a true Self level, we will discover the core motivation for our existence. Although everyone has his or her own unique qualities and intention, it also appears that everyone has several goals in common.

Perhaps **the most significant aspiration of the true Self is simply *to be*.** Every aspect of our energy seeks to exist. Every thought, feeling, belief, and creative impulse wants to be experienced and everything about us desires expression. *Being* is everything.

Nothing must be accomplished beyond the *being*. **To have our experience and to be present wherever we are is fulfilling all by itself**. This is true whether we are experiencing something blissful or painful. The true Self is enriched through the *being* and finds its realization through that experience.

Another ambition of the true Self is to become complete. Full maturity and development require that the true Self experiences every aspect of its Self, resolves its issues, and enhances its Self. To attain the fulfillment of its search for its Self and its ultimate expression, the true Self must evolve through experience. Through its development, the true Self is progressing to become more its Self with an eventual outcome of becoming its fully evolved Self.

While at first glance the ambition to *be* and the ambition to *become complete* may appear to be at odds with one another, they are, in fact, intimately related. **Nothing must be accomplished besides *being present* with whatever is occurring in the moment, which is how our true Self evolves to become complete.** Thus, *being* and *becoming complete* go hand in hand.

Fulfilling the ambitions of our true Self requires an active participation in our experience. A passive presence is inadequate for our true Self's purposes. However, wallowing around in our experience does not enrich our true Self either and it is not useful to indulge in our bliss or our pain. Instead, what is desired is a *movement* through our experience.

The presence that is necessary to fulfill our ambitions is exactly what we have been practicing with our healing process. With our healing process, we are actively involved in our experience by *feeling* it, but we are not attached to the experience. We are moving through it, thus *being present* and *evolving* at the same time.

Even though the Self seeks completion, it has endless possibilities to explore. There is potential to be experienced and realized, and its development may never truly be finished. Since no achievement signifies the completion of our journey, it would be wise to embrace the ever-evolving nature of our existence. This should provide added incentive to replace the *hope* of fulfillment at a hypothetical finish line with the *certainty* of fulfillment that results from being present with our journey. By recognizing and focusing on the importance of *being present* with whatever is occurring, everyone can experience fulfillment *now*.

We must be careful not to confuse seeking completion with the desire to avoid our current circumstances. The quest for the finish line can easily be just a defense against underlying issues for those of us who want to get away from the conditions or challenges that we face. Avoiding our current circumstances does not contribute to the evolution of our Self and cannot possibly lead to completion or fulfillment.

Along with our common goals, everyone has their own unique path to explore. The mastery of each quality that is being explored usually requires experiencing every aspect of its possibilities in order to attain fulfillment and completeness.

A client came to see me because he felt a lack of purpose in his life. Nothing seemed to be that significant or meaningful to him. As we explored his experience, it became apparent that the development of a sense of purpose was part of his true Self's journey. He needed to have the full range of experience from purposelessness to purposefulness, and to heal and integrate those experiences in order to master this aspect of his energy. In a way, his purpose was purposelessness! And being present with his experience of purposelessness contributed to the integration of his experiences, resulting in his finding the inherent flow of purpose within his Self. From that time forward, as long as he remained within the flow of his Self, he always felt purposeful with what he was doing, even if he was simply tying his shoes or walking along the street.

If your true Self wants to explore perfection, every possible expression will need to be experienced. This will require the resolution of false concepts of perfection, which may have meant doing everything right or fulfilling others' needs. It will require the integration of experiencing the perfection of being in the flow of your energy as well as the perfection of losing that flow. It will involve having the experience of the perfection of the moment, while your personality is having an experience of being imperfect. By going through and integrating all of its potential variations and nuances, your personality will come back around to really owning its perfection; your true Self enhances its knowledge of perfection and distills its higher meaning. You evolve your perfection and yet you are perfect at the same time. Eventually, with mastery, you will always experience the perfection of being in the flow of your Self.

❋ ❋ ❋

If we view healing from the perspective of our true Self, we can see that its journey is what determines what is and what is not healing. From our true Self's perspective, healing is simply a means of reestablishing and maintaining its flow; healing is a means of assisting our true Self in fulfilling its goals. Since the evolution of our true Self defines the path of healing, the principles of healing will always reflect what facilitates the journey of our true Self.

The journey of our true Self requires being present with our experience. Thus, healing creates a direct and purposeful engagement with everything in our life.

The journey of our true Self involves both *being* and *becoming complete*. By practicing and developing our healing process, we are learning how to allow our experience and evolve through it at the same time.

Our true Self seeks to grow through every aspect of our experience. By participating in our experience in a way that embodies the principles of our healing process, we fulfill the ambitions of our true Self.

Now, about that experience we were looking for...

The Creation of the False Self

O ur true Self is the eternal part of us that is at the core of our energy. Our true Self is the one *having* the experience. The true Self aspires to become complete. Its full development and expression require the resolution of its issues and the evolution of its Self through experience. Thus, the true Self wanted to come into this life to exercise its intention of gaining experience for growth and learning. Those parts of our Self that we have healed and mastered remain part of our conscious remembering. Those areas that we have not healed must be rediscovered and evolved through healing.

For your healing pleasure, we offer a lovely excursion to the Blue Planet. Please read the microscopic writing at the end of the guidebook listing, as there are several peculiarities to keep in mind regarding your worldly experience...

Your non-stop flight to the Blue Planet is about to land. Will all passengers please return to their seats. Make sure that all carry-on items are safely stowed beneath the seat in front of you. Return your tray tables and seat backs to their locked and upright positions. See that your seatbelt is securely fastened and pulled low and snug across your lap. Flight attendants prepare for landing. This could be a little rough.

We landed here on Earth and found a very compelling experience. Immediately upon entering our physical body, we faced the complexities of functioning in the physical world and dealing with our body. There were emotions that flowed through us and around us. There were other people and creatures with whom we interacted. And we had gained a mind with lots of thoughts that often seemed to have a life of their own. All of these were very intense and certainly seemed real. They demanded our constant attention and required training to maintain and operate. The experience was so involving and took so much time and energy that it was easy to forget our true Self and to forget why we came here.

Initially, our body needed others' care to survive and develop. We learned to depend on other people for help and direction. And we often looked to others to know how to be in the world and to know about our Self.

Frequently, however, the people we relied on to show us around the planet and to teach us about our Self did not even know their own true Self. Many of us were brought up by people who could not nurture our true Self because they did not remember their true Self. Often they were enmeshed in their experience and could not help us remember what we were doing here. As a result, many of us became deeply involved in the local drama and ended up participating in and contributing to the group dysfunction.

The true Self, enmeshed in its experience on Earth, developed all kinds of *blocks* that impaired its flow. Many of these blocks developed because few of us had any idea what to do with our feelings, thoughts, or body. We had experiences that we did not know how to heal and integrate. Blocks developed when being our Self did not receive acceptance. Some blocks were created when we could not do what we wanted to do. Other blocks formed when expressing our Self caused problems. Blocks were also born when we could not grow and learn the way we wanted. And feedback from others that it was not okay to feel the way we felt gave rise to additional blocks. Looking at others, seeing that everyone was suppressed and shutdown, gave us the impression that that was normal.

Few people knew how to go through their own blocks and, therefore, only those few could teach us how to go through our blocks. Most people just accepted their blocks as "the way things are." So we amassed a great number of blocks that kept us from being our Self.

Because the blocks did not feel good, we built *defenses* to protect us from constantly feeling the blocks we had been collecting. Some defenses, such as fear and withdrawal, kept us away from people and situations that would make us feel things we did not want to feel. Some defenses, such as denial and blaming our feelings on others, got us away from the feelings we did not like.

The defenses aided in suppressing our blocks, which diminished our awareness of them and made them less palpable. Still, even though our defenses seemed to alleviate the problems caused by our blocks, they did not eliminate them and only temporarily helped us to cope with them.

We also created a *façade* to present to the world. This was what we commonly used to engage with other people. We learned to act in certain ways even if our behavior was at odds with what we really felt. And while our façade was not genuine or functional, it did get us through the day.

As we grew up, we developed many façades and we learned to present a different one to each person with whom we interacted. We tended to emphasize different qualities depending upon the setting in which we found ourselves and the people with whom we were involved. For instance, we may have presented more of a façade of being nice and responsible when we were at work interacting with customers. Since customers usually expect dependability, courtesy, and fulfillment of their needs, we obliged them to develop our business. We responded to our customers' expectations by adjusting our façade to give them what they wanted.

We routinely absorbed other people's energy and lived with it as our own. This *foreign energy* included others' feelings, expectations, concerns, fears, values, beliefs, and programming. It also included how others perceived us and what others thought about us.

We often absorbed people's energy when they thought we were nice, smart, bad, or inept. We accepted the love and care that we wanted from them. We absorbed others' abuse, panic, pain, fear, scarcity, and isolation. And perhaps we took on their expectations that we should be caring or perfect.

We picked up some energy from other people just by *sensing* it in them. Other energy was absorbed when people *directed* it at us. And we took in some energy by *engaging* with others, such as by opening for their input, through sympathy, or by relating with their issues.

If we did not recognize that the energy belonged to others and separate from it, we incorporated it. The energy became "ours" and our body responded to it as if it was our own. As a further complication, once we identified with it, we acted out the energy as if it was who we were.

People around us gave us constant feedback about our personality, behavior, and performance. Certain aspects of our energy received positive or negative reinforcement, while other aspects were ignored. As we grew up and integrated the input from other people, we developed what I call the *false self* or false identity, which is *not* the same as the façade. Whereas the façade is what we show the world, the false self is our idea of who we are—the character traits *with which we identify*. Often there is only a tiny part of the true Self included in our false self.

The false self is composed mostly of a *façade* such as good, loveable, friendly, easy-going, sensitive, and helpful. But it also has other components comprised of *blocks* such as loneliness, rejection, isolation, and failure; *defenses* such as anger, guilt, intellectualization, over-exertion, judgment, and blame; and

Figure 2: Our Energy Structure

other people's energy such as pain, love, validation, caring, and isolation. And this is what we call our self.

Often, when people describe themselves, the false self will dominate their list. Look at the description of yourself from the exercise at the end of the chapter titled "Energy" and see if you can match each descriptor to a part of your energy—façade, defense, block, false self, foreign energy, or true Self. In my experience, when I start working with people, only about 1% of the true Self is included in what they call the self. Please refer to Figure 2 for a visual representation of the structure of our energy.

Part of the feedback and reinforcement that we received from others has been useful in that it has helped us to function in our society and in the world. But mostly we learned to act and behave in specific ways to function within the *dysfunction* of the people and world around us.

A critical feature of the dysfunction to which we have been exposed involves the way most people handle their emotions. When people do not know how to go through their feelings, they engage with others to get relief from their unwanted feelings. And when people do not know how to create the feelings they want, they engage with others to acquire those feelings. These two motivations explain a great deal of human behavior.

If we grew up in an environment in which unwanted emotions were not handled appropriately, we would have felt and absorbed other people's disowned feelings. We often took whatever they had going on into our space, whether it felt good or not. We soaked up our parents' anger and judgment. We took in our siblings' invalidation and competition. Perhaps we absorbed our friends' hurt and pain. And, of course, we took in other people's praise, love, acceptance, and validation as well.

Growing up in an environment in which people tried to obtain energy from others, it seemed normal to take responsibility for other people's expectations and to give them the energy and feelings they desired. Some of us soothed other people by becoming caring and absorbing their discomfort and pain. We may have become nice to make others feel good. Maybe we learned to behave in certain ways so our parents would feel proud and valid. And we became cooperative and helpful by assisting others with their needs.

Sometimes we developed defenses and façades that seemingly protected us from this liability. Perhaps we created a defense of being rebellious to avoid feeling responsible for other people's feelings. Or we created a façade of being tough, arrogant, or independent to avoid certain people.

If other people were not getting their needs met when we were being our Self, we commonly tried to become something *more* than our Self to fulfill them. If our loving and caring did not take care of people's needs, we became more loving and more caring. If our devotion and loyalty did not satisfy others, we became more devoted and more loyal. We learned that we were inadequate as our Self and tried to be more than we were. We lost our Self to become someone else who could better fulfill others.

In the midst of all of this, we had our own emotional and energy needs and we were doing whatever we could to get those needs met. Perhaps we learned to be nice or kind so that we received acceptance and validation. Maybe we learned to get angry or to control others to get what we wanted. Or we learned to be wild or sexy to get some attention and recognition.

We opened our energy to other people, looking for the feelings we wanted and needed. Sometimes we even actively pulled others' energy into our space to get the feelings that we lacked. We mostly did not care that we were gathering or scavenging other people's energy. We just knew that we had a need and wanted to fill it.

We also had our own feelings that we did not know how to go through. Wanting to get away from our negative feelings, we expected other people to take them on just as we had taken on their feelings. We often directed our feelings at others and even may have developed abusive behavior to dump our issues on them.

Because the feelings we wanted were outside ourselves, we often developed control strategies to keep a steady flow of those feelings coming our way. And because we perceived the causes of our negative feelings to be outside ourselves, we learned to control our environment to minimize undesirable feelings.

Despite all of our efforts to control our environment, the world around us ended up controlling us. Our false self was at the mercy of what happened outside of us because our blocks and issues made us vulnerable to external control or attack— we could be triggered by anyone or anything at any time. And those who wanted to train or program us could use our issues against us.

Outside forces often continue to exert considerable control over us by manipulating our issues and programming. The threat of rejection, embarrassment, pain, or divorce affects our decisions. The risk of being fired, receiving a bad review, or being judged is a strong motivator. Our own fears, insecurities, scarcity, powerlessness, and helplessness induce us to do extraordinary things to avoid them. And the possibility of love, power, security, validation, acceptance, or prosperity inspires all kinds of behavior that is focused on the outer world at the expense of our true Self.

We crafted our false self to cope with the energetic conditions of our family and society. It was formed in response to having energy needs in an environment that, under the pressures of everyone's emotions, tended to take us away from our Self. It was formed to facilitate participation in a huge energy trading system, to take us through each and every day exchanging energy with others. As our false self developed, we learned to take responsibility for others' feelings while expecting others to take responsibility for our feelings. And significant portions of our false self came into existence solely because we identified with some of our own issues and the energy and issues that we had absorbed from others.

Defenses helped to maintain our false self, seeking to stabilize our experience in an unpredictable environment and on a tossing sea of energy. Some defenses sought to mitigate disasters, while other defenses were more actively employed in managing the world around us to minimize possible threats. Patterns of control evolved to sustain our false self and to attempt to fulfill our needs. This all seemed supportive even though our *false* self did not serve our *true* Self. At least our false self was familiar, "comfortable," and somewhat consistent, if not truly functional.

The preservation of our false self turned into a full-time job with low pay, no vacations, and few benefits. All of the activity involved with suppressing our feelings, keeping the defenses well nourished, taking responsibility for others' feelings, getting our needs met by other people, and holding our façade and false self up all day long consumed an enormous amount of time and energy. No wonder a day on the planet can be so tiring! How do people have any energy left for playing?

Furthermore, since we are pretending to be someone we're not and are constantly trying to get our needs met from others, is it surprising that relationships can be so challenging?

Thus, identifying with the false self just does not work. The false self is not in control of anything and needs constant maintenance to sustain it. It is weak, rigid, unstable, and untenable. Yet many of us work like crazy to defend the false self and keep it intact. It is not who we truly are, it is not functional, and it is not fulfilling. Yet many would rather die than change.

The false self has gotten so much practice that it has become an essentially permanent structure. We wake up and jump into it, live in it all day long and perhaps set it aside only when we are asleep. However, during our waking life, it is typically unchanging and enduring. It is so *constant* that it seems real; it seems like it is who we are.

The false self is so resilient and so resistant to change that even after being repeatedly tested and triggered off, it snaps back into shape quickly and quite easily. It perseveres through thick and thin. It persists through an onslaught of constant challenges. It is so *durable* that it seems real; it seems like it is who we are. And if we do not heal, this is what we are left with to negotiate the days of our life.

EXERCISE: *Healing the Loss of Your Self*

One intention of this chapter is to arouse the feelings of losing your Self, if any of those feelings are present. If it elicited *any* response from you, it would be wise to put the book aside and heal every feeling that came up.

Does this chapter bring up feelings of pain, sadness, or loss? Do you feel like you gave up having fun or pleasure to participate in your life? Or are you resisting, denying, or arguing with this discussion?

Even if this chapter appears to bear no resemblance to your history, if there is any resistance or issue that arose, you have something to heal. By healing these issues, you will greatly assist in reclaiming your true Self. Since nothing is more vital than healing the feeling of losing your Self, this exercise is probably the most important exercise in the entire book.

EXERCISE: Exploring Aspects of Your Energy

Using the diagram in Figure 2 as a model, examine how the different aspects of your energy participated in your life recently.

What parts of your energy were involved in your activities?

What parts engaged with the people with whom you interacted?

Did your façade adjust to each person with whom you interacted? How did it adjust?

Can you feel how much energy it took to maintain your façade and false self?

Did you notice any defenses? What was your primary defense?

What conditions were present when you were growing up that nurtured the development of your façade, false self, and defenses?

Finding Your Way Home

The journey home to your true Self is fraught with great peril and many hidden dangers. It is obstructed by numerous obstacles, obscured by many illusions, and crossed by countless false paths.

The first difficulty is, of course, even considering that there might be some part of your energy that is more real than the part that you call yourself. Having a strong sense of identity can easily conceal the reality that you have been your false self for a very long time and fool you into believing that you know your true Self. How is it possible that you could have forgotten who you really are and become someone else?

However, as I have already discussed, it is very easy and quite common to confuse your true Self with your experience. In addition, I brought up the idea that it may be valuable to lose your Self in order to explore an experience that ultimately enhances your Self.

In addition, this issue may be easier to consider once you acknowledge that you experienced enormous pressures from everyone around you while you were growing up. The forces to which you were exposed pushed you towards a place in which *other people* wanted you to exist. To the extent that you absorbed those expectations and responded to those forces, you developed a façade and false self, which then became the most familiar parts of your energy.

Fortunately, this obstacle is not so difficult to perceive once you begin your healing process. When you begin to heal and watch aspects of yourself drop away, never to return, it becomes apparent that you are not who you thought you were. Thus, to verify for yourself that you have to embark on a healing journey to discover your true Self, all you have to do is begin the healing process detailed in this book. Once you go through just one feeling and see your reality change, you will realize that everything is not as it seems.

Once you have begun the journey home, the next difficulty that will arise is how to recognize your true Self. After all, for many people, the true Self did not receive nurturing, encouragement, or support when they were growing up. Since the true Self has rarely been acknowledged by others and may have actually gotten you into trouble, it is not usually a comfortable place to exist. In fact, if you experienced punishment, shame, pain, humiliation, or embarrassment for being your true Self, it may actually be one of the most uncomfortable places in your energy. In addition, if no one connected with you when you were being your true Self, it would have been very easy to feel alone, uncared for, and depressed being your true Self. Then there would have been even more incentive to become someone else in order to connect with other people.

As a result, an essential goal of healing is to resolve the issues that exist around being your true Self. Whatever is uncomfortable about your true Self must be resolved so that you make your true Self the *most* comfortable place in your energy. Then your healing process will be much more successful: it will be harder to lose your Self when you are triggered off, it will be easier to find your Self again after you are triggered off, and you will be more likely to find your way back to your true Self *on your own*. Furthermore, it will be easier to be your Self more of the time. But you must heal every issue around being your true Self to enjoy all the comforts of home.

EXERCISE: *Letting Go of Your False Self*

If you feel threatened or fearful even considering that your identity may be your false self, it would be appropriate to heal feeling insecure, fearful, and lost. Remember that your false self became the most secure, stable, and comfortable place to be as you grew up in this world and, therefore, feelings of insecurity, discomfort, and instability are expected to arise as you move away from your false self.

EXERCISE: *Aspects of Your Energy*

Contrast true Self qualities and feelings with personality, body, and mind aspects of your energy. Say "My true Self accepts its success" and contrast that with "My body accepts its success," "I accept my success," and "My mind accepts its success." While the differences may be subtle, try to discern the various parts of your energy. You may need to practice and enhance your ability to relax in order to move to your true Self and other parts of your energy.

Which aspect of your energy is the easiest to feel? Which is the most difficult to recognize? Which aspect is the most comfortable?

Once you begin to recognize your true Self, you will want to pay particular attention to anything that is uncomfortable about being your Self. Do you feel aloneness, depression, guilt, or pain when you are being your Self? Heal every issue that arises.

❈　❈　❈

Many people believe that they are experiencing their true Self when they are feeling good. However, feeling better or good does not mean that you have found your true Self. From the perspective of your false self, you will feel better when you are *not* feeling your issues. You will feel better when a defense rescues you from your blocks. And prior to developing a healing process, it will feel good to get back to your false self, often a familiar though not totally satisfying place.

It is even possible to feel better by partially healing a block and not reaching your true Self. If you start to relax through a feeling but do not let it go, you will land back at your false self. Some ease and comfort will be present on your return to your false self because a portion of the energy will no longer be present to irritate you or get your attention. And you will be better off because you have accomplished some healing; however, you must *let go* of the entire pattern to arrive at your true Self.

Thus, feeling better and feeling good are not the best indications that healing has occurred or that you have found your true Self. Therefore, you will not want to be attached to these feelings. The trick is to go through your issues and feel better because you have reconnected with your true Self.

An important clue for knowing that you have arrived at your true Self relates to the flow of your energy after your healing work. With successful healing, your focus will shift from *outside* your Self to *inside* and your energy will flow inward and through you.

Feelings of fulfillment and contentment accompany this inward flow of energy. These feelings are not the result of anything occurring in the outer world, but originate within your Self; they are a natural by-product of your healing.

You will also have extra energy but not the need to do anything with it. It will be within you—nothing will have to happen in the world. The energy that was entangled in the issue will be freed up for other uses. And when you do express your Self in the world, it will be because your energy is moving *through* you, not outwards and away from you.

Anytime you feel your energy move outwards, you are moving away from your Self. If, after performing your healing process, your energy is flowing outward, you have not completed your work. You may have gone through some of your feelings but not let them go. You are using a defense to get away from an issue and have not gone entirely through the block. There will be a feeling of moving outward towards the false self and, perhaps, an energized feeling with which to take action in the world. This is the same sensation as when you are avoiding or defending against a feeling.

If, for instance, after "healing," you immediately have to talk to a friend about it or resolve a relationship problem, the issue is not healed. With true healing, the issue is over. There is a letting go, an inner peace. And you will not feel that anything has to be done.

If you look at Figure 2 on page 72, you can see this movement graphically. If, after relaxing through a block, you do not let go of the pattern, you will move outward towards the false self or to something outside your Self. This, of course, is what creates the feeling of your energy moving outward.

Alternatively, if you let go of the pattern after relaxing though a block, you will move towards your true Self, which creates an inward flow of energy. With practice, you will be able to discern this aspect of your energy and know when you have arrived at your true Self.

EXERCISE: Feeling Your Energy Flow

Pay attention to your energy when you interact with other people. What is the intention behind your interactions? Are you trying to get away from a feeling? Or are you reaching out for something?

Feel the *flow* of your energy. Do you feel your energy moving away from you? Or, is your energy flowing *through* you when you interact with others? Can you feel the difference when you stay centered within your Self?

Now look at what your energy does when you are involved in your daily activities. Does your energy move through you or away from you? Are there certain activities that take you closer to or further away from your Self?

The Intention to Heal

M any people *want* to heal; in my experience, however, few actually *intend* to heal. The difference lies in *how* people deal with their life experiences.

When you act to defend your feelings, go outside yourself to fulfill your needs, or project your issues out onto the world, you do *not* have the *intention to heal*.

Having the intention to heal means that the energy behind what you do is focused on moving through whatever issues arise—on healing everything that comes your way and on finding fulfillment within your Self. When you move through an experience or a feeling and fulfill your own energy needs, you shift your identity to your true Self.

An outward movement of energy characterizes the emotional life of the false self, whereas an inward movement of energy characterizes healing. For the false self, the outward flow of energy is created both when you attempt to get away from an undesirable feeling and when you go outside your Self to acquire a feeling you desire. The inward movement experienced with healing is created both by successfully going through a feeling and by looking within for the feelings you desire.

By paying attention to your energy during your healing process, you can discern whether your energy is moving inward or outward. If it is moving outward, you are moving away from your true Self and do not have the intention to heal. If it is moving inward, you are moving towards your true Self and have the intention to heal.

Truly, there is only healing *or* not healing; there is nothing in between. There is no part-time or occasional healing. There is no sort-of healing. Either you have the intention to heal or you don't. Either you go through your own feelings and heal them or you don't. Either you find the source of your energy within your Self or you don't.

Now, having the intention to heal does not mean that you are finished with your work or that you do not have anything going on. It just means that you are traversing your path and that you are willing to heal whatever arises. There may always be issues that require your attention and healing.

And having the intention to heal does not mean that you handle your issues instantly, as it may take time to exercise the intention to heal and apply it to your life. It only means that you eventually find your way along the path to your healing.

And, of course, having the intention to heal does not mean that you handle every challenge perfectly. It just means that your process continues to direct you towards your true Self while you learn.

Because having the intention to heal leads you along a path to your Self, it can be trusted to give truly beneficial assistance and clear direction. The intention to heal can be applied to everything in your life, guiding you to your Self. It can direct your every action and show you how to be in the world and with each other.

Only by being true to your Self can you create what you truly desire. **Only by being true to your Self can you find fulfillment**. How can it be otherwise? How could you possibly create what you want by *not* being true to your Self?

All you have to do to be your Self is to walk the path that unfolds and heal everything that arises. You do not need to make anything happen. Nor do you want to resist what is happening.

It may be difficult to imagine that everything in your life will work out, but that is exactly what happens when you live with the intention to heal. Truly, only through healing will you prove the validity of this statement. Every time you heal an issue, you will demonstrate its truth.

If it is challenging to trust that everything will work out, healing fears or doubts and developing the feeling of Self-trust are the next steps along your path of healing. If dealing with change is difficult, making peace with change and healing any fears around letting go are your next issues to heal.

With whatever comes up, the intention to heal directs you towards your Self. By choosing to live the path of healing, you heal everything you are aware of, everything that comes your way. Every issue, every block, every challenge is a step along your path. Each step shows you what you have to heal to continue your journey and live in the highest possible light.

Without the intention to heal, when you are triggered off, your defenses become active to "help" you get away from your undesirable feelings. With the intention to heal, you allow your issues to bubble up, seeing them as an opportunity to evolve rather than as a nuisance. In time, you may even begin to enjoy being triggered off because it means you can create movement within your energy where it was previously stuck.

Without the intention to heal, when someone wants your energy, you may try to avoid the person, start battling over the energy, or take the "easy" path by giving the person what they want but feel drained afterwards. With the intention to heal, you will evolve how you engage with this person, challenging yourself to evolve how you assert your Self in the face of other people's demands and expectations.

The intention to heal can be impaired in relation to any aspect of healing. You require the intention to heal in order to remember your true Self, to identify with it, to heal your true

Self, and to bring it into your life. Of course, when you are learning about these goals, having the intention to heal simply involves the willingness to move towards these objectives. And in relation to a professional healing practice, the intention to heal means that a client allows their healer to assist them in finding the source within themselves.

One of my patients kept trying to get me to explain things to her. However, no matter what I said, she would reply with some variation of "I don't understand." Her intention was not to heal, but to involve me in her life through her not understanding. She wanted my energy, not my assistance with her healing. Having the intention to heal involves wanting to fulfill your energy needs from within your Self.

One of my friends was always working on his "healing." He never did anything with it, but he was always "healing." Nothing in his life was going the way he wanted: His work was not fulfilling, he had no relationships whatsoever, and he derived no real pleasure from his life. He was using "healing" as a defense to avoid his life and did not have the intention to heal. Having the intention to heal involves bringing your true Self *into* your life, not avoiding your life.

One very capable young woman had a life that seemed to be working perfectly. Successful and respected at work, home, and with peers, she had no reason to pursue healing. Yet, she knew that something was missing. And once she became aware of what to do about it, her intention to heal carried her through to change her entire life experience so that it reflected her true Self. She still has the same job and many of the same people in her life, only now she has her Self as well.

A very important aspect of personal growth involves developing greater awareness of your own and other people's intention. You can use your awareness of the intention to heal to perceive and understand other people's goals and to guide you in how to respond to them.

If people do *not* have the intention to heal, their energy and their actions will be directed at getting their needs met outside their true Self. They will seek to avoid their own issues and direct their issues at other people. They will seek to control others so that the energy they want is available, predictable, and more constant. Whether such a person is conscious of his or her manipulations or not, their intention is the same. They are still controlling and are not aligned with the intention to heal.

The intention behind others' behavior will clearly show you what is really going on with them and clarify what potential exists in those relationships. If you have the intention to heal and the other person does not, the relationship can only go so far. The difference in intention creates a limitation on how close the connection can be. Your behavior will be focused on finding energy within your Self to fulfill your needs, while the other person will be focused on fulfilling their needs through others. You will only be able to walk so far with them.

If, on the other hand, the energy behind what other people are doing is aligned with the intention to heal, you can continue to move through life with them. In this case, the possibility for connection and understanding will be profound.

Practitioners of the healing arts are usually classified according to their academic degrees, specialties, and methods. And it is common to hear discussions about the merits of various healing techniques and practices.

But truly, there is no such thing as a healing *technique* because it is the intention or energy behind the technique, especially the practitioner's intention, that determines whether it is healing or not. I might use a particular technique and achieve healing while someone else may do the same activity and achieve nothing. I have seen many people who were supposedly involved in a "healing practice" achieve little or nothing because the intention behind their practice was to *avoid* healing.

Although one could argue that the emotional process discussed in this book is a healing technique, I see it as an expression of the intention to heal. Thus, what is desirable is the development of the intention to heal for use with whatever technique a practitioner wishes to use. Almost any approach becomes healing when the practitioner is aligned with the intention to heal—when the approach assists clients in moving through their blocks and fulfilling their own energy needs. Of course, certain techniques, by definition, go in the opposite direction of healing. If a technique involves looking for energy, answers, or purpose outside yourself, it cannot be used to assist with your healing.

Everyone can heal and develop their intention to heal. This is directly attainable through the mastery of your emotional process. Practicing the steps outlined in this book will assist in the development of your intention to heal, which you can then apply to every aspect of your life to point the way to health and wholeness.

The intention to heal gives you something concrete to stand on because once you have healed an issue, what is left is the truth. Once it is known, that truth can support the full weight of your life; it creates a solid foundation for all of your decisions and actions.

Significantly, this foundation is not static but moves with you. Because you move forward when you are truly functional, your inner foundation moves forward as well.

With every issue you heal, the intention to heal assists in discovering and strengthening the ultimate truth at the core of your energy: your true Self. Mastery of the intention to heal is all that is necessary to attain the full realization of your true Self.

❋　❋　❋

It is common to have the false self as the reference point for the goals you wish to accomplish. With the false self as your point of reference, it is very easy to use any discussion about healing to maintain your dysfunction. Without the intention to heal, all of your activities support the way things are and "healing" becomes a means of preserving the false self. Perhaps you get a new look or façade by adding another layer to your energy, but no real change occurs.

Since these words can be used to support your false self, it is important to use this material to move *inward* towards the true Self, not *outward* towards the false self. This must be kept in mind when reading and digesting these words and concepts. Without the intention to heal, it is quite easy just to develop a new façade with which to engage other people in novel yet wonderfully dysfunctional ways.

The intention to heal is essential for directing your efforts towards the evolution and expression of your true Self, rather than towards functioning more comfortably with your issues or with your false self. Only now that you have established the appropriate context by discussing the concept of the intention to heal are you ready to explore the benefits and goals of healing with a reduced risk of simply building a better façade.

Why Heal?

Healing has so many benefits that I hope you will be inspired to make healing an integral part of your life. It will affect everything from your sense of Self, purpose, fulfillment, and happiness, to your health and relationships. It will give you true Self control, power, and responsibility. And with healing, you will claim the freedom to create whatever your true Self desires.

An examination of your daily activities, thoughts, and behavior will reveal that emotion is the impetus behind everything you do. Whether you are motivated by curiosity or love or the avoidance of pain or insecurity, the motivation is emotional. The actions you take and your responses to the situations you encounter have an emotional basis.

Without healing, there are two general categories of motivation for your activities—one is the avoidance of feelings that you do not like and the other is the drive to experience those feelings that you desire. When you operate from dysfunctional emotions and needs, your responses do not reflect your true Self. **With healing, you can move beyond the push and pull of your issues and function from the motivation of your true Self.**

Everyone has aspects of their energy that need development to reflect who they really are. The emotions that became blocked or disowned as you grew up require healing and growth to bring them into alignment with your true Self. With healing, you take less advanced aspects of yourself and evolve them to a more mature energy. You are, in effect, parenting yourself, raising your inner child.

Through healing, you learn to take responsibility for your Self. You realize that you can let go of the feelings and experiences you don't want by healing the feelings that don't feel good. You discover that you can create the experiences you desire and generate the feelings you want for yourself. And you find out how to depend on your Self for your healing instead of depending on others. Thus, healing is very empowering as *you* are now the one who is accountable to your Self. If events are not developing as you wish, you have the power to change them through healing.

Healing also empowers you to take back control in your life. You are no longer at the mercy of external forces that can manipulate you through your issues. When you are triggered off, you can use it as an opportunity to heal and thereby both improve your health and well-being and reclaim control of your actions and reactions. You no longer have to react to being triggered off.

When you heal, you no longer have to do anything to create the feelings you desire. You can cultivate those feelings and then they flow through you. If you cultivate the feeling of success, you do not have to do anything to feel successful. It flows through you and you express the success that you have inside you. The same experience can be achieved with any feeling, such as fulfillment: You are fulfilled and everything you do expresses your fulfillment.

Through healing, you can reclaim your health and vitality, which are the natural result of your true Self's energy flowing through you. Often, disease and dysfunction are the direct result of the obstruction or distortion of this life-force energy. Healing removes these blocks and restores the flow of your energy through your life and through your physical body.

Healing physical problems requires the release of every energetic pattern associated with them, as well as bringing the true Self more fully into your body. While this is not necessarily easy and may involve the resolution of many issues on many levels of energy, your emotional healing skills will enable you to evolve through physical illness, dysfunction, and disease.

Healing assists in the development of perception. With healing, you gain clarity about what your issues are and who you really are—your true Self. You become more cognizant of the motivations of your true Self and, therefore, can make better choices—decisions that will be much more fulfilling and satisfying because they reflect more of who you really are.

Mastery of your emotional process also brings clarity and neutrality to your relations with others. Learning to deal with your own emotions and feelings makes it much easier to recognize the difference between your energy and other people's energy. Your clarity will allow you to discern what is you and what is *not* you. You will be less likely to become enmeshed with another's feelings, you will know more about what is going on in the world and with other people, and you will know more about other people's motivation. As a result, it will be easier to respond appropriately to the circumstances you encounter.

Healing presents a completely different option for how to deal with life's circumstances. If, for instance, you use negotiation, force, or fighting as your approach for creating "change," there cannot be any true conflict resolution. The underlying feelings do not just go away, nor can you talk or fight your way out of them.

Without healing, peace negotiations will never result in peace, communication in relationships will never create harmony, and working for a living will never create security, prosperity, wealth, or fulfillment. Without healing, all you have is unrealized potential. Only through healing can you experience all of these possibilities and more. Only through healing, do you introduce a real solution that can create true cooperation and peace.

Some people say, "It's hard to heal!" However, if you do not heal, you replay and re-experience the same issues repeatedly, usually with the same results. It is painful, difficult, and unfulfilling *not* to heal. When you are *not* in the flow of your Self, life is not easy or fun!

Healing is much easier than not healing. It takes less effort and it is more natural to be in the flow of your Self than to be swimming against the current, fighting the flow. It just seems harder to heal because it is different from what you have learned to do. In addition, it does require developing your awareness, and learning and practicing new skills to forge a new way of being. Nevertheless, healing is a much less complicated and less problematic path to follow than the path of not healing.

Some have voiced their concern that this process will deprive them of their feelings. However, while healing clears up any dysfunctional motivation, it does not diminish your ability to feel, nor does it eliminate your true feelings. It actually enhances your ability to feel while resolving your issues so that you no longer have dysfunctional feelings and emotions.

Through healing, you can experience your true Self more of the time. And, eventually, your true Self can be constantly and consciously present in your life. The result is that you get to be your Self—to express who you are, to speak your truth, to interact as your Self, and to create what you truly want.

With healing, you know more about what you really feel and what you really want to do. You know what your life purpose is and that you have nothing to defend. You remember and express the Self within and all that comprises your Self: the joy, the wisdom, the enthusiasm, the peace, the power, the purpose. The possibilities that are available to you through healing are essentially unlimited. Anything that you want to create, anything that you want to experience is possible.

But even with all the practical reasons to heal, perhaps the best reason to heal is that it is so much *fun*! There is so much to discover and there are so many aspects of energy to experience. You can always find something exciting to explore. **Being in the flow of your true Self is the most fun you can have in your body!**

EXERCISE: Discerning Your Motivation

Make a list of your daily activities. On your list, you can put everything from working, exercising, and brushing your teeth to cleaning your home and talking with friends. Then see if you can identify the emotional motivation behind your activities.

Are you looking for success or validation at work? Or perhaps just trying to pay the bills and avoid the feelings of insecurity and not having money? Are you looking for love in a relationship or trying to get away from a feeling of loneliness? Are you eating food for nourishment, for comfort, or to avoid the feelings of emptiness or hunger? Do you do physical exercise to validate yourself, to feel better about yourself, or just for the joy of it? Or do you exercise to get away from the feeling of being overweight or weak? Do you avoid exercise because you do not want to feel your body or you do not want others to see you?

You can peruse the lists of emotions in the *Appendix* at the back of the book to explore some of your possible motivations.

The Problem with Healing

People's first response to the idea of healing is often, "Who wouldn't want to heal?" However, it is not that simple because if you heal, your life is going to change. You cannot heal an issue and have your life go on as if nothing has happened. If your activities have been based on dysfunction and you heal the dysfunction, you are not going to be able to live the same way any longer. This may require changes in your lifestyle, employment, relationships, or recreation. And that is not always attractive or easy.

Some of the changes that result from healing will be gentle and will take relatively little effort to integrate into your life. If you are used to making things happen, healing may show you how to allow your life to unfold without force. If you are used to pursuing your goals with single-minded focus, healing may show you that you have to listen to every part of yourself. You will no longer be able to ignore those parts of your energy and experience that you used to disregard.

Some changes facilitated by healing may not be as simple to assimilate into your life. If, for instance, you are used to taking care of people emotionally in your friendships and relationships and you heal that quality, your relationships will change. Or perhaps your career path developed to please someone else. With healing, you will find your Self—and your path and your life will change.

Many people come to healing with a personal agenda—goals about where they expect healing to take them. However, you may come into healing with one idea of where you are going and leave with a different one. You may have to let go of your expectations and goals to embrace whatever direction your energy wants to take. Healing may show you that you are traveling along a different road.

Since healing evolves your intention, you can expect your motivation and interests to change with healing. Some activities that were previously enjoyable may no longer hold your interest. Or perhaps you have been using your energy to participate in certain activities in order to fulfill your needs. If healing helps you fulfill those needs from within, you may not have the energy or desire to perform those activities any more. While this may be disconcerting, in time, new motivation and interests will surface that will engage more of your energy and enthusiasm than ever before.

When people are healing, it is common for them to experience periods of either reduced or augmented physical energy while their body and energy reorient themselves to a different focus and a different motivation. Once you heal an issue, it may take some time to integrate the energetic changes and for your deeper inspiration to reveal itself. As you evolve, you can anticipate energy fluctuations as the old motivations drop away and your true Self asserts its Self. Eventually, you will have more energy and passion for what you really want to do.

Although you can surround yourself with friends and relationships and keep yourself busy with a myriad of activities, healing makes it clear that you live a solitary life. That does not mean that your life has to be lonely. Feelings of loneliness and isolation are the result of experiencing a separation from your true Self and, therefore, can be healed. Nonetheless, your life is solitary because no one can live your life for you.

Healing itself is a solitary journey since no one can go through your feelings for you. You cannot avoid your blocks or issues. You cannot figure a way out of your feelings, work them out, or talk through them with someone else. When all of the talking and figuring is over, you are still left with your feelings to be felt and healed. Thus, even though there may be many with whom you share your life, you are the only one who can heal and live your life for your Self.

With healing, you will be less willing to connect with other people through dysfunction. If those around you do not heal their issues, the nature of the connection will necessarily change. Therefore, healing and making changes may also require healing the feelings of loss and isolation. However, as you heal and connect more fully with your Self, the feelings of isolation will disappear and be replaced by the excitement and fulfillment of being your Self. As you heal, you are creating new possibilities for connecting in ways that will be more fulfilling and will allow you to be more of who you really are.

Many people, when they read or hear these statements, believe they *have* to be alone or isolated to heal. Instead, these false beliefs are what require healing. Since one of the goals of healing is to be *more* fully involved in life, not less, you want to learn to heal and be present in your life simultaneously. In addition, the more you are your true Self, the more there is to bring into your life.

Another facet of healing is that it is a lifelong process. It does not happen in a few weeks or months. There is no quick fix. While every issue you heal enhances your health and well-being, healing is an entirely different way of relating to your life that necessitates a more profound transformation. You must be prepared for a lifetime of exploration, discovery, and commitment to your discipline. Healing will become a way of life and, truly, a healthy way of living.

Once you experience healing and the understanding, joy, vitality, and freedom that it brings, it is difficult to discontinue healing. Your life will *show* you when you are not healing.

Once you experience being in the flow of your true Self, it is difficult and painful to stop that flow. You will *feel* when you are not healing.

Thus, once you embark on the path of healing, there really is no choice—there is only healing.

And while the path of healing, being a path to the true Self, is worth following to the very end, you have to be *willing* to let go of everything on this path. It takes courage to be willing to let go and to heal what that brings up for you, such as loss, fear, or loneliness. It takes courage to let go of one way of being for another way that is not yet familiar. Nonetheless, all that is involved is a natural evolution. Although it may not initially seem true, you actually gain something while only losing an old way of being. This is the gift and the price of healing.

What Isn't Healing?

Anything that takes you away from your true Self or creates a blockage to the flow of your true Self is the opposite of healing. If you try to avoid your issues or look outside your Self to fulfill your needs, you are not healing. And anytime you direct your issues at others, you are moving in a direction that opposes healing.

There is a common illusion that you can actually get feelings, such as love or acceptance, from other people. However, going outside your Self for feelings does not work for a number of reasons.

First, you cannot run someone else's energy in your space. Everyone has his or her own individual and unique energy that flows through them and fulfills them. Thus, while it may feel good initially to feel someone else's "love" in your space, eventually it will not feel good because it is not your own energy.

In addition, getting a feeling from another person can only be a temporary experience. It depends on the emotional state of the other person. That energy is not your own and can change or disappear at any time.

Another problem can develop when the source of your energy is outside your Self: You may attempt to control that source to make sure you have a steady supply of energy. This can give rise to arguments and struggles in your relations with others as people battle over control of one another.

Since other people cannot function effectively with your energy either, trying to fulfill others' needs is not healing.

You cannot *give* your energy, knowledge, or love to others. All you can really do is *be* your Self. You can *be* love. And you can *be* loving by healing the blocks within yourself and being in the flow of that love. Then everything you do is an expression of love and is truly loving to others, even if other people are not getting what they want or do not understand your love.

Going outside your Self for anything—such as healing, power, knowledge, enlightenment, spirituality, or worth—takes you away from your Self. These qualities are *not* outside your Self.

Seeing a physician or therapist to get a dose of energy, caring, or attention is not healing. No outside energy can substitute for your own energy. Healing is not about going outside your Self for energy; it is about finding the energy *within*.

Because healing is something you must accomplish within your Self, a true healer shows you how to heal yourself, teaching you to find your healing within. A true healer will *not* donate his or her own energy to fulfill your needs. Nor will a true healer bring foreign energy into your space.

You do not have to have a relationship to experience love. You do not need a teacher to obtain knowledge. And you do not need a religious figure as an intermediary to have a connection with God or spirit. Even though other people in your life may guide you to these experiences, the love, knowledge, and connection with spirit are *within* you.

Many popular approaches to "healing" are just ways to cope with problems. Since *managing* a condition only assists people in functioning *with* their dysfunction, these approaches are ineffective for real healing. While management will always have an important role in health care, it does not change the underlying causes of people's health issues, which require healing to be resolved.

If I smoke cigarettes or eat junk food to deal with emotional issues, changing my habits may be beneficial for my health, but the underlying issues will require emotional healing to resolve the real cause of my habits. If I smoke or eat to soothe, love, or nurture myself, I still need to learn to find those feelings within my Self and not just go seek them somewhere else. Likewise, if I eat or smoke to cover up feelings, I still must relax through those underlying feelings and heal them to resolve the issues.

Healing is not *only* about getting over an illness. Even if you alleviate pain through drugs, surgery, massage, spinal manipulation, or acupuncture, you still have to clear up any related issues to accomplish healing. You have to resolve all of the energetic issues associated with an illness in order to heal it.

Many turn to "healing" in an attempt to get away from their pain and depression. This creates an inherent problem in that true healing does not take you *away* from your feelings. Instead, healing takes you into them and through them. There is no way around your feelings and your true Self is waiting on the other side of your issues. Either you integrate them now or you are waiting to integrate them later. Not healing simply means that you are delaying your process.

If you do not master emotional healing, it is very easy to become involved in other people's issues and to project your issues onto others. This complicates and delays your healing and that of others. Getting energetically involved with others through dysfunctional issues is the opposite of healing.

As healers, if we do not master emotional healing, it is very easy to misuse our energy skills. Becoming entangled with other people's issues and projecting our own issues onto others have ramifications that are more significant in a healing setting. And, if we use our energy skills to take others away from the challenges they face, we impair their healing and possibly compound their original problems.

It is common to use the mind to avoid healing. You may use your mind to talk yourself out of your issues, such as by saying to yourself, "I'm really a good person. Look at all of the good things I've done," when you are actually feeling bad about something. It is also common to project issues onto others through arguments, through a third party (triangulating), or through a strategy to avoid a feeling, such as figuring out how to blame someone else for your feelings.

Every time a disaster occurs in the world, people attempt to make sense of what happened and often try to determine who or what is to blame. There is the illusion that if they can learn from the experience and change something, they (or someone) will avoid this experience in the future and not have to feel the way they do now. The real purpose of this activity is solely to get away from the feelings that have been activated. Or else, as a slight variation, people are projecting their current feelings into the future and trying to avoid them at a later date. Their energy is focused on getting away from and keeping away from their issues, instead of feeling their pain or loss and healing it.

Once they establish who is to blame, they can then direct their unprocessed emotions at the guilty party. They may even be able to get others to agree with them and add their energy to making the perceived culprit into the problem. People can try to force the "problem" person to take on their issues and carry their unprocessed emotions.

Then there is the difficulty of a media-induced sharing of emotions in which many people are exposed to feelings that are not their own. This gives the illusion of being helpful when all it does is distort, delay, distract, and increase the difficulty of healing. The dissemination of unhealed emotion does nothing to assist those people who are the subjects of the media presentation in the healing of their issues. Furthermore, it can instantly increase the emotional burden for the people participating in the media experience as observers. This occurs both through the increased quantity of unprocessed emotion triggered off in any observers and through the absorption of foreign energy by those observers.

There is also the response from those observers who are now triggered off, projecting their issues back at the people who were directly involved in the incident. It is common to put ourselves in other people's shoes (Watch out for the fungus and cramped toes!) to imagine what we would be feeling and then to direct our imagined feelings at those involved in the actual event. I have assisted many people in the resolution of their own issues when someone close to them dies, only to watch as they were buried under a deluge of other people's projected pain and grief.

Much time and energy go into evading feelings when it would take just a tiny fraction of that time and energy to heal. Strategies to avoid feelings confuse the issues and can even become social events to feed dysfunctional patterns!

The Department of Defense

P art of your energy keeps you away from your blocks and directs your issues out at the world and at other people. This part takes you in the opposite direction of healing and prevents you from finding your true Self. It seeks to protect you from having your issues activated and tries to get your needs met outside your Self. It may even attempt to control the world and other people to fulfill its goals.

This part consumes vast quantities of energy, resources, time, focus, and effort yet does nothing for your healing. It keeps you from looking at your issues even at the risk of adversely affecting relationships and creating disease and dysfunction. You invest a lot in it and yet there is absolutely nothing to show for it.

Can you guess what part of your energy fits this description? It's your personal defense system! Is it any wonder that there is such an element in the government? The Department of Defense is the perfect manifestation of everyone's individual patterns of behavior.

If you do not have a healing process, you are vulnerable to outside forces. Consequently, most people have a strong defense system that is designed to minimize this vulnerability and to protect them from their "adversaries." However, no matter how much people defend and attempt to control the world around them, they risk being triggered off by external forces.

Furthermore, if you go outside your Self for the feelings that you want, you will easily be controlled by these outside influences. You defenses cannot give you the power that you have already given to others. If your feelings of worth, validation, security, or success are dependent on other people, those people have the power to control how you feel.

Defenses will assist you in avoiding feelings that you do not want to feel. Yet, while they may support you in temporarily getting away from your underlying emotions, the emotions are still present and affecting you anyway. Even when you are not conscious of your feelings, you are still experiencing them and interacting through them.

Sometimes defenses will keep you from taking part in the activities in which you really want to participate. By keeping you from those activities, they "protect" you from feelings that you do not want to experience, such as pain, failure, invalidation, embarrassment, inadequacy, punishment, blame, or responsibility. You defenses assist in minimizing the risk of activating your issues by limiting your participation in the world.

Finally, to maintain your defenses and to engage through them takes a great deal of energy. It also takes great effort and a large amount of energy to suppress your feelings and to try to control them. And, it takes energy to constantly monitor your surroundings for risks and threats.

So, let's see if I have this right. The defenses do not protect you from being triggered off. They do not guard against being controlled. They engage you in ways that do not feel good. They may prevent you from doing the things you really want to do. And they drain your energy. They don't work very well, do they? Healing sounds a lot better.

By having a healing process, you are no longer vulnerable to external control. Even when someone or something triggers you, you can choose to heal and disengage from your adversary. Your healing process gives you *real* control in your life. While you are not always in control of *when* you are triggered off, you can choose to heal and respond in a healthy way instead of engaging through the triggered emotion or defense.

Through healing, you can resolve any issue that comes up in the pursuit of your goals and desires. You will not need protection from anyone or anything. You will have your healing process to help you deal with whatever arises.

And, by healing, you won't waste your time and energy defending against issues. You will do your healing work, be free of your issues, and joyfully continue with your life.

There is no need to defend the feelings, behaviors, or knowledge of your true Self. Who you are, your true Self, is valid and has nothing to defend. Therefore, if you are defending, you have something going on that you can heal. The task in healing is to dismantle your defenses, go through the blocked emotions underneath them, and rediscover your true Self.

Anything that takes you away from a feeling is being used as a defense. Thus, any activity, including any thought or behavior, is potentially a defensive activity if that is the intention behind it.

There are numerous defenses that you readily have at your disposal. Many beliefs function as defenses as they assist you in avoiding various feelings. Judgment is a huge defense that blocks healing. Loyalty can be a defense if you are loyal to avoid feelings, such as loneliness or insecurity. If you go shopping or talk with friends to avoid your feelings, you are using those activities as defenses. Impatience is an expression of unfulfilled expectation and is a defense against feelings such as discomfort, defeat, scarcity, failure, or not being good enough. Even practices like meditation and activities like reading *can* function as defenses when they are used to avoid feelings.

Other responses that are *always* defenses include figuring everything out, becoming angry, competing, feeling guilty, shutting down, denying, resisting, giving up, trying harder, watching television, contemplating suicide, overworking, being aggressive, rebelling, numbing out, lying, being "independent," being critical, and indulging drugs, alcohol, cigarettes, cravings, or addictions. There are, of course, a great many other prospective defenses in your arsenal.

How can you tell when you are defending? You will experience tension and a feeling of resistance in your energy. Many people will feel this in their body first. **Tension and a feeling of resistance are the ways your body lets you know that you are being defensive.**

Once you recognize that you are defending, you can be sure that there is a blocked emotion underneath. On the path of healing, when you notice a defense, you are going to want to heal whatever is going on underneath it.

With denial, for instance, you are obviously trying to get away from a feeling. It reduces or eliminates awareness, which is relatively easy to accomplish by overriding or ignoring your feelings. Nonetheless, every feeling must be felt and honored. It does not work to deny a feeling. Denied feelings do *not* go away, and all blocked feelings must eventually be reclaimed and healed.

The mind comes into play as perhaps the most imposing defense. For many people, it is constantly trying to "understand" everything in order to protect the false self and to keep them from feeling their blocks. Whenever you find yourself figuring something out, you will want to heal the feeling from which your mind wishes to escape.

Fear is a defense to help you avoid feelings that you do not want to feel. If you have unhealed insecurity, fear will attempt to keep you from going into experiences in which you might feel insecure. However, there is no need for fear. Once you have healed your insecurity and invalidation, you can rely on your perception to tell you what is going on. You do not need to fear dark streets at night, for instance. Rather than hold onto a fear that may keep you from danger—but may also take you into danger!—you can heal yourself and use your perception to tell you what is and what is not safe.

Guilt is another familiar defense. It tells you that it's wrong to feel the way you feel and it is commonly used as a way to control you. However, guilt is neither helpful nor useful in any way and, like all defenses, stops the flow of your energy, thereby preventing healing.

Some people believe that a little guilt is good, but that belief is based on a misunderstanding of healing and of emotions. You do not need guilt to tell you how to feel or what you should or should not do. That's why you have feelings! When you are in touch with your feelings, you know how you want to be. Your feelings tell you how to respond to the situations you face. Of course, you can always evolve your feelings to reflect more of your true Self. However, to evolve them, you need to have your feelings and heal them, not block them.

It is relatively common for people to seek medical care, counseling, and "healing" as a way to *avoid* their issues. Many popular medications, including pain medications, nutritional supplements, and antidepressants are prescribed and used to *avoid* healing. Of course, all of these methods can be used to support true healing, but "healing" *can* also become just another defense to support the avoidance of feelings.

Shopping is a common way to avoid various feelings, including emptiness, worthlessness, loss, failure, insecurity, pain, inferiority, and feeling unattractive. It is a great way to create the illusion of prosperity by buying things, especially on credit, when the underlying feeling is actually one of scarcity. I remember a friend buying an entire case of canned peaches when she did not have any money. She was so happy to have that food even though she now had even less money with which to handle her affairs. But now, at least, she had all those peaches!

Another common defense is to go into effort to make things happen. It is common to misuse the ability to take action by making things happen that are in alignment with the false self or in alignment with the defenses. It is also common to make things happen to defend against issues that are triggered off. This is how many people try to avoid feelings of failure and inadequacy. With healing, you will learn to align your effort and actions with what you really want on a true Self level—in alignment with your healed feelings.

Since defenses are meant to help you avoid your issues, they block awareness of your real feelings. The more "successful" the defense, the less aware you will be of your issues and your feelings. Therefore, it may take some practice to notice when you are using a defense.

Although tension and the feeling of resistance are the hallmarks of every defense, many people are so adept at numbing out or are so out of touch with their body that they do not feel their tension. Many people are so accustomed to their tension and resistance that they do not discern them. And some defenses are either so good or so habitual that people do not even know they are defending. Furthermore, people defend against their defenses and that makes it even more difficult to spot them.

I commonly hear people say, "I'm not going to let it get to me. I'm not going to let it bother me," but that is not possible. If you have an issue and the appropriate trigger is present, it will be activated. No one has the ability to prevent something from triggering them off. Since you cannot successfully guard against being triggered off, trying not to let something bother you is just another useless defense. **There is only one practical approach to life and that is to heal every issue that arises**. If you have an active issue, you have something to heal. And if nothing is active, you don't have anything to process.

Another frequent comment that I hear is, "I just let things go." Most of the time, the speaker has just denied or ignored their issues. Pretending that nothing is going on, numbing out to issues, and using your mind to "let things go" are merely defenses. Again, you are either triggered off or you aren't, and there is no way to ignore an issue if you truly seek healing. While you have no power to control the world and, therefore, when and what is triggered off, **what is in your power is to heal whatever is triggered off**. Healing is the only effective way of dealing with your issues.

With practice, you will develop more of an awareness of when you are defending. When you detect a defense, you can search for the deeper, underlying issues that are waiting to be healed. Pay attention to when you are defending, go to the feeling that is underneath the defense, and heal it. You are applying your tools for healing specifically to remove anything that generates new defenses and to unplug anything that feeds existing defenses. Then your defenses will start to drop away and your Department of Defense will eventually be closed down due to disuse.

Your true Self is moving *through* its experience; it is not the experience. A feeling of resistance and tension develops when you have stopped moving and have identified with your experience. Whenever you notice that you are resisting the flow of life and, therefore, using a defense, you will want to heal the feeling underneath the resistance so that you can continue with the flow of your true Self. Non-resistance is the path of your true Self, the path of healing.

If you do not think you do much defending, you may want to pay particular attention to those times when you think that nothing is going on and look at yourself more deeply. If you feel tension and resistance when you focus on yourself, your body and energy are telling you that a defense is active.

EXERCISE: *Defensive Behavior*

Throughout the day, pay attention to how you react to people in your life. Do you notice times when you are defending against feelings you do not want to feel? Try to become aware of the feelings that may be defenses such as anger, judgment, denial, guilt, or fear. You may wish to refer to Figure 2 on page 72 or look at the lists of emotions in the *Appendix* for additional possibilities to consider.

Then look underneath the defenses to see if you can discern the feelings that underlie those defenses. Relax through any feelings that you perceive.

EXERCISE: *Healing Defenses*

Imagine having a conversation with a co-worker in which the co-worker insinuates that things are not up to par and that the issues are related to your work. Perhaps you respond with *anger* as a defense against feeling *invalidated* or *incapable*. Or maybe you are in *denial* that the co-worker's comments have anything to do with you because there are feelings of *failure* or *appearing stupid* that you do not want to face. Or perhaps feelings of *guilt* come up that you are *not doing enough*. To heal this encounter, you would relax through every defense that arose and look for the feelings underneath them. Then you would relax through those feelings as well.

EXERCISE: *Speaking for the Defense...*

When you *talk* with others about issues that are active, it is likely that you are defending against your underlying feelings. You may be trying to get agreement from others or you may be talking to avoid your feelings. Notice how talking about issues often prolongs their presence rather than helping to resolve them.

Sometimes people talk about their issues to try to get rid of their feelings by "sharing" them with others or directing their feelings at another person. Notice that when someone does this to you, they may appear to feel better while you often feel worse.

When you are triggered off, experiment with *not* talking about it for a few days. Keep it to yourself and practice your healing process. Notice that when you heal an issue instead of talking about it, it loses its significance. This process can assist you in developing connections with others that are not based on your issues.

Turning Blocks into Virtues and Treasures

Without a healing process, emotional issues become a real dilemma. We can stay in touch with our issues and feel lousy all the time. We can suppress our issues and adapt to them, which means they are still present and affecting us anyway. Or, we can turn our issues into virtues so that they almost feel good. With these choices, it is not surprising that we are remarkably adept at creating a virtuous experience where none exists.

Any feeling can be transformed into something that seems good. For instance, rather than feeling powerless, with a little remodeling, we can call it compassion. We can transform feeling uncared for into feeling carefree. We can spiritualize not getting our needs met into not having needs. We can convert invalidation into feeling special. We can change feeling inferior into appearing unassuming. We can become a nurturing person even though we desperately want nurturing for ourselves.

We take a feeling that most certainly does not feel good and make it into something to be proud of, a treasure. Many emotional issues can be converted into what we call nice and good. Suppression, fear, insecurity, uncertainty, invalidation, failure, helplessness, unworthiness, and inadequacy can easily be converted into what appears to be niceness.

"Relaxation" is another catch-all feeling that is usually something quite different from genuine relaxation. Usually it is a version of suppression or apathy. Or it can result from having a temporary reprieve from responsibility. The key to tell whether it is real relaxation is whether it flows for you when you feel it. If it is not flowing, you are stuck in something that is definitely not real relaxation.

"Patience" is often just an adaptation to suppression. "Tolerance" is usually just suppressed judgment. "Peaceful" is often just being shutdown or suppressed. "Love" is commonly just feeling wanted and serves as an antidote for feeling alone, empty, or unwanted.

It is no surprise that we have so many false virtues. Transforming a block into a virtue makes us feel better. Now we have to watch for those so-called virtues and reveal their true identity so that we can heal them properly and become more genuine.

EXERCISE: Healing Your Virtues

Look at the qualities of your personality. Are they really what they seem? Especially examine the "good" traits that you exemplify. Relax through them to see if they are truly what they appear to be.

Judgment Day

From school tests and the legal system to social etiquette and religious beliefs, we are inundated with judgment. Judgment is such an integral part of our life that we commonly categorize everything as right or wrong. There are right ways to behave, right ways to think, right ways to feel—and wrong ways for each of these.

By making certain behaviors right and others wrong, we support our false self. We often judge being nice, caring, altruistic, and unselfish as "right" and being rude, tough, and disruptive as "wrong." Of course, some of us make the opposite judgments or rebel against these judgments with the identical goal of supporting our false self.

If we have the right thoughts and beliefs, we believe that we are better people. Therefore, we change our thoughts and beliefs to align with the right way of thinking.

If we do everything right, we are perfect. Then we can feel good, successful, valid, or loved. And we do not have to experience feeling bad, not good enough, or failure.

We want to think in certain ways and judge feelings to try to force an alignment of our thoughts and feelings. For instance, if we want to think of ourselves as kind, we judge any mean or harsh thoughts and feelings that do not agree with how we want to think of ourselves. If we want to believe that we are nice, we may judge and deny parts of ourselves that aren't nice so we can maintain our belief.

We may try to improve ourselves by having the right feelings and getting rid of the wrong feelings. For instance, we may judge jealousy and anger to try to eliminate them. If only it were that easy! The judged feelings are still present even if we successfully remove them from our conscious awareness.

We judge other people as a defense to avoid our own issues. If someone triggers us off, it often seems easier to make the other person wrong rather than feel our own feelings.

To avoid the feelings we have labeled "wrong," we may try to avoid experiences in which we might feel them. We may even make rules or enact laws in an attempt to avoid various feelings.

We judge behavior to get people to act in a socially acceptable manner. For example, some people judge stealing and truancy to try to get people to stop misbehaving. At the same time, we judge that doing well in school and being responsible at work are right in order to encourage people to behave "properly."

Judgment may be used to justify our actions, even when our actions are abusive or inappropriate. Therefore, some of us can justify violating other people's boundaries because we perceive a slight or grievance. And, perhaps, while we go to war and kill people out of anger or revenge, we may try to justify it through righteousness.

We judge behavior to create goals and to establish priorities. For example, we may choose a "right" career in business, law, or medicine instead of pursuing our heart's desire in the arts that were judged to be less valid.

The material presented in this book can also become just another judgment. While the concepts presented here are real for me, without the requisite emotional healing, they may simply become the latest "right way" of thinking. This merely makes them into another defense against healing and emotion.

It is important to distinguish between judgment and perception. Our ability to perceive has nothing to do with making what we perceive either right or wrong. While accurate perception has its own challenges, judgment and perception are two unrelated qualities.

The problem with judgment is that it stops the flow of any feeling being judged. Since we only experience feelings when they are flowing, judgment keeps us from feeling them. However, judgment does not change our feelings, it does not get rid of them, and it does not heal them. We must feel our feelings to heal them, so judgment can only help us to escape them temporarily. Thus, **judgment only functions as a defense** against feelings.

And judgment is not selective. It stops the flow of both positive feelings such as joy, validation, and love, and negative feelings such as invalidation, loneliness, and rejection.

By judging our positive feelings, we lose the experience of them because they stop flowing. For instance, we may have been taught *not* to make other people feel bad by being too happy or joyful. Or, perhaps, *not* to validate ourselves so we have some motivation to try to do better. When judgment blocks the flow of these feelings, either we stop noticing them or we only experience their lack of flow. The judged energy remains in our energy field blocking our normal flow and self-expression. **Positive feelings only feel good when they are flowing.**

By judging our negative feelings—the ones we want to get away from—we stop their flow but remain immersed in them. Judging the feelings of rejection, failure, or inferiority may insulate our conscious mind and decrease our ability to feel them, but they are still present in our energy field and, therefore, are still affecting us. With judgment, the best we can achieve is the clouding of our awareness of them.

Judgment also makes our healing more complicated. Once we have judged a feeling, we have to heal the judgment and then we still have the original feeling left to heal anyway. Therefore, judgment is an obstacle to healing.

If we have a feeling of hatred and we use judgment to make it wrong, we have just blocked and suppressed the feeling of hatred. The hatred has not gone anywhere and it will have to be felt and healed eventually. In addition, because we have used judgment to block the flow of the hatred, we now have to heal the judgment as well.

Blocking our experience of a feeling stops our movement through that experience. We become anchored where the flow is stopped and cannot move forward again until we let go of the judgment and feel the underlying feeling.

If we act out on our feelings and others use judgment to make our actions wrong, our actions may cease, but the underlying feelings will still be present. Perhaps we suppress and consciously ignore our motivation for "misbehaving," but healing is not accomplished. Even if we express our feelings differently, the original feelings still have to be felt and healed, and the judgment of our actions now requires healing as well.

Some people insist on holding onto their judgment. Perhaps they want to blame someone else for what they are feeling. However, everyone will eventually realize that they have to let go of their judgment to continue on the path of healing.

To heal, we must have our feelings. We have to be able to feel them so that they can flow through us. Once they are flowing and we have let them go, we will have reestablished our presence on our true path.

EXERCISE: Rights and Wrongs

Make a list of all the things you have done "wrong" recently and another list of all the things you have done "right." Did you eat the "right" foods? Say the "right" things? Obey all of the driving laws? Behave properly? Brush your teeth? Did you do *everything* "right"?

Which list is longer: The list of the things you did "right" or the things you did "wrong"? Most people in my classes have made longer lists of the "wrongs."

Then practice healing your feelings of judgment. Focus on the events listed and relax through the feelings of "right" and "wrong." What do you notice about your feelings? Both "right" *and* "wrong" block the flow of the energy! When you have healed the feelings of both "right" and "wrong," you will discover that a more evolved quality exists beyond judgment.

Beyond Judgment

By healing the feelings of both right and wrong, we move beyond judgment. When we have achieved some healing of our judgment, we will begin to experience that there really is no right or wrong. We move to a higher level of energy where everything becomes *all right*. What this really means is that we are now open to learning from our experience. Functional learning can only occur when everything is all right.

When we stop judging feelings, we can, of course, become stuck in them in other ways, such as through other defenses or by identifying with them. However, now we have the option of healing them and truly evolving them. When we let negative feelings flow through us, they are gone! Instead of judging them "out of existence"—which really means that they are still present but out of our awareness—healing allows us to be completely free of them. In addition, healing makes it apparent that only blocked feelings cause harm and that their unobstructed flow is healing.

When positive feelings are no longer judged, they can also flow through us. Blocking the flow of positive feelings, such as joy and validation, obstructs our life and causes harm just like blocking the flow of negative feelings. With healing, we can experience their unobstructed flow. Then, they will either dissipate when they are complete or continue if that is the flow of our true Self.

Judgment blocks the exploration and the necessary healing of feelings and behavior. This is the opposite of healthy learning and does not resolve anything.

If someone uses stealing to deal with his or her feelings, judging the behavior may end the stealing but also tends to make things worse. It does not resolve the underlying motivation for the action and adds another layer of blocked emotion to the pattern. It can further suppress the real issue and contribute to a more insidious expression of that issue. Thus, rather than judging stealing, one may wish to explore what is behind it.

Perhaps people use stealing as a cry for help by nabbing our attention. Or maybe people steal to cover up their lack of self-worth with something of "value." If "rule breakers" allow their feelings and explore them, they *learn* that acting out on their feelings does not work. They *learn* that they still have to reclaim and heal their underlying feelings. And, of course, they *learn* about the feeling itself and the healing process that is required to resolve it. By exploring their behavior, they become aware of what is really going on, heal whatever issues are involved, and become significantly more functional.

When we learn, we simply participate in an experience and heal the issues that arise. We want to pay attention to our experience, to the consequences of our choices, and to our healing process. If appropriate, we can make new choices in relation to what we want to create based on what we learn through our healing.

Some people rebel to get away from rules, judgments, and restrictions; however, rebellion is just another defense that does nothing to resolve the patterns and feelings of limitation. Rebellion cannot possibly assist anyone in moving beyond judgment. It is a reaction to the causal issues and even if people do the opposite of what they are "supposed" to do, they are not acting independently. Their programming still controls them and they are not free to be their true Self.

We cannot get beyond judgment by judging it, so we do not want to judge judgment. Two wrongs do not make a right! Two judgments just make two blocks that we then have to heal.

There is nothing wrong with judgment; it just does not work. Judging feelings and behavior does not get rid of them. And we cannot get very far with judgment before our development and progress are stopped. Through healing, we can move beyond judgment and embrace that there is only learning and that everything is truly *all right*.

EXERCISE: The Mechanics of Judgment

What is the intention behind your judgment? Can you feel that it is a defense to get away from your feelings? Can you feel that judgment blocks the flow of your underlying feelings? Can you feel your energy move away from you when you are judging?

EXERCISE: Healing Judgment

Continue to heal all of the judgment you are aware of during your daily activities. With practice, there will be less and less judgment in your life and more and more learning and staying in the flow of your life. With the resolution of judgment comes the new feeling that everything is all right. You'll know what I mean when you get there.

Shutting Down

If we stop doing what we want to do, we impair the flow of our Self or *shut down*. We may be aware that we are holding back and there may even be a physical sensation of tightness, resistance, or blocking.

Most of us learn to shut down during the molding of our personality. We are taught how we should behave and how we should express ourselves. We have programming about what activities are acceptable and when we can be in our flow. And we are rewarded for shutting down and behaving "appropriately."

We are taught when to feel good about ourselves and when we should stop our flow to accommodate others' expectations and feelings. We shut down to express our façade by being "friendly" and "good." Maybe we shut down because it is not "polite" or "nice" to be upbeat when someone else is feeling down. We may shut down out of "respect" for others' feelings or because it is not "kind" to express our true feelings. We may shut down to avoid triggering others' issues or to support other people's feelings. It may be out of sympathy or "caring" that we shut down to match others' pain and discomfort. It may be out of "compassion" or "consideration" that we shut down to wait for others instead of moving on with our life.

Sometimes we shut down as a defense against feelings such as insecurity, rejection, or invalidation. Since shutting down stops the flow of our energy, if we have an active issue, it may temporarily block our experience of that issue.

Shutting down is also a common defense to "protect" us from energy that is directed at us. We may shut down to avoid others' anger or to minimize the risk of being hit, either physically or energetically. We may shut down when others disapprove of our behavior, to avoid engaging with people in ways that do not feel good, or as a response to others' judgment. And, shutting down becomes an especially well-developed defense when it is reinforced with pain or punishment.

Shutting down is a very common strategy when we cannot separate from others and we want to avoid the assault of energy that we experience in the world and with other people. And some of us shut down as a defense to avoid certain incidents, such as conflicts or arguments.

Sometimes we shut down to acknowledge that we did something wrong in order to get other people to back off. We might also try to get others to leave us alone by shutting down to signal that we will not express ourselves or cause any further problems.

Many of us get so accustomed to being shut down that we do not notice it. We feel "comfortable" shutting down in our relationships. And we commonly shut down when we go to school or work. At some point, it may feel "natural" to be shut down all the time. And once we feel that shutting down is "normal," it is difficult to recognize the pattern's presence and to perceive other options for how to deal with life.

As a practical matter, shutting down does not work. By shutting down, we do not learn how to heal our issues and we do not evolve our true Self to function in healthy ways in the world. Instead, we lose touch with our Self and learn how to sublimate many of our desires and real feelings.

Shutting down prevents us from being our Self and, at best, *temporarily* avoid dealing with our issues. However, it does not help us heal and truly feel better. Shutting down does not stop or change whatever issues are present. Instead, it stops the flow of our energy and it makes us feel worse. Shutting down is painful!

With healing, we are not going to want to shut down any more. We will want to be in the flow of our Self and never stop our flow. Does that bring up feelings of rejection or loss? Does it bring up fear of judgment, pain, or others' anger? If so, those are important issues to address through healing.

Since shutting down is a defense, we will want to heal any underlying feelings. If, for example, we learned to shut down to accommodate others' expectations, we will have to separate from those expectations and heal the underlying feelings, such as failure, insecurity, invalidation, or judgment.

With healing, our intention is to be our Self and for everyone else to be themselves. We will not go out of our way to trigger others off. Nevertheless, if being our Self triggers someone else off, he or she has an opportunity to heal and to connect with us in a healthier manner.

Not shutting down means that we always maintain our flow. It means that we are free to be our true Self and to express our Self.

There is a big difference between acting out of the false self and expressing the true Self. While we do not want to squelch or shut down the expression of the true Self, the false self requires healing to evolve it to the level of true Self expression. Shutting down simply blocks our healing and impairs our necessary evolution.

It is, of course, a challenge to know how to assist others with their healing so that they can express more of their true Self. Children and students, in particular, require assistance in learning to maintain the flow of their true Self while becoming truly functional within society. We can assist them in developing their awareness of their true Self and in healing their issues as they arise. In this way, they become more their true Self and express more of their true Self in their life. Rather than shutting down, which blocks the flow of the Self, they can heal and evolve to become their true Self.

EXERCISE: Healing Shutting Down

Shutting down for another person does not resolve your issues or theirs and, therefore, does not help you or them. What is your motivation for shutting down? Those are the feelings that require healing.

In The Darkest Hour

D epression commonly accompanies shutting down and results from being mired in a feeling that we do not know we can change. While depression can be triggered by anything from environmental or physiological conditions to personal, professional, or social situations, it develops when we are too deep in our own emotions and often involves having someone else's energy in our space.

Minor and often unrecognized forms of depression, such as apathy and boredom, are associated with a mild impairment to the flow of our energy. More severe forms are associated with being more deeply involved in our own or other people's issues. The more shut down we are and the more deeply we are stuck in an issue, the more severe the depression.

Those of us who experience chronic depression are used to shutting down, being constantly too deep in our energy, and going deeper as a defense against dealing with the issues we face. We do not seem to know how to lighten up and move towards healing. As a result, the compass for finding our way home takes us deeper into our issues and away from our true Self, rather than *through* our issues and towards our true Self.

We are trapped in our patterns and programming, which often engage others' issues and leave us inundated and entangled with the foreign energy. There is a separation from our Self and a feeling of not being able to reconnect with our Self. Without the awareness that we can change our circumstances, it is easy to feel helpless and powerless around our issues and outside forces. The darkness seems pervasive, and it is easy to fall into a black hole that is laced with fear, powerlessness, and helplessness. The downward spiral into darkness seems inevitable and irreversible. It is very difficult to see a way out of inner collapse and withdrawal.

The element that is missing is the knowledge of healing: We have the power to separate from foreign energy and reverse the downward spiral. Instead of going deeper and deeper into our own issues and into the foreign energy, we can learn to get lighter and to relax through the issues. With healing, we can resolve how we engage with other people's energy and extricate our Self from the pit of despair. We can free our Self from being submerged in other people's issues and remobilize our shut down energy, reestablishing the flow of our true Self.

Regardless of the depression's origin, a healing process can assist in the resolution of its cause and its symptoms. This requires diligence and honesty with ourselves. If withdrawal and going too deep into our issues are a part of our pattern of depression, we must be careful not to surrender to those tendencies. Expert professional assistance is strongly recommended to successfully negotiate these issues.

Every part of an energy pattern requires healing to resolve it. Perhaps we feel powerless or helpless. Maybe we feel that we cannot change how we feel around certain people. We may have to deal with our shutting down around others' anger and other energetic threats. And we have to resolve the issues through which we engage with others' energy. All of these feelings can be healed, and we will then be free of depression.

dAnger

Anger is a common and valid response to a variety of situations. However, while anger is not *dangerous*, it is a defense. Therefore, you are going to want to notice whenever you are angry and do some healing work with your anger. This includes subtler presentations of anger such as frustration, irritation, impatience, annoyance, and resentment.

If you have any judgment around anger, you will have to heal that first. You have to make it acceptable to have whatever feelings you are experiencing. There is nothing wrong with anger; it is just another response. Since judgment impairs healing, you will have to heal the judgment before you can work on the anger.

One common reason for becoming angry is when you want something that you are not getting. Anger acts as a defense when your needs are not being fulfilled and can be directed at other people to try to get them to give you what you want. Now, instead of getting angry and stomping your feet, you can use your healing process to deal with your issues. If there is something that you want, you can give it to yourself and resolve the cause of your anger.

Another reason you may get angry is that you have a feeling coming up that you do not want to feel. The anger may be directed at another person in an attempt to push the unwanted feeling onto that person. Now, if you have an unwanted feeling, you can use your healing process to resolve both the unwanted feeling and the anger by relaxing through the undesirable feeling.

You may also get angry when you are trying to push someone else's energy away from you. When someone directs their energy at you, anger is a natural response to try to move their energy out of your space. However, no matter how justified your anger, the only way for someone else's energy to get in your space is if you engaged with their energy. Thus, if someone's energy is in your space, you will need to look at that issue and heal it to resolve your part in the exchange and truly separate from the other person's energy. This concept will be developed further as we progress through this book.

If you do not get angry, either you have healed your anger and the issues discussed above or, more likely, you have learned to suppress your anger. Suppressed or denied anger is just another blocked emotion that requires healing. Perhaps there is some judgment against anger that keeps it hidden. Or maybe anger feels out of control and is, therefore, suppressed. The suppressed anger will have to be reclaimed before it can be processed and resolved. Without healing, some people respond with explosive, violent, and often unexpected outbursts when their denied anger is triggered.

If you do not get angry, either you have mastered separating from other people's energy or you are responding inappropriately to boundary violations and abuse. Without anger, you will *not* be trying to push other people's energy out of your space. And if you do not move foreign energy out of your space, it will just sit there having an adverse effect on you, negatively affecting your health.

Anger is a natural and normal response to dysfunctional engagements. Until you heal every issue, other people can engage with you through those issues. When a dysfunctional engagement has occurred, there may be some anger that gets your attention and lets you know that healing is required.

EXERCISE: Healing Anger

A very useful exercise for improving relationships is to heal any anger associated with them. You can start by making a list of the people with whom you are angry.

Next, go down the list and ask yourself what feeling is underneath the anger. For instance, it might be rejection, embarrassment, hurt, or insecurity. Perhaps you will want to look at the list of negative emotions at the end of the book if you cannot identify the feeling. Then relax through each of the feelings that you find underneath the anger.

After that, go down the list of people one by one and ask yourself what feeling you wanted from each of them. Then you can generate those feelings within yourself. To generate a feeling that you are looking for, you can either remember an experience from the past in which you felt that feeling or you can just imagine what that feeling would feel like. If you start with a feeling that is attached to a person or event, you will want to separate from that person or event once you get the feeling flowing and just stay focused on the feeling itself.

It is not necessary to *name* the feeling that you are trying to give your Self in order to resolve your anger and to accomplish healing. Just feel what you want and relax into that feeling more and more until the unobstructed flow of the feeling is moving through you.

If you are trying to push someone else's energy out of your space with your anger, you will have to identify what issue or quality allowed their energy into your space. By healing that quality, you raise its vibration and separate from the other person's energy. Were you supportive, generous, caring, understanding, or accepting? Relax through the qualities of engagement. We will go into this concept and process in much greater detail in the upcoming chapters titled "Separations" and "Avenues of Engagement."

You can test your progress by thinking of the same person again. As long as there is a reaction, you still have some healing to do. You will want to keep doing the healing work until the anger is resolved and you are free of it.

Competition

Competition is present in almost every aspect of our world. It is a significant element of a great number of interactions between people, companies, and nations; we compete for energy in the form of approval and validation from parents, teachers, bosses, and friends as well as for societal worth in the form of money and status.

Much of the energy around competition is dysfunctional. It is often a defense against feeling worthless, insecure, inferior, invalid, or unfulfilled. It involves a comparison in which someone comes out feeling better than another and someone comes out feeling less than another. As a defense, competition is ineffective since we can only temporarily avoid our underlying feelings by competing. We can be better than another person today, but then we have to prove ourselves again in the future. To heal competition, we have to heal the feelings behind it.

Competition is just the externalization of our internal blockages and limitations. Then we try to overcome our externalized limitations to gain the feelings we desire. While we compete to get better grades, get ahead, make more money, run faster, and look better than others, it is our internal limitations that need to be healed to have the feelings and experiences we desire. Even when people say that they are only competing with themselves, they are still externalizing their issues. They are in resistance to their invalidation, they are comparing and measuring their performance, and they are looking *outside* their true Self for validation.

When we attempt to fulfill our needs in the outer world, we make use of our internal energy. The activities in which we participate consume our energy in trying to obtain those feelings and experiences in the world. Taking part in activities, such as work or recreation, to prove our worth wastes our valuable energy on those pursuits. And using physical exercise or athletic competition *to validate ourselves* depletes our body's energy.

If we perform tasks or activities to validate ourselves, our invalidation becomes an element of those tasks. Our work carries our invalidation if that is how we validate ourselves. A musician's invalidation will be conveyed by their music if they attempt to validate themselves through the music they make. Other people who participate in the activity are then exposed to that invalidation and may absorb it if they engage with the invalidation through their own issues.

When we identify with our physical body—as most of us do—it is common to attempt to validate ourselves through it. We may wear certain clothes or jewelry, get a new hairstyle, or get cosmetic surgery, for instance, to try to get away from the feelings we resist. It may make us look and feel "better," but the underlying emotions remain.

If we identify with our body and participate in sports or exercise programs, it is common to use those activities as a defense. If we exercise for its supposed health benefits, for example, we may be defending against the feeling of vulnerability, weakness, or aging. If we exercise to lose weight or to make our body look a certain way, we may be defending against feeling unattractive. It is also common to try to validate ourselves through sports and exercise programs. Often we will push our body to play better, get stronger, and go faster in order to validate ourselves.

The drive to win aligns two parts of us against healing: the part that is trying to escape from the feeling of invalidation (false self) and the part that is aiding the escape (defense). But pushing ourselves to overcome invalidation and battling that feeling do not get rid of it. Even if we win a competition, our invalidation remains until it is healed. And while they may be able to create external validation, the false self and our defenses are incapable of generating internal or true Self validation.

Some people use steroids and medications to enhance their athletic performance and try to outsmart the drug testers in a game of cat-and-mouse. They are trying to push their body beyond its perceived limitations, but the price they pay is enormous. Their physical body can be ravaged by their obsession with results and they will be even further removed from the issues that need to be addressed. Again, the underlying feelings are still present no matter what the outcome of the competition and those feelings are what need to be healed to move beyond their limitations.

Many people judge competition. But we must remember that there is nothing wrong with competition and that judging competition cannot possibly evolve it or help us get beyond it. Judgment will only block the flow of our energy, preventing its healing and adding another layer of defense that is going to have to be healed later. We do not want to avoid competition and we do not want to judge it. It is present and we must acknowledge it and heal it.

Many behaviors are actually competition in disguise. For instance, *not competing* and *not participating* are forms of competition when they are used as defenses against underlying feelings. Anything we do to avoid feeling invalidated or not good enough *is* competition.

Other variations on the non-competition theme are to be *better than* others by *not* competing with them or by not participating in competition because we are *better than* that. These are obviously just alternative forms of competition!

Believing our feelings of invalidation and buying into not being good enough are a part of competition as well. They can be defensive maneuvers to avoid overt competition. Or they can result from a genuine agreement with those beliefs. Nonetheless, winning and losing are two sides of the same coin: Both are competition. A belief in being a loser is just as much a part of competition as a belief in being a winner.

Competition will never be a successful way to avoid feelings of invalidation, worthlessness, or not being good enough. The limitations and feelings underlying the competition require healing to evolve beyond them.

EXERCISE: Healing Competition

Take a few moments to look at the activities in which you participate. Do they have an element of competition in them? If they do, feel what is underneath the competition and heal that feeling.

Go through your day looking at what people do in terms of competition. Take note of how many activities are expressions of competition. Once you learn to spot competition, you may be surprised by how many ways people compete just to avoid their feelings.

EXERCISE: Exploring Competition

On a recent weekday visit to the local zoo, all of the human mothers I saw were in competition over who had the best baby carriage! How do you compete with other people? Who has the best car, the best spouse, the best job? Who makes the most money? Who is more important, more loving, more skilled, or more accomplished?

Make a list of the things that you are better at than others and the things that you are not as good at as others. Then relax through the feelings of being better than and being less than others.

Notice when you respond to an interaction by competing. Check out whether the underlying issue is yours or whether you are simply responding to the other person's competition. If you are experiencing your own issue, heal your feelings. If you are engaging with another person's competition, you must separate from that person's energy. This will be discussed more fully in "Separations" and "Avenues of Engagement."

EXERCISE: *Feelings of Worth and Security*

What are you worth? Are you secure? Look at the feelings that come up when you ask these questions. Perhaps it brings up feelings in your façade that are related to accomplishment, finances, status, family, fame, or what others think about you. Perhaps it brings up defenses, such as competition, comparisons, judgment, or defensiveness. You might have feelings that come from your blocks, such as inferiority, worthlessness, insecurity, invalidation, or not feeling good enough. And if you respond from your true Self, you may feel an inner sense of worth and security for no apparent reason. Heal every feeling that comes up.

EXERCISE: *Self-Validation*

How do you validate yourself? Do you validate yourself through your career, work, relationships, looks, money, success, skills, achievements, family, or contributions to society? With each way that you validate yourself, feel the validation, separate from its stimulus, and relax through the validation. Now you are cultivating your Self-validation!

Beyond Competition

To heal our competition issues, we have to resolve the underlying motivation for the competition. The motivation usually stems from feeling invalid, inferior, worthless, not good enough, less than others, or unfulfilled. We can learn to notice when we respond to a situation with competition and, instead of just acting out on it, we can refocus on the underlying feeling and relax through it.

Then we will want to nurture our feelings of Self-validation. We can learn to recognize the feelings of validation within our Self, relax through them, and own that we are valid just the way we are without having to do anything.

When we heal our invalidation and can validate our Self, our activities become an avenue for expressing that validation. We no longer take part in activities to validate ourselves. Instead, we bring our validation *into* those activities.

When we participate in activities to express our Self, our participation enhances our energy instead of consuming it. The flow of our Self is augmented and there is a greatly reduced expenditure of energy. We are not wasting our internal energy to obtain external feelings or experiences.

Beyond the dichotomy of winning and losing—and beyond the striving to achieve—is the state of *being*. When we no longer engage through invalidation or through the avoidance of invalidation, when we do not engage through worthlessness or trying to prove our worth, we get to *be* our Self in the world and participate in activities to express our Self. Beyond competition, we do things to express who we are rather than doing things to avoid what we feel and identify with.

With competition, there is a tendency to resist whatever appears to obstruct the completion of our goals. With *being*, there is more of a going with the flow of whatever develops. When we are *being*, we create and take action in the flow of our true Self. We do not need to make things happen.

When we are operating from a place of *being* and not engaging through competition, *cooperation* becomes a real possibility. Cooperation has nothing to do with compromising our Self or meeting others' expectations. It is *not* about shutting down, being something we are not, or being more than we are. **True Self cooperation means that we are willing to be our Self with others.** It is not necessarily easy to be our true Self with other people, but that is the challenge of cooperation— to bring *everyone's* energy together at a level where they get to be their true Self.

With cooperation, we are working with other people to attain personal excellence and explore untapped potential—to experience new possibilities, to expand awareness, to move beyond limits, to perform at our highest level, and to experience something beyond ourselves. This does not mean that we always have to be achieving greater and greater results or breaking records, which is just using competition as a means of validating ourselves. Instead, we get to face whatever condition we are dealing with today and benefit from the challenge, whether that condition is an obstacle or unobstructed expression. We get to *be* right where we are.

With healing, we will no longer wear clothing and jewelry to create a façade and to get away from feelings in our body that we want to hide from others and ourselves. We will select and wear clothing, hairstyles, and jewelry to express who we are and to demonstrate our enjoyment of our body.

With healing, we will participate in sports for the pure joy of experiencing our body in motion. Athletic pursuits will engage our physical body and inspire its enthusiasm. Physical activities will express our body's happiness and pleasure.

Any number of activities could speak to you in this way. It could be tai chi or yoga. Running, hiking, volleyball, rowing, tennis, soccer, or bicycling could call to you. Or perhaps rock climbing. Or dance or ballet. Or weight lifting. Tune into your body and feel what engages its enthusiasm. Feel what your body looks forward to doing to express itself.

For me, it is cross-country skiing that brings great joy to my body. The inner feeling of grace and beauty with each gliding step. The sheer pleasure of the movement, the balance, and the dynamic weight shift from leg to leg. Every stride slightly different, adapting to the snow conditions, the terrain, and my strength and fitness. Up and down hills, around corners, flowing with the landscape, in contact with the elements. With cross-country skiing, my body feels especially alive and actively engaged in the moment.

Exercise gets our own energy running through our body. We physically experience energy in motion in a way that is very similar to our emotional healing process. In addition, it is a great way to move others out of our space—by revving up our own energy and getting it moving, exercise helps to expel foreign energy.

Athletic training and performance have another value as well. Once we heal our competition, there is no reason to run hard up a hill—except to experience it! This is not about making something happen. It is about aligning with what we really want to do and asserting ourselves to do it. This is true assertiveness and athletics is a very good way to train this essential quality.

We need to revive our assertiveness and heal it so that we can be our Self in the world. Our assertiveness can be aligned with our true feelings and engaged in asserting our Self. We must use our assertiveness to take care of our Self. And it takes an act of assertiveness to exercise regularly and to do other activities that we know are beneficial for our well-being.

By paying attention when we exercise, we can become aware of blocks that affect our assertiveness. We can note anything that comes up that obstructs the expression of our Self and heal it.

If we participate in competitive events—which can be a lot of fun!—we can be observant of what transpires and how our energy interacts with the other participants. We can heal anything that arises from our experiences.

It will not be a matter of mind over matter or drug-induced enhancements when real breakthroughs occur. When we heal our blocks, we create greater alignment of our energy and we will attain new levels of excellence. Through healing, we can dissolve the limitations that we come up against and experience more of our true capabilities.

Beyond competition, there is the possibility of transcendence—of moving beyond our sense of body and self. Previously unknown potential can make itself known and expand the horizon of our possibilities. We can glimpse the energy behind our body and perhaps experience the miracle of energy itself. We can be transformed through the experience of performing at the threshold of our ability.

EXERCISE: To Develop Genuine Validation

You could do well in a competition and yet feel bad about yourself if you did not get the validation, recognition, or love you wanted. You could also lose and still feel fantastic about yourself if you can validate your Self. To test yourself, first imagine winning a competition. How would you feel? Then, ask yourself if you would feel fulfilled and happy *with the same performance* if you finished last instead of first? If the answer is "no," the source of your validation is outside your Self. If the answer is "yes," you are validating your Self.

EXERCISE: Healing Winning and Losing

If you follow an athletic team, try switching sides during a competitive event or root for the opposite team. Change allegiances when your team is winning and see what feelings arise. Do the same when your team is losing. Heal all of the feelings that come up.

Mind Games

Look out! Our mind has taken over the world! And as interesting as the mind can be, it can also be a serious obstacle to healing. This is because we have learned to use our mind as a defense *against* emotion and healing.

Because we did not know how to heal our feelings or body, our mind became involved as a way to experience control. We learned to use our mind as an external controller of our feelings instead of developing the internal control of our Self that results from healing our feelings. We figured everything out as a way to *manage* our life instead of *healing* our life.

As a practical matter, the thought process has become so dominating that for most people, it is what they identify with as themselves. This is truly horrifying! As a result, whatever is outside the mind—which is most of our energy, including our true Self—is living a separate life.

For many, even the idea of a true Self seems invalidating to the mind. "I am King!" it proclaims and believes that when we say, "true Self," we are, of course, referring to the mind. It is quite a stretch to recognize that there is something else besides the mind in our energy. And an even more significant step to consider strengthening the true Self at the expense of King Mind.

If we identify with our thoughts, it is easy to think that we can change ourselves just by changing our thoughts. We can think more "right," more "spiritual," or "better" thoughts and believe that we have actually done something. However, if we have only changed our mind, we have not accomplished anything positive. In fact, we may have further obscured our true feelings and, thus, created a further fragmentation of our energy. Instead, we have to heal all of our feelings, especially those that conflict with our "better" thoughts, to align our energy with our higher goals and ideals. This is not done in the mind.

The concept of "mind over matter" is a common theme in many therapeutic approaches. However, even though our mind can push our body beyond certain limitations, the underlying conflict that causes bodily problems remains unresolved without emotional healing.

I had a client who was experiencing a fever, coughing, and malaise. His complaints resulted from liver stagnation and inflammation caused by his not doing what he really wanted to do. The impaired flow of his true Self was accompanied by irritation and frustration. One day he commanded his body to stop coughing, to which his body responded immediately; however, within the next 36 hours, he had his first experience of hemorrhoids. The causal issues were unresolved, and the liver stagnation and inflammation simply expressed themselves differently. His mind had merely altered the path of the expression of his dysfunction.

Some of us use affirmations, positive thinking, and various forms of mental control to try to "heal" our body, beliefs, and other issues; however, all too often this simply creates another barrier to real healing by creating a greater separation from our body and emotions. Sometimes there is an illusion of healing *because of the separation* of the mind from the rest of our energy. That is, we do not feel our problems any more. Nevertheless, just because the mind can separate from the other portions of our energy does not mean that those portions are gone or that our issues have been resolved. We have only complicated the situation by diminishing the awareness of our issues that is required to accomplish healing.

Thought patterns can, of course, instigate emotional issues and, in those cases, we will want to deal with our thoughts directly. The mind has its share of dysfunctional programming that requires healing for optimum health and well-being. Our mind does make faulty assumptions, faulty conclusions, erroneous associations, and so forth.

In these cases, it may be useful to use mind techniques and mind reprogramming to attain healthier function; however, underneath any undesirable thinking lies an emotional issue. Thus, the emotional process that we have been developing is the most effective approach to healing our mind. Our emotional process can be used to relax through the feeling of the thoughts themselves. Any other associated thoughts and feelings will need to be healed in this manner as well.

Sometimes changing or reprogramming our mental patterns can *appear* to be effective because our mind can seemingly overpower the body and emotions in those of us who strongly identify with our mind. Still, our mind can only temporarily subdue the rest of our energy and only with great effort. While the mind can drown out the voices of our body and emotions, unless the underlying emotions are resolved, no healing is accomplished. The emotional issues that gave rise to the programming require an emotional process for resolution. And for those of us who identify strongly with our emotions or energy other than our mind, simply reprogramming our mind will not even appear to be effective.

Many approaches to "healing" actually assist us in developing defenses and *adapting* to our problems. Adapting to problems is a very common occurrence and may seem to be healing because it tends to remove the problems from our awareness; they blend into the background and become less noticeable. However, once we adapt to a problem, we then have to reawaken our awareness of that problem. And after we reclaim our awareness, the new defense requires healing while we still must address the original underlying issue. Thus, we do not want to adapt to our issues, which is the opposite of healing—we want to heal them and let go of them.

Furthermore, disease and dysfunction develop *without* our awareness when we are not conscious of our issues. Thus, we will always want to move in the direction of enhancing our awareness, rather than adapting to issues and reducing our awareness. Conscious awareness of our issues is a prerequisite for healing them and resolving disease and dysfunction.

We can gain valuable insight by viewing thoughts as *symptoms*. Thoughts related to our issues are often either an expression of the underlying issues or a defense against those issues. If they are defensive, they are symptoms of our defensive intent and attempt to take us away from our issues. If the negative thoughts relate to our underlying issues, they are simply expressing what is already dysfunctional in the body, energy, or emotions. The thoughts are not causing the problems; they just reflect the underlying issues. If, for example, we think that someone is a "pain in the neck" or that something is "killing" us, our thoughts might actually be true; however, our thoughts only express the underlying cause of our concerns.

By only addressing our negative thinking, we are attempting to treat our symptoms. Although this may appear to resolve an issue, it does nothing for its underlying cause and does not heal any disease, disorder, or dysfunction. To resolve an issue, we have to heal the causal element and that is most commonly on an emotional level. Changing a negative thought is like altering the image on a mirror when you do not like what it reflects. Negative thinking merely expresses our emotional issues and changing our thinking does nothing for those issues. Even if we completely obscure the object's reflection, the original object is, of course, unchanged. Overpowering our body and emotions with our mind is ineffective for healing.

If talking through problems, figuring everything out, using mind control, and reprogramming our mind were valid approaches to healing, emotional issues would be eliminated with these approaches. However, if we really examine our experience, we will see that after using these methods, the problematic emotions are still present and essentially unchanged.

True healing is about resolving conflict and creating unity; it brings our mind, body, and energy into harmonious oneness. This can only occur through healing, which is not a thought-based process.

If we feel jealous, for instance, it is not enough to use the mind to talk ourselves out of the feeling. Or to suppress the jealousy with judgment. Or to overwhelm the jealousy by affirming that we have or can get what we desire.

To heal jealousy, we have to heal any feelings of lack, emptiness, and inequality. We have to heal feeling left out, not good enough, and that others have what we want. We may have to heal a belief that we cannot have what we want. Then, we have to nurture the feelings of equality, abundance, prosperity, love, connection, and completeness within ourselves.

We can use affirmations to assist in our healing by relaxing into the *feeling* of the affirmation itself and letting it flow through us. Then we will want to pay attention to what feelings come up in response to the affirmation. We will want to heal whatever feelings arise in order to create complete alignment around the affirmation. Every voice must be heard and healed to create alignment.

Now don't get me wrong. The mind is wonderful; it is just not intended to be the center of our universe. It is supposed to serve our true Self, not the other way around. And it requires healing and retraining just like every other aspect of our energy.

We can bring stillness to our mind by doing a silent meditation. Inner silence and quieting our mind can assist in the realignment of our energy by reducing our identification with our mind. While this does *not* move us towards our true Self and we still must pursue a healing process in order to become our true Self, it can be quite useful in achieving a shift in our false self identity.

Another important step is to redirect our mind to support our healing process. We can teach it the tools for healing and give it new tasks to occupy its appetite—to be alert for opportunities to heal and to apply our healing tools to those opportunities.

If we want to be actively involved in healing and quieting our mind, we can work through any blocks that engage our mind. That way we cut off the energy source for the mind. If we go through the associated blocks every time our mind engages in defending, we will quiet our mind through healing.

Together these steps help to create a peaceful mind and to allow the rest of our energy to take its rightful place in our experience.

Slowly, with continued focus and healing, we can teach our mind to be a powerful ally in our healing work. There, there mind... nice mind... attentive, clear mind... calm, helpful mind. But the mind can be a terrible thing... and we always have to watch out for its bite!

EXERCISE: Healing Thoughts / Mending Minds

Jot down any negative thoughts that you have been having. Take them one at a time and relax through them as feelings. Learn to heal your negative thoughts through your emotional process.

Now take note of some of your positive thoughts. Relax through them one at a time. What do you experience after you have healed both your positive and negative thoughts?

As a reminder, if you cannot relax through a particular thought, it probably belongs to someone else and you will simply want to separate from it.

Good Grief! Beliefs!

With our creative energy, we build a framework for experience. On the canvas of the universe, we can create marvelous artwork with our energetic brushstrokes. We can construct concepts and creations with our mind and imagination. We can explore possible futures and outcomes. And we develop and gain knowledge and understanding through specific growth experiences.

Because energy is real, these constructs have a reality all their own. They are a creative playground for exploring energy and possibilities.

A problem develops, however, when we no longer experience our constructs as what they are—that is, as just constructs. Then they become fixed within our energy and turn into beliefs.

Because we create beliefs, they are artificial structures. Yet, once present, they become solid and constant fixtures in our energy. They are experienced as real because their relatively stable form lends a "reliable" structure to our experience. Their reality is further supported by their seeming permanence; once formed, they appear to be difficult to modify or remove.

Beliefs create and support a framework within which we live and *through* which we experience life. Because we experience life through our beliefs, they have the power to shape our experience. They become a foundation for our experience, whether they are true or not and whether we are aware of them or not. Their power over our experience increases the more we are attached to them.

We may develop our own beliefs individually or take on other people's beliefs by matching their energy patterns. We often match others' energy patterns to fit into the social structure in which we find ourselves. Matching other people's energy is so easy to do that we frequently adopt their beliefs without knowing it.

There are so many beliefs with which we operate that it is difficult to outline the scope of their influence except to say that they affect everything in our life. We have been saturated with the beliefs of our family, community, and planet since the time of conception. We also have managed to create some of our own beliefs along the way and brought many with us from our past lives. There are beliefs about right and wrong, good and evil, the afterlife, God, science, disease, lifestyles, relationships, sex, money, values, and purpose. We have beliefs that we are separate from the whole, that there is not enough, that we cannot take care of ourselves, that the source of our fulfillment is outside ourselves, that we cannot trust ourselves, and that we cannot do what we really want to do.

Some beliefs develop as a result of creating a particular experience that we want to explore. Perhaps we want to expand our understanding of abandonment. To have a complete experience, it is useful to be totally absorbed in it; however, that makes it easy to forget that we are experiencing an artificial energy pattern and to begin believing in our abandonment.

It is common to create beliefs to fill in gaps in our knowledge. Beliefs about what occurs before conception and after death often demonstrate this pattern.

Many beliefs develop from experiences that we have not healed and integrated. If we have an experience involving scarcity and do not heal it, it can easily become a belief about the way things are in the world. Unhealed insecurity is a feeling that is often turned into a belief about ourselves or the condition of the world.

Other beliefs can develop around these distortions and obstacles for defensive purposes—as a defense against feelings that we do not want to experience. They create a structure that allows us to function *with* our blocks. In other words, they support our false self and impair healing.

If we believe in scarcity, for example, we may develop additional defensive beliefs to try to function with that feeling. Perhaps we start to believe that we deserve our scarcity in an attempt to get used to the feeling. Or perhaps we create a belief that we are victims in an attempt to direct the feeling of scarcity at someone else and get away from it.

I recently treated a client for a belief that he could not trust his father. That belief "protected" him from the feelings of isolation and rejection that were underneath it. It also "protected" him from the risk of trusting his father in the future and experiencing further isolation and rejection. He had created a defensive belief to avoid his issues.

It is a frequent experience *not* to feel love from one or both parents when we are children. That does not necessarily mean that they did not love us—although that may be the case—but that we did not *feel* it. It is then common to create a belief that agrees with our experience, such as that we are unlovable. It is also common to create defensive beliefs to try to avoid the core belief that we are unlovable. This might include a belief that we do not deserve love, that we are not good enough, that we do not matter, that our parents do not care about us, or that our parents are mean. We will then live out our beliefs and experience them as true.

If we experience a separation from our Self, instead of feeling the pain and fear of our separation and healing it, we may develop a defensive belief to support us in avoiding our feelings. We may choose to believe that there is no Self. Or perhaps, if we feel unworthy of connecting with our Self, we may create a belief in a Supreme Being who judges us.

If we have fears of the unknown, we may develop a defensive belief of trust or faith in something outside ourselves or a belief that everything is going to work out. And we may join a compatible group to gain support for our beliefs.

For many of us, beliefs are like dreams. Often, when we are dreaming, our experience seems congruent even when the most outlandish things are happening. Yet we continue to participate in the dream without full realization that we are dreaming until we wake up.

Being immersed in our beliefs makes it very difficult to perceive anything outside those beliefs. Everywhere we go, our beliefs go with us. Since they are always present, they quickly fall out of conscious awareness and become part of the background of our experience. Thus, the significant impact that beliefs have on our life is often hidden from view.

Group beliefs may be more difficult to become aware of than beliefs that only we hold. The greater the number of people who share a particular belief, the more it tends to be a constant in our experience, which can make it harder to discern. The greater the energy behind a belief, the more compelling it can be to participate in and the more difficult it can be to notice its presence.

Many groups develop their own set of beliefs that are adhered to by the group members. If we surround ourselves with people who share our beliefs, it is often more difficult to recognize them as beliefs.

While beliefs form a structure based on a core issue, their structure usually involves many aspects of our energy including emotions, thoughts, mental constructs, and other more abstract parts of our energy.

Because beliefs are composed of more than just thoughts and mental constructs, we cannot heal them just by changing our mind. Every belief has an emotional component, which is the key to healing the belief. Defensive beliefs in particular require emotional healing before any movement will occur in the defense.

To heal beliefs, we simply exercise our emotional healing process. We want to feel the belief itself and the feeling underneath it. Then we want to generate the feelings that we desire.

In the example above, in which my client had a belief that he could not trust his father, the belief dissolved after he healed feelings of rejection, isolation, and distrust. Healing was enhanced further when he generated feelings of acceptance, connection, and trust.

In the example about not feeling love from a parent, we would want to heal feeling unloved and generate our own feeling of love. We would also want to heal any associated beliefs by processing them as feelings. This might include feeling and healing that we are unlovable, that we are undeserving of love, or that we do not matter. We would also want to *generate the feelings*—not just the thoughts—that we are lovable, that we deserve love, and that we do matter.

When we experience what is real, there is no distortion or obstruction of the energy. We have pure and direct perception.

When we have experiences that we do not heal, they begin to distort and block the purity of what is real. Once these experiences are set, they become enduring obstacles to our direct interaction with energy and to our understanding of that energy.

If, as children, we do not receive the *care* we desire, we may get used to not receiving it. This will often become a barrier throughout our life to being able to experience care. It is unlikely that we will be able to give care to ourselves or even consider that as a possibility. Even if caring people surround us, we may not perceive their care or let ourselves have it. We might even push people and their care away because we are not comfortable having it. Feeling uncared for will be our constant companion.

Once a belief is created, it has a reality all its own that alters our perception, inducing an alignment of our experience. Any energy that does not conform to our beliefs is often distorted, denied, or just plain deleted. Thus, our beliefs maintain themselves, providing "stability" while being nearly invisible.

If we believe that there is no love, we will not experience it in our life. We will not notice its presence. Our world will lack love and we will not perceive evidence to the contrary.

If we believe that we are separate from nature, our experience will reflect our lack of connection with the natural world. We will not notice imbalances that develop in our body. We will not sense the connection between our energy and any illness that we experience. And we will likely not be aware of the feeling of disconnection within ourselves.

Because beliefs become the filters through which we experience our life, all of our observations are potentially tainted when we are operating within a belief system. Often, our observations are simply by-products of our beliefs. And usually, the interpretation of our experience simply supports our beliefs.

A belief in scarcity means that we will experience insufficiency in our life and find evidence that there is not enough in the world. It will be true, and we can prove it! Yet we often will *not* see that the evidence we gather is the result of our belief in scarcity.

Without a belief in scarcity, we would observe that some people *experience* scarcity. We would understand that it is a valid experience, but that it is an experience that can be changed through healing. We would see that there are other ways to experience "reality."

If we believe in powerlessness and do not recognize alternative options for how to deal with our circumstances, our experience will support our belief. It is, nonetheless, not necessarily valid within the context of different beliefs or outside of beliefs. From a different perspective, we may see other possibilities.

Because we experience the world through our beliefs, they can appear to be in the world instead of only within our energy. Then we experience our beliefs happening in the world when they are really just our own experiences.

I recently had a discussion with a couple who were trying to educate me about what was wrong with the world. When I mentioned a particular restaurant, they informed me about how poorly the food was prepared there. When I referred to certain performing artists, they enlightened me about what was wrong with them and their music. Everything that was wrong with the couple's lives could be traced to something or someone else. They were perceiving through their own judgment, yet experiencing it in the world. And they could not see that their lives were not working because they were filled with judgment.

If we believe in right and wrong, all of our observations are made through judgment. All of our thoughts, feelings, and behavior are experienced through judgment. Our world and everyone in it is seen through our judgmental eyes and, therefore, our judgment is projected onto the world. Everything has judgment on it and that will be our experience.

Once again, our experience seems to validate our beliefs. We experience our beliefs as reality instead of seeing them as participants in the creation of our experience.

Because all beliefs alter our perception and understanding, they distort and obstruct the truth. Our experience becomes an interpretation of reality, one that has been altered by our beliefs. We become separate from the real world. Because beliefs represent a separation from what is true, **there are only limiting beliefs.**

While beliefs have built-in limitations, they serve a purpose. **Every belief supports experiences that lead to our growth and development.** This includes the group beliefs that are rampant in our social structures, which foster group experiences and learning. Thus, even though beliefs distort our experience, they are useful and have an important function.

In fact, their function *requires* that they distort reality. Thus, while beliefs exist as a separation from what is true and are, therefore, inherently inaccurate, there are no right beliefs and there are no wrong beliefs. **Every belief is valid within its own context** and that is how it fulfills its purpose.

Thus, a belief in victimization supports our growth and experience. Within the context of this belief, it is valid and we can easily substantiate our position. Yet, with healing, we will discover that a broader view exists beyond this belief and its perspective. It is for us to integrate its perspective to make us more whole. Once that purpose is fulfilled, it is time to let the belief go and return to a bigger, truer, and more real world.

I worked with an 11-year-old boy who was being harassed at school by a bigger boy. This had been going on nearly daily for a number of months. Not surprisingly, he felt like a victim and was sure that he was powerless to change the situation.

In our first session, my client healed issues of feeling insecure, feeling like a victim, and feeling hurt. He also practiced feeling self-love and self-acceptance, and felt better about himself immediately. Without ever saying a word to the other boy, he has not been harassed by him since that time.

Without a belief in victimization, we would observe that some people *experience* victimization. We would understand that "victims" can free themselves from their experiences and reclaim their power by healing all of their feelings. Through healing, they can take steps towards resolving the dichotomy of power and powerlessness and master the illusion of helplessness.

Beliefs are an important element of society and, to be functional in the world, we must understand the framework of beliefs within which society operates. Nonetheless, *participation* in those beliefs is not essential for functional involvement in the world and, at some point, those beliefs become confining. A bigger picture lies outside of our belief structure. That larger perspective is necessary to make sense of our total experience, to take meaningful action in our life, and to thrive. Since beliefs are separate from what is true, they do not directly support the true Self. Once we have mastered how to operate within our society, we need to move beyond its belief structure to be able to experience and express our true Self.

Without beliefs, we are freer to perceive without distortion and without preconceptions. Healing allows us to dispense with beliefs, perceive the truth, and ascertain real knowledge. By applying our healing process to everything we encounter, illusions drop away, leaving the truth as the only remaining alternative.

By now you are probably wondering why I have only discussed negative beliefs. You may be thinking, "If negative beliefs have these effects, then certainly positive beliefs must have related beneficial effects."

The problem here is that all beliefs distort the truth, what is really going on. So positive beliefs are not beneficial for accurate perception or healthy engagement with the world. Furthermore, if you really examine what appears to be a positive belief, you will find a blocked negative emotion underneath. A positive "belief" is usually just a defense against a deeper negative belief and associated emotion. We cannot counteract those deeper beliefs and emotions with positive thinking. We must heal them to be free of them.

Beliefs appear to make everything more stable and predictable; however, because of their nature, they are not functional, flexible, or true. Beliefs are false constructs that require a great deal of energy and a strong defense for their support. They do not hold up under the scrutiny of healing.

Truth requires no energy and no defense to support and sustain it. Because the truth reflects what is real, it is practical and dynamic. The truth stands on its own.

With healing, beliefs dissolve and truths deepen. When you accomplish your healing, you will not have to rely on beliefs to support your world. Instead, you can rely on the truth of the knowledge and perception that you gain through healing.

Do you believe that the source of love is outside your Self? Then you will always be seeking that source and, even if you think you have found it, the source will still be outside your Self. With healing, you will remember the truth. You will remember that the source of love is within and has always been there, waiting for your return.

EXERCISE: Transforming Beliefs

Make a list of the core beliefs in your life. Do you believe in any of the following?

- There is not enough of something—money, love, food, housing, caring, connection.
- You cannot do what you want to do at work, for recreation, in relationships, in life.
- Your body is defective and subject to dysfunction and failure.
- You aren't safe or secure.
- You are separate from everyone else. You have no connection, no understanding, no love.
- There is a Creator. If "yes," are you part of the Creator or separate from the Creator? If "no," what is the source of your life-force energy?

- You are your mind. You are your physical body. Or what?
- You must control others to get what you want, such as love, peace, order, security.
- Truth, knowledge, love, and freedom are outside of you.
- You are powerless, helpless, uncared for, useless, or worthless.

Beliefs can only be rectified through an emotional healing process and through the resolution of their underlying intention. What is the motivation behind the belief? Is this belief a defense against feeling fear, pain, insecurity, or loss? Relax through the underlying feeling.

Then you can heal your beliefs by relaxing through each belief as a feeling. Beliefs can be dissolved by getting out of resistance to them, feeling them, and letting them go.

You can then generate the feelings you want by relaxing into them. If you believe there is *not* enough of something, pretend that there is an abundance of it and imagine what that would feel like. Let the feeling flow through you. Relax more and more into the feeling.

Once you get the flow going, pay attention to when the flow is disrupted during your daily life. Go through your healing process whenever you notice that you are no longer feeling what you desire.

Look more deeply at your daily experiences. See if you can discern any hidden beliefs. Pay special attention to difficult or draining situations and look for the beliefs behind them.

Control

When we believe that the origin of our experience is outside ourselves, we typically attempt to control that source. If the feelings we desire, such as prosperity, health, security, or love, appear to have an external source, we may resort to using control to make sure we get the feelings we want. If our problems, such as loneliness, emptiness, pain, or invalidation, are perceived as coming from outside, we may try to control their perceived cause. If disease and dysfunction seem to originate in the world, we may attempt to control the world to try to avoid them.

Control is, of course, just a defense against an underlying feeling, usually some form of insecurity, powerlessness, or scarcity. There is an illusion of being in control when everything around us is in order and we do not feel our underlying feelings. Nevertheless, **if the source of our experience is outside our Self, we are *out of control.*** The rest of the world controls us because our feelings are in someone else's hands.

We can exercise our inner control by using our healing process every time we experience something happening in the world that we want to control. If it is something that we want to hold onto, we can relax through the feeling and give it to our Self. If it is something that we want to get away from, we can relax through it and resolve the feeling within ourselves.

Letting go of the need to control what is going on around us is the most functional way to live. By healing whatever arises in our life, we develop true Self control and realize that we can only gain control of our experience through healing.

Many people make decisions and take actions to gain control over their feelings and to feel in control of their life. To avoid insecurity and scarcity, people are often motivated to accumulate money, friends, and (other?) possessions to create the illusion of security and abundance.

Of course, security and abundance cannot be measured by the amount of money that we have in the bank or the number of friends that we have. I have known people who had many friends and were financially independent but who did not experience abundance or security. And I have known people who had no money, yet they felt secure and prosperous.

Insecurity can be associated with any part of our experience. We can experience insecurity in relationships, with finances, with self-expression, and with mental skills. When we become aware of insecurity, rather than attempt to avoid it by controlling the world around us, we can relax through it and heal it.

Then we can complete our healing by generating feelings of security within our own energy. We create security when we feel our true Self energy flowing through us.

EXERCISE: Creating Security

Are there things in your life you would change if you felt totally *secure*? Are you holding onto a job or relationship because of *insecurity*? Imagine that you feel totally *secure* about yourself. Relax through the feeling of security to assist with its flow through you. Then heal any feelings of scarcity and insecurity around those things that you would like to change in your life.

❋   ❋   ❋

It is common to believe that there is not enough: not enough love, not enough food, not enough money, not enough care, not enough security. Any experience can be accompanied by the feeling of scarcity. However, if we experience scarcity, it is not in the world, it is within ourselves. Therefore, rather than trying to control the world to avoid feelings of scarcity, we will want to heal our feelings. Every time we experience scarcity in our life, we can focus on that feeling and heal it within ourselves.

Then we can complete our healing by generating feelings of abundance within our own energy. We experience abundance when we are in the flow of our creativity.

EXERCISE: *Creating Abundance*

Are there things in your life that you would change if you were sure there was an *abundance* of everything? Are you holding onto a job or relationship because of *scarcity*? Imagine that there is a *wealth* of everything and that you can *create* what you want. Relax into those feelings to encourage them to flow through you more strongly. Heal any feelings of scarcity that you have around those things that you would change.

❋　❋　❋

Control is commonly used in an attempt to obtain the feelings that we desire from others, such as obedience, devotion, loyalty, comfort, cooperation, and respect. We may try to get others to behave in specific ways so that we experience those feelings.

Parents often try to control the flow of their children's energy by moving into their children's space to direct their behavior. While this often appears to be effective because the desired behavior can be reinforced and often achieved, the altered behavior is attained at quite a steep price. It creates an internal conflict within the child who is then more removed from the flow of his or her true Self. I have treated many teenagers for rebellious behavior that was simply the result of their trying to separate from their parents' controlling energy.

Trying to teach care, responsibility, or cooperation through external control will never be truly effective. One way to observe that controlling others does not work is that once control is used with someone, those control issues remain to disrupt his or her energy and behavior until they are resolved. Every adult that I have ever treated was wrestling with these issues and they were unable to establish the natural flow of their true Self until such healing was accomplished.

The goal of healing is to assist our children with the removal of their blocks so that they experience their inner respect and responsibility. People can be taught to develop these qualities in their own energy, thereby experiencing Self-respect and Self-responsibility. Then they will not need external control to behave in a healthy and functional manner. They will express genuine respect and responsibility from within.

One of my clients was having difficulty pursuing her goals and wanted some assistance. We discovered that she was seeking fun everywhere but within her Self. This had developed when she was growing up and her father had control of when she could have fun: when her homework was completed, when she behaved properly, and when her chores were done. There was resentment at this controlling energy and plenty of rebellion. Because she was rebelling against her father's control, she also resisted her own natural self-control and self-discipline, which contributed additional resistance to doing what she really wanted to do. She was in resistance to pursuing her deepest desires because she felt like she was being controlled by those desires.

By separating from the controlling energy and finding the flow of fun within her Self, she began to experience the joy of expressing her true Self discipline and responsibility. Her rebellious personality disappeared and was replaced by passion for her work and the fun of being her Self. Now she pursues what she truly wants to do with great joy and playfulness.

Stability & Movement

Stability and movement are two qualities that are essential for being functional in our daily life and for successfully negotiating the path of healing. Any aberration of stability or movement detracts from our healing and from the full expression of our Self in our life. Instability, forced stability, lack of movement, and dysfunctional movement are all impediments to a healthy, normal existence.

When we are healthy, there is a natural movement and flow of our Self through its experience. There is a need for movement so we can let go of blocks and dysfunctional ways of being and move towards new, healthier ways of being. Responding to changes in our world and creating a dynamic progression in our relationships necessitate the flexibility and adaptability afforded by movement. The natural movement of our Self allows for growth and a healthy response to the world.

A stable foundation is essential for consistent function in our life and in our world. For stability, it is necessary to establish a solid and dependable platform within our Self. That platform forms a base from which to create the desired movement in our life and to take action in the world. Its stability also supports the movement we create through our healing work and is vital to being functional with the changes that result from our healing.

Without stability, we will find it challenging to get through a day on the planet. When we cannot create stability, our reality will constantly shift so that nothing is dependable. The shifts can be unpredictable, unsettling, and sometimes even reckless. Often, instability is a defense that "protects" us from our feelings and keeps us from being present in our life.

A lack of focus is one form of instability. Since focus is an integral step of our healing process, a wavering focus impairs our ability to heal. A lack of focus and difficulty paying attention also fight against learning. This is frequently noted in people diagnosed with attention deficit hyperactivity disorder (ADHD).

Sometimes we try to compensate for a lack of internal stability by creating what appears to be a stable environment; however, controlling our environment is simply a way to *adapt* to internal instability. A management strategy does nothing to address the cause of our problem; a permanent solution requires healing the issues underneath our defensive instability.

Another strategy for dealing with a lack of internal stability is to create an artificial or forced stability for support. To create the illusion of stability, either we identify with some part of our energy—typically the false self—or we identify with some part of our reality, such as our home, partner, or family member.

Those of us who identify with our false self appear to be some of the most stable people around. However, the false self by its nature is unstable because it is based on an artificial construct in our energy. Its lack of flexibility also makes it vulnerable to outside influences. It is fragile and brittle like an eggshell.

When we identify with our false self, our identity is often well-defined and quite rigid. Unfortunately, this also means that we are quite stuck. While we are predictable and consistent, there is no real growth or change. Activities will be repetitive and monotonous and relationships will tend to stagnate.

Because of our fixation on the false self and our inability to let go of that attachment, there is no healing. Although we experience something constant as a point of reference, it does not provide a functional focus for our life and is incapable of supporting healthy growth. Instead, we have created another defensive pattern that will require healing.

Sometimes people use medications to create the illusion of stability in their life. Using a medication in this way either blocks a fixation on our negative feelings or creates a fixation on feelings or aspects of our life that are more positive. The medication then becomes another layer of defense against healing the underlying blocks themselves and against finding real stability within our Self.

Many of us squelch our movement through life to maintain the illusion of stability. We attempt to control, suppress, or minimize movement by screening the experiences we have to deal with, by managing the events we participate in, and by controlling the world around us. Through this false sense of control, we create an illusion of stability and maintain it even when it is not functional. Our need for control creates difficulty in responding appropriately to changes in the world, in relationships, and in the workplace. It consumes our energy and impedes our desired responses. We are also vulnerable to the forced movement caused by unanticipated events.

This kind of control is the antithesis of healing because it hinders the movement that is necessary for healing. Healing requires going through our experiences, rather than blocking, avoiding, or denying them. It requires the movement of relaxation and letting go.

Another form of control that thwarts healing is when we resist making changes until we know what our life will be like after we heal. But, healing *requires* the letting go of a known in the present for an unknown in the future. It requires the uncertainty of change. Thus, if we need to control the consequences of making a particular change, we will interfere with the healing process.

We are *not* in control of what is triggered off, when it is triggered off, or what it will be like when we have healed an issue; however, by healing and going through the issues that arise, we *are* in control of ourselves. This includes healing any issues around our process, such as feeling out of control or feeling afraid of change. With healing, we experience true Self control.

Movement just for the sake of movement is not useful either. It is often used as a defense to keep us distracted and off-balance so we do not experience our immediate feelings.

While healing requires movement *through* our pain or discomfort, movement away from our Self is painful and causes discomfort. Many people attempt to avoid their issues through behavior and activities that take them further away from their true Self. This kind of movement does nothing to heal the underlying issues and actually promotes and prolongs their pain and discomfort.

Many of us attempt to avoid our pain by taking drugs, using medications, or by drinking mind-altering beverages. The consumption or inhalation of substances to avoid focusing on negative aspects of our life and our world, and the use of medications to alter our fixed sense of self, are simply ways of defending against underlying issues.

Even though it may be difficult to watch as other people avoid their issues and move away from their true Self, we have to separate from their energy and simply own the compassion that we have been evolving with our healing process. Our inner stability and healthy movement can be maintained no matter what transpires around us, and it may even assist others in finding functional stability and movement within their true Self.

A valuable metaphor for the dynamic interplay of stability and movement involves imagining that we are standing on a large ball and that we want to move somewhere. If we attempt to maintain a rigid stability, we waste a lot of energy, do not move where we want to go, and actually create instability. If we attempt to make a leap, the ball will probably go in the opposite direction and we will go nowhere. However, if we use the ball as a base and move with it, we can maintain the stability that is required to create the movement we desire.

The only constant in our experience is our true Self. Therefore, stability can only be based on our sense of Self. It provides a focus and point of reference from which we can fully participate in our life. We can thrive on the movement in our life with our Self as our stable platform.

Energetically, this is an aspect of the intention to heal. We intend to move towards our true Self and we intend to function there. The Self is not static, so it takes continued application of the intention to heal to continue the flow of movement and stability.

Stability does not come in the form of a pill, a belief, a book, a diet, a teacher, or a friend. Only our true Self can provide the stability that is required to be truly functional.

Movement, or a lack thereof, does not provide a refuge from the issues we face. Only when movement is aligned with the flow of our true Self is it truly functional.

Instability, forced stability, lack of movement, and dysfunctional movement are defensive patterns that impair the discovery, evolution, and expression of our true Self. Their resolution entails experiencing and healing the emotions underneath the behavior. Only healing allows us to attain both healthy stability and healthy movement in our life.

The Inverted Self

While the true Self is at the core of our energy, many of us do not function like that in our life. In fact, for a great many of us, the true Self is nowhere to be found!

Instead, we function as if the false self is who we really are. We live as if this fabricated part of our energy—consisting of those parts of our mind, façades, defenses, blocks, foreign energy, and the tiny bit of our true Self with which we identify—is at the center of our personal universe. We perceive the parts of our energy with which we do *not* identify as being outside of ourselves. This means that we perceive the true Self as being largely separate from ourselves as well.

In contrast to the actual structure of our energy, which has the true Self at its center (See Figure 2 on page 72), we attempt to function with the false self at our center. This gives rise to a distorted structure that I call the *inverted self.* Figure 3 on page 175 depicts what this looks like. **Identifying with our false self causes our energy to appear to function in nearly the opposite way from how it truly is.**

The inverted self develops when we do not have the intention to heal. Without the intention to heal, everything we do strengthens our identification with our false self and supports the structure of the inverted self.

A great many of us go through our life so fixated on our false self that it seems real, secure, and constant, and our inverted self seems functional. This illusion is often maintained through the control of everything that goes on around us so that we do not experience our issues. In truth, the illusion of our stability *depends* on our ability to control our surroundings. And it takes an enormous amount of energy and control to maintain the inverted self and to sustain any semblance of steady function.

Although it is not always evident, the inverted self is a highly unstable configuration that leaves us in an untenable position. In spite of the huge energy expenditure and the focus on controlling our world, those of us who function as our inverted self are out of control of ourselves and totally at the mercy of what happens around us.

Those of us who operate as our inverted self often have trouble with unexpected turns of events. Our responses are often the opposite of what is really desirable and are inappropriate for healthy energetic function. When we are triggered off, we are quick to defend ourselves and try to regain control of what is going on around us. We do not use healing to find our true Self and, instead, will scramble to get everything in our world back in "order."

When we identify with our false self, the other parts of our energy with which we do *not* identify become disowned. Thus, those of us who are living as our inverted self experience many of our own issues as being outside ourselves, either as other people's stuff or part of the world around us.

Since those of us who are living as our inverted self experience our own issues as being outside ourselves, we tend to have a poor perception of boundaries. Where do we end and where does someone else begin?

And because the false self tends to be highly defended, the disowned parts of our energy are thrust outward when they are activated. We project our issues out onto the world and other people. Our own stuff is projected across others' boundaries and into other people's space when we are triggered off.

Figure 3: The Inverted Self

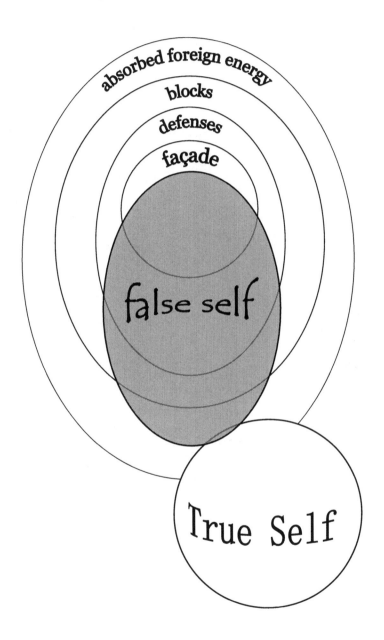

If, as our inverted self, we feel insecure, we project our insecurity onto the people around us. Then we react to the people around us as if those people are the origin of our experience of insecurity.

Recently, I was running along a logging road in an archery range near my house. I came up behind a couple walking in the same direction that I was running. I had not attempted to be quiet and was, in fact, quite noisy on the trail so that they would hear me. Nevertheless, they had not heard me and jumped with surprise when I ran by them. Instead of acknowledging her fear and insecurity, the woman threw them right at me with a threat, saying, "It's a good thing I don't have my bow and arrows! You shouldn't sneak up on people like that!" The woman had been triggered off but would not own her feelings. Instead, she tried to project them onto me and was still peeved about it a half hour later when I ran by the couple again.

It is impossible for such a person to heal as long as she is attached to her false self. She could not own her fear and insecurity, which is the first requirement to begin to heal it. Even if I had taken responsibility for her issues or taken "care" of her, she would have only felt better temporarily. Her fear and insecurity would have still been there to be triggered off at a future time.

People who have the intention to heal function in almost the opposite fashion of those who are attached to the structure of their inverted self. Individuals who are healing own their issues and seek to heal themselves. They have nothing to defend. They are in control of themselves through their healing process and, consequently, have no need to control what goes on around them. They are capable of recognizing and respecting another person's space and boundaries in their relationships.

People who are healing do not expend any energy on maintaining their false self or on supporting the illusion of the stability of their inverted self. Instead, they find greater and greater stability within their true Self, which allows them to handle their life with greater ease and purpose. They use their energy to express their true Self, a truly dependable foundation.

EXERCISE: Mistaken Perceptions

Pay attention to situations in which your experience of what is happening turns out to be incorrect. For instance, if someone has not returned your phone call promptly, do you wonder if they are ignoring you or avoiding you? Then later, when you find out that they were sick or out of town or did not get the message in a timely manner, you have an opportunity to process your response to heal it.

Separations

Earlier in the book, we discussed a basic concept of separation that involved shifting the focus from the trigger of an issue to the issue itself. A practical and relatively easy approach, this maneuver facilitates our healing process and initiates our separation from other people's energy.

Now let's expand on that concept to gain a deeper understanding of what is involved with disengaging from other people. We will want to develop our process to effectively handle the entire spectrum of issues related to engaging with other people's energy.

We need to be able to separate from other people's energy for a number of reasons. First, **no one can heal another person's issues.** If you have an issue, such as unhappiness or pain, no one else can go through it for you. If I take on your issue, it just sits in my space—and ferments! ☺ Only an issue's owner can go through it and heal it.

To reiterate, we cannot heal anyone else's feelings and no one can heal ours. We cannot unload our issues on anyone else and no one can hand us their struggles. Thus, **we are all going to have to *separate* from other people's feelings and heal any feelings that we are trying to evade.**

At the same time, **no one can give others the feelings that they want or need.** If I have a need and get it filled by someone else, eventually I have to let it go, returning the energy to the "benevolent" person who gave it to me, because I cannot function properly with someone else's energy.

To repeat, no one can give us the feelings we want and we cannot give anyone else the feelings they want. **We are all going to have to look *within* for the feelings that we desire and *separate* from what others want.**

In addition, we frequently *open* to other people to find out about ourselves. We check with others for feedback on who we are, how we are doing, and whether we get validation and approval. Am I good? Am I smart? Did I perform my tasks well enough? Am I behaving properly? Did I understand you correctly? Do you like and accept me? When we open to others, we pull their energy into our space. ***Separating* from other people's energy is essential for remembering who we are and for knowing how we feel about ourselves.**

Significantly, we often exchange energy with other people and are used to having others' energy, blocks, and agendas in our space. If we do not recognize the foreign energy and *separate* from it, it is likely that we will act and react in the world based on the absorbed energy. ***Separating* from foreign energy allows us to respond based on our own energy and motivation.**

And, finally, everyone has his or her own energy. We each have our own little piece of the whole, which is our only responsibility. All we can do, and all we have to do, is evolve *our own* energy to the highest level of vibration that is possible. We cannot evolve another person's energy and we cannot directly assist other people in the evolution of their energy. Furthermore, no one else's energy is truly functional in our space. Thus, our only healthy option is to *separate* from their energy.

It is common to respond to other people's competition with competition when we cannot *separate* from their energy. I remember my years in college as being a very invalidating experience. Imagine my surprise, after having done some healing work, when I discovered that much of this invalidation originated from other people. College students are busy polishing their wonderful façades as a way of avoiding their feelings of invalidation. And having no idea how to heal their invalidation, they push it out onto the rest of the world through competition. Of course, at the time, I had my own invalidation to contend with as well, and it was all very confusing. But once I began to heal my own invalidation and competition, I was able to recognize other people's issues and *separate* from them.

In health care practices, it is common for people to project the responsibility for their health issues onto their physician. They expect their physician to take responsibility for fixing their problems. If physicians do not *separate* from their patients, they take on their patients' energy. This does not help the patients resolve their issues and it impairs the health and well-being of the physician. Unfortunately, this is a frequent occurrence. Furthermore, if a patient's health issue is not resolved, the patient may blame the physician for the outcome! The challenge for physicians is to *separate* from their patients' energy while providing a service to the best of their ability.

The areas of money and finance are rife with examples of *separation* issues. A large percentage of people have issues with money. When people play games with you around money, they are playing out their money issues but not owning them. These issues are then directed at you and, if you do not *separate* from the energy, they can easily appear to be your issues. You may even begin to act as if they are your issues!

Let's imagine that you perform a service for someone and the other person doesn't pay you when they had agreed to pay you. Perhaps this drags on, and they do not communicate their intentions about the payment that is past due. They do not bring the topic up for discussion if you do not bring it up. It gets to a point where you have to remind them to pay you. If you bring it up, it looks like it is your issue instead of theirs and sometimes they will even say so. It is common to think of the other person's issue as your own because you took their issue on when they first played their money game with you and you did not put an end to it at the outset. Nonetheless, the money issue belongs to your client. *Your* issue is *not separating* from the client's money game.

In business, there are potential *separation* issues with every customer interaction. If you own a business, customers often expect you to take responsibility for fulfilling their emotional needs as well as their business needs. For instance, some people want to feel that they have worth, while others may want to feel important or special. They will often project these emotional needs onto you and your associates. If you *separate* from their needs, your customers may get upset and perhaps not do business with you. But if you don't *separate*, you and your co-workers are essentially taking responsibility for fulfilling your customers emotionally. Ultimately, you need to learn how to address your clients' needs without bringing their energy into your space.

Separating from other people's issues is particularly important when we are trying to assist them. When I work with clients, I must engage with them to gather information and to understand their concerns. At the same time, I must *separate* from them to accurately perceive their issues, determine the cause of their experience, and assist them with their healing.

Although people tend to feel most comfortable when someone engages with them *through* their issues, I have to *separate* from my clients' issues for healing to occur. I must maintain an environment in which my clients feel comfortable enough to have their issues and, at the same time, be separate enough so that they can heal and let go of their issues.

In addition, to truly be able to assist others, we need to be aware of our own issues so that we do not make them other people's issues. If, in a health care setting, we perceive people as being victims of their problems, we are making it harder for our clients to take responsibility for their healing and to feel empowered to accomplish their healing. This may be the most difficult aspect of *separating,* as we may not be aware of our own issues and, therefore, not be effective in keeping them separate from those with whom we are interacting.

How do you know what is your issue and what is someone else's issue or energy? Ultimately, you will be able to recognize the difference between your own and someone else's energy just by the feel of it. With more experience with this healing process, you will know how your own unique energy feels.

However, in the beginning of your development, try to relax through all of the feelings that you notice. Try to heal everything. Normally, when you relax into a feeling, you can find a level of ease at which the feeling moves through you and is gone. If, when you relax into a feeling, it feels heavy and immovable, you are most likely experiencing another person's energy. If it gets heavier and feels worse as you attempt to relax further into it, it is even more likely to be someone else's feeling. This is true for both negative and positive feelings.

If you are experiencing pain and insecurity and try to relax through those feelings, you will become stuck in them if they are not your feelings of pain and insecurity.

If someone wants your love to get away from his or her pain, you might feel their pain and think that it is yours. You may then respond by wanting love from another person, sometimes the very person who wants your love.

If you have trouble relaxing into a positive feeling, such as love or generosity, it is most likely someone else's feeling. Thus, if you are experiencing a feeling that you call love, you might want to feel more of it. However, if you try to relax through it and it does not flow, it is probably not your love.

If you are feeling generous but realize that you are giving your energy away or that it does not feel good, try to relax through your feeling of generosity to heal it. If the feeling does not flow when you attempt to relax through it, it is not your feeling. It may be someone wanting you to be generous with them or it may be someone else's definition of generosity. You could have absorbed this form of generosity long ago even though it is coming into play now.

As a caution, you must be sure that you are relaxing properly before you can be certain that you are dealing with someone else's energy. Many people become stuck in their own feelings because they are not finding the optimum level of relaxation.

How do you *separate* from another person's energy? Sometimes simply recognizing that the energy is not your own is enough to create a *separation*. At other times, once you recognize the energy as foreign, you will have to heal the issues through which you engaged the other person's energy in order to create a *separation*.

You may have engaged with the other person through a feeling that you were trying to avoid. If this is the case, you can heal your feeling by relaxing through it, which will create a *separation* from the other person.

You may have engaged with the other person if there was a feeling that you wanted from him or her. In this case, you can heal your issue by giving yourself the feeling you wanted and that will create a *separation*.

Another way you can engage with someone else's energy is through the qualities that you contribute to the interaction. These are typically façade or false self qualities with which you engage with other people. For instance, you can easily engage with other people by being helpful or friendly. These qualities either bring other people's energy into your space, such as when you accept their pain or loneliness, or give other people energy, such as when you validate someone to fulfill their need for success. Healing these qualities will not make you less friendly or helpful; it will make your helpfulness and friendliness more functional.

While your façade and false self were developed specifically to engage with other people's issues and to engage others in your issues, now you know that the qualities that comprise your façade and false self are dysfunctional when you connect with others in this way. Once you become hooked into another person's energy, you will have to heal the quality that you contributed to the interaction in order to successfully separate from him or her.

To heal what you contributed to an interaction and to separate from the energy you engaged with, you will want to relax through the quality that you brought to the connection. If your cooperation, responsibility, helpfulness, caring, openness, or love engaged someone's energy, relaxing through the feeling of that quality will heal it and create a *separation* from the other person's energy.

If your caring pulls someone's pain into your space, your caring needs to evolve. You must heal your caring to separate from their pain, because you cannot help them by carrying their pain for them. You heal your caring by relaxing through your feeling of caring. This does not make you uncaring. It makes your caring healthier and you will actually be more truly caring.

If you suddenly feel the need to talk with someone on the telephone, try to relax through that feeling. If you cannot get through the feeling, it is most likely the other person who wants to talk with you. To separate from the other person and their feelings, you will have to find out how you engaged with them. Perhaps you were being friendly and pulled their energy into your space. In this case, you will have to heal your friendliness to separate from the other person's wants.

If you discover that your feeling of being courteous or nice is not your own feeling, you will have to address how you assumed someone else's definition in order to separate from it. Perhaps you were taught how to be courteous and nice when you were growing up. If you could not validate your behavior, you probably embodied other people's concepts of nice and courteous. In this case, you will have to heal your invalidation before you can personify *your* definition of these qualities.

I had a client who was feeling someone else's pain and tried to heal the pain by relaxing through it. When she kept getting stuck in the pain, she realized that it was not her pain and began to look for how she had engaged the other person's energy. She could feel herself caring for her friend and thought that she had engaged with his pain through her caring. She then attempted to heal her caring by relaxing through her feeling of caring but kept getting stuck in that as well. Realizing that the caring was not hers either, she began to look for how she had engaged with her friend's need for care. She discovered that she had taken responsibility for her friend, pulling his need for care and his pain into her space. She had to heal her sense of responsibility to separate from her friend's issues and evolve herself.

Later, the same client discovered that she was still engaging with her friend's desire for care and feelings of pain. This time she had to heal her feeling of being loving. By healing her loving, she separated from her friend's issues and evolved the quality of her loving. She also attained a greater sense of inner peace and a healthier state of being.

Everyone has the power to separate from other people's energy. You must simply ascertain how you engaged with their energy and heal your part in your connections.

Separating means that you are not enmeshed with other people's issues and that you do not interact through dysfunction. When used successfully, *separating* assures you of having only your own energy in your space.

Separating from another person's energy is not necessarily the same as disconnecting from that person. Disconnecting from someone means that there is no longer any energy interaction. If your connection with someone is only through dysfunction, then making *separations* will be the same as disconnecting. If, on the other hand, your connection with someone has other healthy aspects, then separating and healing the dysfunctional aspects of your interaction will result in a much more enjoyable connection.

Commonly, people attempt to disconnect from others when they are trying to get away from an undesirable interaction. However, **when an interaction is mediated by an issue, that issue and the dysfunctional engagement continue until there is healing**—even if you never see the person again! Attempting to disconnect is simply a defense against the underlying issues and will not end the energy connection. If your connection with someone is through an issue, only healing will allow you to move beyond the issue and create the possibility of a healthy connection.

Once you have successfully separated from another person, do not expect them to be thrilled that you are healing, though that may be the case. If you have been carrying their issues around for them and you effectively separate from them, they will now be feeling their issues and, in fact, you might find them more upset with you than before. Then again, if they have been carrying your issues and you separate and heal those issues, there will be an immediate release of tension from your relationship and a noticeable improvement in the flow of that relationship.

Many people try to disconnect from *themselves* as a way to defend against their own issues. However, they remain engaged in their issues and defending only takes them further away from their true Self. This pattern contributes to the development and maintenance of the inverted self. Disconnecting *cannot* assist you in reclaiming your true Self.

When you are *separate* from your true Self, you experience feelings like pain, loss, isolation, and loneliness. From this place, you could easily reach out to others to cope with your feelings. However, since these feelings signal a loss of your Self, only healing can resolve them and cure the *separation* within you.

As your connection with your true Self grows, all of your other connections will flow from this inner connection. From this vantage point, you will discover that *separating* from everyone else is normal; it is the healthiest way to be and the most evolved way to relate with other people. From this place, truly functional and mature connections with others are possible.

With healing, you will find it easy to be around people from whom you can *separate*. In healthy relations, there is a constant flow of connecting and letting go. You connect in healthy ways and let go when the interaction is complete. You maintain a state of wholeness within your Self and experience the true inner fulfillment of such a state. Then your relations can flow from wholeness and healthy creativity instead of need.

To the false self, which is so used to having constant interactions with others based on needs, the idea of being totally separate from others may be frightening. For many people, feeling comfortable and complete requires constant engagement and connection with others as a defense against their underlying feelings of loneliness or emptiness. And because the path of healing takes people to a place where they only have their own energy in their space, some people may experience feelings of isolation, anxiety, or discomfort when they separate from others. All of these issues will require healing to **become comfortable with not always being connected with others.**

With healing, you will discover the contentment of not engaging with others as well as the joy of connecting with others in healthy ways. You will realize your natural state of wholeness.

Several people have suggested that we are all mirrors for one another. This involves both positive and negative aspects of our experience. In particular, they suggest that conflict with another person and negative experiences are a reflection of our own issues. Unfortunately, this model for understanding human behavior does not reflect a true understanding of what is going on.

For sure, it is common to get other people's energy in our space. And, if we do not recognize it as such, to act as if it is our own. It is equally common for other people to be doing the same thing in relation to us. But the actual phenomenon of mirroring requires a combination of someone projecting their issues out into the world and someone else engaging with those issues. That is, someone acting as their inverted self and someone else being complicit with the first person's worldview.

Of course, being a mirror for another person is neither functional nor desirable. We do not want another person's energy in our space, let alone his or her issues. This is another reason to master the essential skill of separating from other people's energy.

EXERCISE: Practice Separating

Next time you cannot stop thinking about someone, practice separating from him or her. Are you engaging through a feeling that you are trying to get away from, a feeling that you want, or a quality of your energy that you are contributing to the interaction? Heal your part in the engagement and separate from the other person's energy. When you have successfully separated, you will no longer have that person on your mind.

Relationships: The Energy between People

We are interacting with people all the time. Some of it is overt and obvious like when we are on the telephone talking with friends or clients. And much of the time it's not so obvious, such as when we are thinking about other people or have feelings about them. We are actually interacting with other people nearly 24 hours a day, even when we are asleep.

We previously discussed how our false self or personality developed. Now let's explore more fully how energy and emotion flow between people. Then we can apply our healing skills to what we learn so we have healthier and more fulfilling interactions with others.

While this discussion focuses on intimate relationships because they often involve the greatest demands and expectations, it applies to all kinds of relationships, including work relations, friendships, and even relationships of an adversarial nature. Even though we have different expectations in our various relationships, many of our issues will arise in all of them. We still have to discover the true Self within and function from that place. Our issues still require healing and cannot be resolved by a relationship. Even in an intimate relationship, for instance, we still have to heal our feelings of isolation and aloneness. And sometimes those feelings are even more noticeable in an intimate relationship!

Let's begin by stating the obvious: Every relationship involves an engagement with another person's energy. This gives rise to a series of questions that will be the focus for the rest of this chapter: What part of your energy engages with other people? What part of the other person's energy engages with you? What is happening between the two of you energetically? Is the engagement truly healthy? Is this kind of energetic engagement the way you want to be with other people?

When we bring two people into relationship with each other, there are a variety of interactions that are possible (see Figure 4). We bring different parts of our energy into relationship with others. And we often have an assortment of different types of energetic interactions going on at the same time.

Some of the interactions that are possible include façade to façade, defense to defense, defense to block, block to façade, block to false self, false self to false self, false self to true Self, and true Self to true Self.

Façade to façade connections occur frequently at work between employees and clients.

Defense to defense connections develop when someone directs his or her issues at another. This occurs when people are angry at each other, when people compete with each other, and when people abuse one another.

The people we do not like to be around are often those who trigger off our issues or dump their issues in our space. These are often defense to defense or defense to block connections. Often there is a defense to block connection when one person is judging another for a particular behavior.

If we feel insecure or lonely and call a friend on the phone, there is frequently a block to façade or block to false self connection. If we are "helpful" to someone in need, there is a false self to block connection.

Figure 4: Energy Connections in Relationships

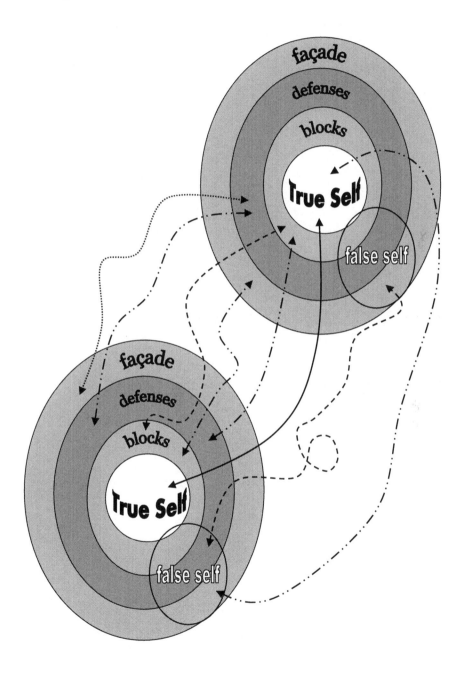

When we are interacting with friends, our "best" friends will often support the parts that we like about ourselves. These are often façade to façade or false self to false self connections.

The intention behind our interactions determines their energetic dynamics. As a result, the true Self interacts with the world and with others in a very different way from how the false self interacts. Using our knowledge of intention as our basis for our evaluation, let's explore some of the different kinds of interactions to develop a greater understanding about what occurs in those interactions.

First, we will take a deeper look at false self to false self interactions because they are a good model for demonstrating how energy flows between people in all *non*-true Self interactions. Later we will look at true Self to true Self relations, followed by a look at false self to true Self interactions.

False Self to False Self Connections

Every type of connection other than a true Self to true Self connection is based on either trying to obtain feelings we want or trying to get away from feelings we don't want. Both people in these interactions have the intention of trying to fulfill their needs outside themselves and, therefore, do not have the intention to heal.

Because these interactions are based on either getting away from feelings we don't want or getting feelings we want, we will gravitate to those people and scenarios that fulfill these needs. Our needs dictate what will catch our attention and be of interest to us and, therefore, what we will find attractive.

People who give us the feelings or energy that we seek will be attractive to us. If we do not experience our own security, we may be attracted to someone who gives us the feeling of security. If we do not feel our own beauty, we may be drawn to a particular look or façade. If we feel invalid, we may look to others to find validation.

People will find us attractive if we fulfill their energy needs. If someone wants inspiration and we are "inspirational," they will be attracted to us. Or, perhaps someone is attracted to our loyalty if that is the feeling they want.

Whoever grows up in an abusive household may find themselves attracted to abusive relationships. This kind of relationship will often feel comfortable to participate in and may even seem loving to the participants. They often get some energetic benefit from the relationship and, even if it is a negative experience, it is still a form of attention.

Because everyone who is acting out the false self has energy needs, they often engage in energy trades to try to fulfill themselves. They will tend to surround themselves with people who fulfill at least some of their needs while they are fulfilling other people's needs at the same time.

They may give someone a feeling of love and in return get a feeling they want, such as feeling valid, wanted, or desirable. They may engage in façade to façade interactions by acting nice and supportive in order to get their need for validation satisfied. They may give someone the feeling of security in exchange for having a connection, feeling appreciated, or perhaps feeling respected.

Another kind of attraction relates to our negative feelings. **We will be attracted to people with whom we do not feel our negative feelings.** These people do not take our feelings away, but we do not have to feel our feelings when we are around them. If, for instance, I do not feel my invalidation when I am around you, you will be attractive to me. Not having to feel our issues is a common expectation regarding relationships.

Attraction also develops towards people who absorb our blocks, issues, and defenses. They will be attractive to us because they help us maintain the "comfort" of the false self. We will feel better when we are around people who take our negative feelings away. Perhaps we are feeling lonely and, when we are around friends, they listen to our problems and absorb our loneliness. Then we no longer feel lonely. Isn't that what friends are for?

When we are not the source of our positive feelings, we look for them outside our Self. There is a tendency to project what we want onto others. It is common for others to accommodate our needs by absorbing our projections and reflecting them back to us. This creates attraction. **We become attracted to our own positive projections that have been absorbed and reflected by other people.**

Perhaps we project that someone is caring and, because that person absorbs our expectation, he or she becomes caring towards us and we get to feel cared for. Or, we become friends with someone because that person projects that we are friendly and we absorb that energy.

Or, let's say that we don't feel secure and maybe someone who is successful and wealthy gives us the feeling of security. We might be attracted to such a person because we cannot generate the feeling of security for ourselves. We are attracted to something that *implies* security for us. However, since success and wealth are not equivalent to security, we are projecting what we want onto someone else, and then we are attracted to and fulfilled by our own projection.

Perhaps we do not feel powerful and someone who is big and muscular gives us a feeling of power. We might be attracted to such a person because we cannot generate the feeling of power for ourselves. Once again, our projection directs our experience and behavior.

Often, we absorb other people's expectations and give them the feelings they desire. That makes us attractive even if it is not who we really are. As our false self, we are often just acting anyway, so why not? If we sense the possibility of getting our needs met, we are all too happy to oblige.

We may even fall in love with someone who absorbs the projection of our expectations and who then turns around and fulfills our needs and expectations. If we end up falling in love with someone who has absorbed our projections and reflected them back to us, we have just fallen in love with our own projections!

To summarize, the false self will be attracted to people who:

1. Fulfill its energy needs.
2. Take it away from its (-) energy blocks.
3. Absorb its (-) energy blocks and (-) projections.
4. Absorb its (+) projections and reflect them back.

When our false self or personality becomes involved in an intimate relationship, the source of our energy is outside our Self—we look to others for our fulfillment. Our needs form the basis for our idea of what a relationship should feel like, and we are attracted to people who meet those criteria or at least some of those criteria. To a large degree, the greater the need, the greater the potential attraction.

The combination of specific needs and need fulfillment, along with individual programming about relationships, will create the desire and attraction for a relationship with a particular person. Our needs determine what is attractive to us and this can develop into what we call love.

Love for the false self is energetically defined as the fulfillment of specific needs and the absence of certain negative feelings. Some of the needs that we confuse with love in our culture include support, control, power, acceptance, caring, understanding, validation, and sex. Sometimes we confuse love with the *absence* of feeling alone or empty. We are used to connecting through these issues and these connections are the basis for our ideas of love. Popular music is filled with expressions of false self love, such as, "I can't live without you," "I need you," "My world is empty without you," "Everything I do, I do it for you," and "I can't make it without you."

We can create a mathematical equation that describes this kind of relationship and that is ½ + ½ = ½. We enter this kind of relationship being incomplete and seek an external source for our fulfillment. We look outside our Self to complete ourselves, but cannot gain anything by connecting with other people in this way. The relationship does not complete us and we are still just the fractional people that we were prior to the relationship.

Our blocks are still present, though we may not experience them when the other person absorbs them. However, this can only be a temporary reprieve. Alternatively, we do not feel them because of what the other person is giving us, thereby fulfilling our needs—again temporarily.

In this kind of relationship, we only have the fraction of ourselves that we started with. Eventually, the emotional blocks and distortions that keep us from experiencing wholeness will raise their ugly heads and have to be healed. Or else we can run off with another person who will do a better job of fulfilling our needs! After all, when our false self feels lonely, we often interpret it to mean that we miss someone else.

With false self connections, there is a premature merging with people through unhealed issues. There is an illusion that there is completion in this kind of relationship. There is an illusion on the false self level that we are getting fulfillment and that this is intimacy. But actually, intimacy is completely absent here because intimacy comes from bringing our true Self into relation with another person—it has nothing to do with the false self or with bringing unhealed issues into the relationship.

What do we need to do to sustain a relationship like this? Primarily, each person is going to be providing some energy that the other person needs. We are going to give the other person validation, acceptance, and security if these are the feelings that are needed by that person. We can become very specific, tailoring our conduct to match other people's expectations. We can match other people's programming about the meaning of particular actions and behavior to give them the feelings they want. We can get very sophisticated with our patterns of tiptoeing around each other's stuff to stay in our false self and feel as good as we can in this kind of relationship.

Typically, neither person in a false self relationship knows how to go through a block. Therefore, to sustain this kind of connection, we will also try to avoid upsetting (triggering off) the other person. We may stop the flow of our energy (shut down) to avoid triggering the other person. We do not want to rock the boat (or tip the boat over!) because we want to stay in our false self. Furthermore, if the other person is triggered off, we will often help them get back to a "comfortable" place by absorbing any negative emotion that arises and by feeding them the positive feelings they desire.

If we are not getting what we want, we can try to get the other person to give it to us. This might be through some kind of direct negotiation, manipulation, or control game. Or we might try to get the person to give us what we want indirectly by going through a friend, family member, or pet to manipulate the relationship.

What is involved with communication in a false self relationship? **Without the intention to heal, communication will never support healing.** Thus, in this case, communication will be used as a defense—it is *not* going to facilitate healing or getting through issues. It will be used to negotiate for the other person's energy, to find a way out of our blocks, and to get back to the original, but dysfunctional, false self to false self connection. It is going to do everything *except* assist us with healing.

Many people in false self relationships try to minimize communication with the intention of avoiding their issues. This defensive maneuver may diminish the overt friction in the relationship, but it does nothing to facilitate a healing process or a real resolution of issues. These people may hope that their issues will just go away if no one acknowledges or talks about them; however, not acknowledging issues is the opposite of healing and not talking about issues is *not* what we want to create. We are interested in creating healing and in developing communication that is functional and open.

When we define words like care, love, and friendship in the context of the false self, they all support the false self. If we are triggered off and we want to be comfortable, a friend who is caring and loving is going to help us return to our false self. Our friend may absorb the feelings that were triggered off and give us energy. While it does not help with our healing, a person who is a caring or loving friend to our false self is someone who supports our dysfunction.

For our false self, it is common to mistake the avoidance of our issues for fun because running away from those issues seems to feel better. Thus, for the false self, activities that seem fun involve defenses that take us away from our issues. But truly, **there is no such thing as an *activity* that is fun; it is the *energy we bring* to an activity that determines whether or not it is fun.**

In false self relationships, the blocks, façades, defenses, and foreign energy that we identify with are the parts of our energy that form the basis for our connections. We are connecting *through* the qualities of our false self, which include some of our dysfunctional issues. Since we are interacting with others and with the world *through* our issues, those issues intervene in the connection.

Because our issues form the basis for false self connections, it makes it very difficult to heal any of our issues when we are attached to or committed to these connections. In the previous chapter, we discussed the need to separate from other people's issues because we can only heal our own issues and other people are the only ones who can heal their issues. However, now we are connecting with each other *through* the issues. If we try to separate from the other person's issues and heal our own, we have just started to disconnect from the other person. Thus, there is really no room for healing in a false self relationship! Yet, without healing, there cannot be any growth or movement in a relationship.

Furthermore, our true Self cannot participate in a relationship in which we are connecting through our issues. If we attempt to be our true Self, we have to separate from the other person's issues. By separating from the other person's issues, we will appear to be cold, uncaring, unloving, and heartless because their issues come up and we do not bail them out. The other person will often experience distress because they are used to merging with us and never having to feel anything. Unhealed issues that were temporarily hidden because of the relationship are now palpable and the other person loses the illusion of completeness and friendship.

Other dysfunctional elements accompany our relationships when we are not being our true Self. For instance, being separate from our Self is what gives rise to feelings of isolation, aloneness, and insecurity. Therefore, when we interact through our issues and do *not* bring our true Self into our relations, feelings of insecurity and isolation will be inherent features of those interactions. And they will be intrinsic aspects of every relationship until we become our true Self.

With healing, we can slowly but steadily move out of identifying with our false self and move towards identifying with our true Self. Our relationships will then reflect an increasing presence of our true Self.

If we are involved with others during this time of change and growth, it can be quite unsettling as we separate and go through the healing that is required. It may feel like a loss or disconnection to one or both people involved. If the feelings of loss or disconnection arise, those feelings will require healing as well.

We can also go bouncing in and out of a particular relationship. We may separate and heal something but become enmeshed again because of a different issue. Perhaps we are missing a particular feeling and go back into the relationship to get it. If we merge energy with the other person again, the issues temporarily submerge and we do not have to feel them. Then a new cycle of dysfunction begins.

True Self to True Self Connections

With healing, we become our Self. Then relationships become an opportunity to bring our *Self* into relationship with another person instead of just bringing our *issues* into relationship with another person.

A true Self connection is *not* going to be based on need. This may seem unusual since we are so familiar with connecting with people out of need. Nevertheless, we can connect with people through other energy besides our needs.

True Self connections are based on who we really are. Thus, on a true Self level of relating, we are attracted to who a person really is and we connect as our Self. In these interactions, we connect Self to Self without anything intervening; they are mediated by the qualities we have mastered *within* our Self. This may include connecting through the love, success, or peace that is within us. We may connect through the wisdom, expression, or validation of our Self. We may engage through the joy of being our Self or the creativity that flows from our connection with our Self. Or a connection may simply involve enjoying who the other person is and having a companion who is our equal, someone who is operating on a similar energy level.

These connections feel completely different from false self connections because they are not based on our issues. For one thing, there will not be a battle over who gets their needs met and whose issues are whose. Both people will know that if they are triggered off, they have something to heal. Also, it will be okay to have issues going on because the participants will know that they have to have issues arise to continue on the path of healing. True Self to true Self connections are not about the issues and both people focus on taking care of themselves. This creates the possibility of a truly mature connection with another person because the connection is not about completing ourselves or merging through unhealed issues.

The intention to heal provides direction and guidance for staying on the path of our Self and for continuing to evolve our true Self while in a relationship. There is a dedication to personal growth and to healing our Self. There is a commitment to strengthening the connection with our Self and to healing whatever issues arise.

The qualities that were attractive in the false self to false self scenario will *not* be attractive to the true Self. As we heal and become more our true Self, our needs will begin to drop away. As we fulfill our own needs, our expectations of others will diminish. The attraction of need fulfillment disappears.

Furthermore, we realize that it is not possible to give anyone the feelings that he or she desires. We recognize that emotional healing does not work in this manner and that the feelings people desire must come from within.

For the false self, it will often feel attractive to have someone needing us or needing our energy. As we become more our true Self, when others come to us and need us, we will initially feel repelled by their grabbing at our energy. We will know that we cannot give others anything and that they have to find it within themselves. The grabbing will not feel good anymore because we will know that we cannot fulfill their needs, but are not totally separating from them yet. Eventually, with more healing, we will not be attracted to the grabbing and we will not be repelled or repulsed by it either because the grabbing at our energy will not touch us at all. We will have mastered the ability to separate from other people's needs.

Most of us are familiar with connecting with others to avoid feelings of loneliness and isolation. If we are functioning from our false self, we may call a friend or create a relationship to avoid our feelings.

If, on the other hand, we are functioning as our true Self, loneliness means that we miss our Self. It tells us that we have lost our true Self connection and that we have to go through the feeling of loneliness to reclaim our Self. There is nothing to run away from and the solution is not out in the world. With healing, the experience of loneliness or isolation dissolves to be replaced by the fulfillment of a connection with our Self. Then we feel whole and complete.

As our true Self, we realize that love is not somewhere out in the world and it is not a feeling that is generated through our interactions with other people. We realize that love is something that flows *through* us and, therefore, it becomes a part of us and a part of everything we do. True Self relationships are not going to be based on a need for love because we already have it within our Self. Instead, relationships become an opportunity to express and create with our love *with* someone else.

For our true Self, qualities like caring, loving, and friendship have a different meaning from what they mean to our false self. Our true Self friends support us in being our true Self. If we are triggered off, our friends are not going to jump in and drown in the feeling with us. If we're feeling down and wanting them to share in our horror, our true Self friends do not take our energy on, give us sympathy, or shut down and match our energy. If we call them up wanting to get some "caring" energy, our true Self friends do not feed us the energy we desire: the forms of "caring" and "friendship" we are familiar with in false self to false self connections. True Self friends do not participate on this level.

True Self friends support us in our healing, which means *not* connecting with us through dysfunction. It means they remind us that the source of our fulfillment is within and that the true Self is who we are. When we connect with someone who honors the true Self, who cares about the true Self, and who isn't going to get into our junk, their true Self caring, loving, and friendship support who we really are. A true Self friend is someone with whom we can be our Self!

A mathematical equation that describes our interactions with others on the true Self level is $1 + 1 = 3$. And I don't mean a baby, although that is a perfectly legitimate creation! What this means is that we are no longer looking to complete ourselves through somebody else. We bring our wholeness into the relationship, someone else brings their wholeness, and instead of battling over energy—as in the $\frac{1}{2} + \frac{1}{2} = \frac{1}{2}$ scenario—we are freed up to create something more than our Self in the relationship.

For the false self, communication is commonly used to negotiate an energetic settlement. People attempt to talk themselves out of their issues and into the feelings that they seek. Unfortunately, false self people often negotiate themselves into greater dysfunction and further away from their true Self.

Communication for true Self people is very different. When they communicate, they strive to align their spoken words with the intention to heal. When they express their true Self, they *respect* other people's space and energy. True Self people own their issues and do not direct them at each other. And any assistance given by a true Self person to other people supports them in moving through their issues and towards their true Self; it supports the intention to heal in others.

While healthy communication can occur regarding any topic, there is no way to talk ourselves out of our feelings. No matter how much we talk about issues and no matter how much we understand about a problem, we still have to go through our feelings. Thus, true Self people do not attempt to talk their way out of their issues or bargain for feelings they desire.

Even though we cannot negotiate our issues away, many things are negotiable within a functional relationship. In fact, the only aspect of our life that is not negotiable is our true Self. And one of the gifts of healing is that it can show us what is the true Self and, therefore, non-negotiable, and what is outside our true Self and, therefore, negotiable. Only through healing can we discern the difference.

Although healing is a solitary process and everyone has to go through his or her own feelings, there are, of course, many ways we can facilitate healing through communication. Since it is essential to acknowledge that an issue exists before we can heal it, it is useful to set up healing through communication— we can talk about what is going on and have a better idea of what the problem is. Many people do not realize that they are wrestling with an issue until someone brings it to their attention or until they talk about it. Thus, it is a good idea to discuss most issues as they arise until the healing process is well established.

There are also certain things we can do to facilitate the healing of our communication. For instance, it is essential that we take responsibility for our own process and feelings, and not try to tell other people what they have going on.

Furthermore, if a barrier or defense is forming between people, it is useful to do what we can to take that barrier down. Anything that reduces barriers and defenses facilitates healing, and we can effectively use communication for such a purpose. For instance, by owning and expressing our own feelings, conceding when we may be wrong, admitting when we are stuck, and acknowledging when we do not know what is going on, we can diminish or remove barriers to healthy interactions in relationships.

In a true Self to true Self connection, separations are the rule. Your issues are your issues and my issues are my issues. I cannot go through your issues, and there is nothing I can do to help you evade your issues. If we are connecting through issues, we must separate and heal on our own. Then we can reconnect at a higher level of energy, moving beyond connecting through the junk. Again, because we are seeking a connection that is not based on issues, separations are the rule. We want to connect true Self to true Self, and our issues are going to be separate and individual.

In false self relationships, issues are shared and we forget whose issues are whose. It's all one big mess and it is very difficult to heal. We are either connecting through the issues and are unable to separate to heal them, or we try to separate to get away from the energetic morass. To separate from the other person's feelings, we often end up disconnecting from that person.

In true Self relationships, the connection is coming from a different part of our energy and the connection is what we want to continue to nurture. We are going to want to heal and let go of the issues.

While the false self appears to have the option of disconnecting from others and from issues that it finds uncomfortable, the true Self recognizes that our dysfunctional connections with others require healing to be resolved. If there are aspects of our interactions with others that involve engaging through issues, we will separate on those levels and heal the issues.

Even if we could disconnect to try to avoid an issue, at some point in the future we would have to reconnect to heal the original issue. And even if it appears that we have disconnected, that is an illusion. Once we have engaged through an issue, that engagement persists until it is healed. Disconnecting is not possible, nor is it desirable. Either we heal our issues now or we have to heal them later. Thus, attempting to disconnect is not a viable option—healing is the only way to go.

Fun is the natural result of being in the flow of our Self. Anything can be fun when we are in our true Self flow. And when we are with others, being in that flow together.

Even work can be fun when we work in the flow of our true Self. In fact, it is normal to work in alignment with our Self and to work together with others in that flow. And being in the flow of our true Self *includes* having issues going on. Thus, we can have fun even when we have active issues, whereas the avoidance of our issues is what makes things not fun. Our healing process is an integral part of being our Self and, therefore, an integral part of having fun.

The fun only stops when the flow of our true Self stops. Anything that takes us out of our flow takes us out of our fun. If we stop being true to our Self, try to avoid our issues, or leave our path to engage with others, we lose the flow of our fun. If we engage with someone to give them energy or to take on their issues, we lose the flow of our fun.

Genuine fun involving other people can only occur at the true Self level of connection. Everyone involved has to be in the flow of their true Self to have genuine fun together.

True Self to False Self Connections

True Self to false self interactions happen more often than we might think. Every time someone heals an issue, they become more their true Self. And if other people have not healed their issues, they are going to be functioning as their false self. They are going to attempt to engage through their issues.

We can have fun and enjoy other people even when they are being their false self. We do not have to engage with their issues. We can be our Self and honor the true Self in others, whether they identify with that part of their energy or not. Even though everyone involved in an interaction will have to be in the flow of their true Self for everyone to have fun together, by remaining in the flow of our true Self, we can always have fun.

It is very beneficial to accept, allow, and enjoy true Self to false self interactions. A true Self level of connection is not a prerequisite for fulfillment, development, connection, or enjoyment. If we are looking for that *from* an interaction, we have some healing to do.

Nonetheless, a problem develops when one person wants to become his or her true Self and has the intention to heal, and the other person wants to remain as his or her false self and does *not* have the intention to heal. These two people are going in very different directions. All the person intending to heal can do is continue to heal and go through whatever is coming up, and one of a few things will happen.

One possibility is that the person who is attached to their false self remains attached, and the true Self person continues to move away as a result of the healing process. In this case, there will be more of a separation *and* a disconnection between the two people.

On the other hand, when one person has separated and gone through their own issues, the other person may have an easier time going through their issues. It only takes one person performing their healing work to create changes in a relationship. If we heal our part of a dysfunctional connection, we are no longer playing that game, and the other person may let go of their issue.

Part of the difficulty is that all of the words we have been discussing—friendship, loving, caring, and support—are going to mean the exact opposite things for these two people. For one person, caring means, "Go through your stuff, and I'll meet you on the other side." While for the other person, it means, "Get involved in my stuff with me and help me get back to where I was." This could give rise to disagreements because these two people have divergent motives and goals.

Although it is helpful, it is not necessary for both people to be engaged in a healing process for a relationship to be successful. Nor do we have to jump in and try to heal the other person for the relationship to move forward. We can use the relationship to continue our healing and to assist our progression towards our true Self. If we are not engaging with the issues that the other person has going on, it should facilitate positive movement in the relationship.

EXERCISE: Examining Relationships

Look at every relationship you participate in and identify which part of your energy is involved in those interactions. Do you use a façade at work or with friends? With whom do you feel most genuine?

Energy Traders

If we do not experience the source of fulfillment within ourselves, we will seek the fulfillment of our energy needs from the world. The motivation for our actions and interactions is based on our desire to fulfill those needs outside our Self.

We may spend the entire day exchanging energy through our constant interactions with other people, even if it is just through thoughts and feelings without any direct contact with them. We can easily go through our life absorbing other people's expectations and trying to give them what they want, while at the same time trying to fulfill our own energy needs. And other people are often absorbing our expectations and trying to give us what we want, while trying to fulfill their energy needs.

Thus, we are constantly engaged in trading commodities with other people. We trade goods and services, we trade energy, and we trade feelings. We are all energy traders!

If we look at what occurs in our interactions with others in the context of exchanging energy, several patterns become apparent.

We may give others something to get something in return. Perhaps we give someone security in exchange for companionship. We might give loyalty to obtain love or security. We are generous so that we get some recognition or give acceptance in exchange for attention. We please others to get some validation. We might give love when another person really needs us. Some people trade sex for love and validation.

And we can be very devoted to another as long as we are getting what we want!

We might try to get our needs met by behaving in specific ways. To get some attention or validation, we can call a friend on the phone, make a scene, flirt, throw some sex energy, drive a unique car, achieve something noteworthy, or win a competition. We may act helpless or be a victim to get some caring or sympathy. To get a feeling of power, we can boss people around at work, be demanding with our co-workers, be controlling at home, be pushy with our family and friends, or exude toughness from our façade.

We may give up certain feelings to get other feelings. Perhaps we want to get away from a feeling of insecurity and are willing to give up our freedom to experience the security of a job. Or we might want to escape a feeling of isolation and be willing to give up our independence for the connection of a relationship. And it is common for people to give up their true Self in exchange for the love and security of a relationship.

If we would like something from a certain person, it is common to read their energy to see what they want. Then **we may try to finagle a trade by fulfilling the other person's desires.** By providing the other person with what he or she wants, we are attempting to create a connection and to obtain the desired energy in exchange.

Sometimes when we desire some energy from another person, we may just take it. This often occurs when we think that it is owed to us or that we deserve it. We may make a trade without any agreement from the other person and give what we think the other person wants. Then, if we don't get what we desire, we may just go and grab it. And even if there is an agreement regarding an energy exchange—or if we do not get what we expect—we may try to take the energy that we had anticipated receiving.

In many interactions, we exchange energy in a programmed manner through the roles we choose to

play. Whether it is a professional or a personal relationship, we contribute energy in agreed upon ways. It is common to play out roles that engage us in ways we believe fulfill our energy needs. And it is also common to seek out people who are willing to play the complementary role with which we wish to engage.

Sometimes it can appear that the roles are working when everyone maintains their game. However, watch the fireworks if we try to get real or if we are tired of playing our role and just stop. And what do we do if our role doesn't achieve the goals we desire? While some of us will attempt to change our way of being, many will simply find someone else with whom to play our game, even though it fails to accomplish our goals.

When we exchange energy through the roles we are acting out, we expend a lot of energy. The more acting that is involved and the less genuine the role, the more energy it takes to play.

At work, for example, many people are just acting at their job. But sustaining the illusion of trying to be someone we're not requires a considerable amount of energy. And taking on other people's expectations and giving them what they want takes energy. The more we are our true Self, the less energy trading we are going to do and the less tired we are going to become when we are living our life. The more tired we are at the end of the day, the more energy trading we engaged in that day. It is very draining to be giving our energy away, and we are not paid enough for it anyway!

Furthermore, when both people in an interaction want to get their energy needs met, there is often a battle about who gets whose energy. Someone wins the battle if they get the energy they need from the other person. Of course, it is quite draining to be battling for energy throughout the day.

Since energy trading is so pervasive, it is no surprise that many people carefully monitor all of their trades. They keep track of the credits and debits involved with all of their energy exchanges. With this accounting of their trading, they can balance their books, keeping an eye on who they owe energy to and who owes them energy.

Furthermore, many people view their energy exchanges as investments. They make decisions about how to invest their energy and judiciously calculate the costs and benefits of participating in any given energy exchange.

Of course, some people will use your integrity around energy against you. They may pretend to have integrity to take advantage of you and obtain your energy without any intention of reciprocating. Thus, you cannot assume that everyone shares your perspective when it comes to energy trades. On the other hand, did anyone promise that their energy trading was going to be handled with honor and integrity?

When we seek the fulfillment of our needs outside ourselves, our issues are validated because we use them to meet our needs. Creating energy exchanges with our issues actually supports those issues. For example, if I trade my loneliness for your nurturing, it supports my loneliness *and* your nurturing. If you trade your insecurity for my understanding, your insecurity *and* my understanding are supported. In these exchanges, there is an illusory benefit of a temporary connection that dulls the experience of loneliness or insecurity, and there is validation for being nurturing or understanding. And more generally, the trades engage us with other people, which is an important reason we participate in energy exchanges in the first place.

Furthermore, in our system of energy trading, it seems validating that someone wants our energy. Often we feel *honored* when someone accepts our energy. This is crazy! Would you feel *flattered* if someone came up to you on the street and asked for your money? Would you be *grateful* if someone wanted you to give them your home or car? Then why do you give your energy away so readily?

Moreover, we feel complimented when someone wants to dump their energy in our space. Would you feel *privileged* if someone wanted to dump their garbage in your house? So why do you joyfully welcome other people in to unload their invalidation, pain, and grief in your space?

If exchanging energy with others really worked, we would be fulfilled *by* our relationships. Our needs would be met by the energy donated to us by other people. Clearly, this cannot lead to fulfillment, and eventually we will have to look *within* to fulfill our own emotional and energy needs.

Thus, we must conclude that energy trading does not work. The energy we trade away is only useable by us and it only temporarily assuages another's needs. And by giving our energy away, we are bankrupting ourselves.

Furthermore, if we pick up someone's negative energy, we just feel bad. And even the positive energy for which we trade can only temporarily fulfill us. While we may feel content temporarily, the energy does not stick. It is *not* our energy and eventually it goes away. Then we need to go out and get some more of the same energy to fill our needs.

Fortunately, the habit of trading energy is curable. We can connect without trying to fill our emptiness, without trying to escape our loneliness, and without giving energy to each other. We can connect and keep our issues in our own space. We no longer have to connect through blocks, needs, dysfunction, or deficiency.

By healing, we create the possibility of connecting Self to Self through our fullness, our wholeness. Then, rather than engaging through the dysfunction of energy exchanges, we can truly co-create something that is greater than the sum of the parts.

EXERCISE: How Do You Get Your Needs Met?

What do you do to get feelings of worth, validation, love, and security? Notice what you are willing to trade to get these feelings.

EXERCISE: *Awareness of Energy Exchanges*

Energy exchanges occur with everyone with whom we make contact. To check this out in your own life, look back at your interactions with other people over the last few days. Did you look outside yourself to get acceptance, validation, security, approval, or sympathy? Were you giving energy to those people in the form of attention, sympathy, validation, caring, love, acknowledgement, or agreement? Did you absorb any pain or discomfort? Did you exchange sympathy?

Watch your interactions with others over the next few days. After each interaction, ask yourself the following questions: What did I want from this person? Did I get what I wanted? How did it feel? What did the other person want from me? Did they get what they wanted? How did it feel? Acknowledge and observe whatever energy exchanges occur.

Then evaluate for yourself whether or not energy exchanges really work. For how long does exchanged energy seem to endure? What do you and other people do when the exchanged energy dissipates? Does absorbing others' feelings really help anyone? Are you willing to play a role in someone else's life just to temporarily get some energy in exchange?

❊   ❊   ❊

All energy is a tradable commodity. Consult the lists of feelings at the back of the book for some trading ideas. ☺ Try them at home with your family! Use them to amaze your friends and even people you don't know! Make new friends wherever you go!

The Energy of Engagement

While we connect with others through the qualities that we bring to our engagements, **our interactions are always *motivated* by our intention,** the energy behind those qualities. Even the most minor, insignificant, or apparently random connections have intention as their initiating force.

Although interactions can be motivated by a variety of specific intentions, they can be classified into the three general categories we have been discussing: trying to get away from a feeling, wanting to fulfill a need, and, with healing, just *being* our Self. This underlying intention determines how we *energetically engage* with others.

With true Self connections, we connect true Self to true Self through the qualities that we own *within* our true Self without anything intervening. We interact or *energetically engage* through the qualities of the true Self without an agenda and without an energy exchange.

For connections other than those of our true Self, we must *complement* the other person for there to be an *energetic engagement*. If I am trying to get away from a feeling, such as pain, someone else must accept my energy, such as by being caring, to create an engagement. If I want to fulfill a need, such as success, someone else must give me some energy, such as through validating me, in order to create an engagement. Without a complementary pattern, no engagement can occur.

While these relations may seem attractive and enjoyable, it takes a lot of energy to maintain them—and there are healthier, more fulfilling ways of relating. In addition, a dysfunctional engagement occurs whenever someone gives energy to another or absorbs another person's energy. This is due to issues that we have already discussed: No one can go through our feelings and no one can give us the energy we want on a permanent basis. **An energy transfer or energy exchange *always* creates a dysfunctional connection.**

Some people act "powerfully" in their relations to get other people to absorb their insecurity. Some people get validation for being cooperative. And most people feel good about themselves when someone appreciates their assistance. Unless you engage with others as your true Self, there is *always* an energetic payoff or agenda behind the qualities that you bring to your interactions.

Since the evolved true Self is *never* involved in energy transfers or exchanges, contributions to our interactions can only originate from other portions of our energy. Our defenses, façade, and false self were developed specifically to avoid blocks, to get our energy needs met, and to participate in energy exchanges. Thus, either we interact as our true Self and engage through the qualities within our Self, or we engage through other aspects of our energy and participate in energy trades and exchanges.

Because we connect with others through the qualities that we bring to our interactions and because intention is always the motivating force behind those interactions, all of the qualities of our energy carry that intention. And **the qualities that we bring to our interactions always communicate our intention.**

If my intention is to get some help, my personality may portray neediness and victimization, or friendliness and love, but my energy will always articulate my desire for help. If my intention is to get away from a feeling of pain, my energy will always assert my intention, even if I am defending against it by denying it or engaging with others to try to avoid my feelings. And if my intention is to contribute enthusiasm to others to give me a sense of worth, my support and confidence will exude enthusiasm while I'm reaching for a feeling of worth.

Our personality traits and other qualities that we bring to our engagements convey the real purpose behind our behavior. No matter what the appearance of our behavior, if there is an underlying agenda, it is always active and expressed. While we may engage with others on a façade or false-self level that often appears to be pleasant, innocuous, or, at worst, uncomfortable, there is always at least one other level of engagement that relates to the intention of the communication. Since intention is the real energy of engagement, that is the energy to focus on to understand what is really going on with a particular interaction. It is this level of energy that lets us know whether we are interacting on a true Self level or participating in a dysfunctional connection.

EXERCISE: Energy Contributions

What qualities do you contribute to your interactions? Support? Success? Validation? Caring? Love? Understanding? Acceptance? For each quality that you can identify, what is the intention behind it? By healing the underlying motivation, you evolve the energy of your contribution.

If you feel defensive about any quality of your energy, please make use of this opportunity to heal your defense and whatever issue lies beneath it.

Dysfunction Junction:
A Place to Meet

While we can engage with other people with the motivation of *being* our Self, we can also engage with others through trying to get away from feelings or through trying to get some energy that we desire.

Let's say that I have feelings I am trying to get away from, such as loneliness and insecurity. If I connect with another person based on that motivation, I engage with him or her *through* the feelings that I am trying to get away from. In this event, connecting is a way to avoid or defend against my feelings.

If you are my friend, I may call you on the telephone or get in touch with you. Perhaps you are sympathetic, nice, or caring. Or perhaps you are understanding or helpful. Or perhaps you feel lonely, too. So, you respond to my call. We have just engaged *through* your sympathy, for instance, and my feelings of loneliness and insecurity.

If you are caring, nice, or sympathetic, you will feel my insecurity and loneliness. If you understand or feel lonely, you will commiserate with me, and I will not have to experience them by myself. If you are helpful, you may try to talk me out of my feelings or help me figure out a way to feel better. When I interact with you, I do not have to feel my feelings as much. My loneliness and insecurity are temporarily reduced because you interact with me and share my feelings.

If I do *not* have the intention to heal, I just want to get away from my feelings. I am not interested in healing them and I will do all kinds of things to try to avoid them. If you won't engage with me through my issues, I may get mad at you and tell you that you aren't nice or caring in an attempt to get you to help me carry my emotional issues.

As long as I am experiencing feelings that I want to get away from, I will not feel better. While you may be trying to help me, I may get frustrated if I don't get what I want. I may continue to attempt to engage you until my feelings are reduced or until I get the feelings for which I am looking. And if you do not meet my needs, I may storm off to find someone else who is more caring or who is a better friend to fulfill me.

On the other hand, if you engage with me the way I want, I might feel some relief from my issues and you get to validate your façade of being a good friend and a caring person. And we both get to experience a connection—not a truly healthy or fulfilling connection, but a connection nonetheless. However, that connection is the result of engaging through our issues— my loneliness and insecurity and your sympathy and caring. Is this how we want to connect with each other?

Though it is not wrong to engage with my loneliness and insecurity, it does not heal anything. Engaging with my issues does not resolve them; it only delays the possibility of my healing. And, no matter how hard you try, you cannot go through my feelings. Even though I may get a brief reprieve from my issues because of our connection, I still have my feelings to heal, as our interaction only temporarily dulls my discomfort. While I may eventually get used to the feelings and adapt to them, they will be there forever unless I heal them.

In addition, having my loneliness and insecurity in your space cannot feel good. If your caring engages with my issues and it is painful or uncomfortable for you, your energetic definition of caring requires some healing to take it to a more functional level. How can healthy caring be painful? Consequently, you have proof that your caring does not work and requires healing.

Figure 5: Engaging through An Emotional Block

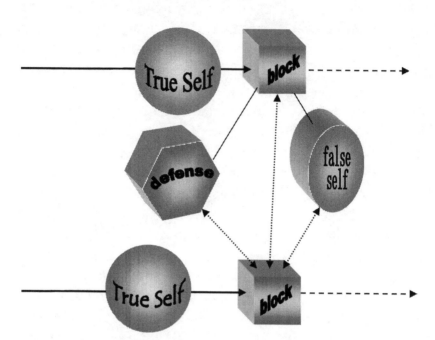

Figure 5: Anything that obstructs the flow of the true Self is a block. Dysfunctional concern and cooperation are blocks just as a feeling of invalidation is a block when we identify with it. Positive feelings, such as joy or peace, block the flow of the true Self when they are suppressed, obstructed, or held onto.

When we engage with others through a block or issue, it takes us off our true Self path and keeps us trapped in the engagement until it is healed. If we connect through our mutual loneliness, we connect block to block. If you have "compassion" for my insecurity, we connect false self to block. If you are angry that your "friendliness" engages my isolation or pain, you are defending against a block to block connection, and we experience a defense to block engagement. Many other possibilities for dysfunctional interactions exist.

Healing separates us from the other person's issues, takes us through our blocks, and restores the flow of our true Self.

Furthermore, if you engage with my issues, both of us lose the flow of our true Self (See Figure 5). By engaging with my loneliness and insecurity through your caring, you stop your true Self flow to engage with my blocked feelings through your false self. Again, you have proof that your caring does not work and requires healing. In this example, caring is *your* issue. **Healthy personality qualities do not stop the flow of our Self and do not engage with other people's issues.**

At the same time, I stop the flow of my Self when I engage with you through my feelings of loneliness and insecurity. **Staying in the flow of my Self would involve going *through* my feelings.**

A diversion from our true Self flow is readily palpable as an impairment of our movement through our experience. By paying attention to our interactions, we can be more aware of any engagement that takes us off our path. Then we will know that a dysfunctional engagement has occurred that requires healing.

Another problem with these interactions is that every quality that engages us in each other's issues creates difficulties with personal boundaries and with making separations from each other. Whose issues are whose? Once we have engaged, we have the complex task of discerning our own issues and disengaging from the other person.

Many of us stumble from one dysfunctional engagement to another without making any perceptible movement on the path of our Self. We look and act as if intoxicated, staggering from person to person, leaning on each in turn for support as others lean on us as well. This is the result of avoiding our issues and continually looking outside our Self for what we need.

The compelling nature of these kinds of connections relates to the intensity of our underlying feelings and our resistance to those feelings. And, until our blocks, issues, and dysfunctional personality qualities are healed, we will always use them as our avenues of engagement.

Avenues of Engagement

ny quality of your energy can be used as the basis for interacting with another person. You might connect *through* pain, *through* sympathy, or perhaps *through* true Self caring or validation. **The specific qualities that you bring to your interactions *mediate* those interactions;** you engage with others *through* those qualities.

Many of your personality traits were developed purposefully to engage others. If you have a façade of being supportive or friendly, it engages others through those features of your personality. If you are competitive or controlling, you engage through those defensive traits.

If you look back at the description that you wrote for the chapter titled "Energy," you will probably see some of the qualities that you *automatically* bring to your interactions with others. Every one of my clients—and probably every one who reads this book—can say that he or she is a nice, friendly, kind, understanding, loving, and caring person. That is what most people identify with. It is who they think they are. Thus, while you have your own unique definition of these qualities, you engage with everyone *automatically* through your niceness and friendliness. You do not even have to think about it or contemplate whether you will be nice to another person. You *are* nice and, therefore, you routinely respond in that manner *energetically*.

The actual mechanics of your engagements depend upon how you *define* the qualities that you bring to your interactions. Every quality that you possess has its own unique **energetic definition** with its own individualized function.

Your energetic definitions evolved in response to your own needs and issues and to those of the people around you. And they evolved based on your intention, as I discussed in "The Energy of Engagement."

Your energetic definitions delineate how your interactions develop energetically. They characterize the specific manner in which your energy engages others.

If your energetic definition of being cooperative or generous involves *giving other people what they want*, you will engage with others' wants through giving your energy. And if your definition of cooperation entails *compromising* your Self for others, you will shut down or block the flow of your true Self to engage with those people.

If being helpful involves *fulfilling others' needs*, you will find yourself giving people the energy that they desire. You will engage others' needs through being helpful.

Your responsibility engages with other people's issues if being responsible means *taking on issues that others cannot handle or that they blame on you.*

If trusting someone means that *you believe what they tell you*, your trust will engage with other people's agendas.

You engage with other people's opinions and judgments through your acceptance if your energetic definition of acceptance involves *accepting other people's energy into your space.*

If understanding involves *matching other people's energy,* you will engage with features of their blocks, defenses, façade, and false self to understand them.

You will engage with other people's issues through your caring if your definition of caring includes *feeling their issues.*

If your definition of devotion involves *taking what others direct at you,* you will involuntarily engage with any energy that they want you to take care of or that they blame on you.

This is often part of the energy behind people's wedding vows when they state their commitments to each other "for better or for worse."

Often, having an *interest* in other people engages you in their life and issues. And if you take other people *personally*, their issues become your issues. You engage with them through their issues and life even when those issues have nothing to do with you.

Instead of creating abstract ideals about what trust, generosity, and other qualities should be like, **you can evolve functional energetic definitions that reflect what truly works.** To evolve the qualities that you possess, you can simply use your daily experience to show you what is functional and what is dysfunctional.

While engaging with other people in ways that feel good is fun and natural, when you notice that an interaction does not feel good, it means that you have engaged in a less than ideal manner. **Any quality that engages you in other people's issues, engages other people in your issues, or engages other people in ways that do not feel good is *not* functional and requires healing.**

If you want to change how you engage with other people, heal the energetic definition of the qualities you use to engage with them. You can evolve the qualities you bring to your relationships to a truly healthy level of function. To evolve an energetic definition, use the healing process from this book to heal any undesirable quality of engagement and to disengage from other people. Simply pay attention to how you feel when you interact with others. ***Feel* how you open to other people. Then relax through those feelings to raise the vibration of how you engaged.** You do not even have to name the quality of engagement. Simply feel it and relax through it. This is valid whether the quality that you bring to an interaction is positive, negative, or neutral.

Dysfunctional energetic definitions involve energy exchanges in one of two forms. Either they direct you to give energy to other people or they direct you to absorb other people's energy. Let's look at how this transpires.

Your energetic definitions may dictate *giving* energy to other people in your interactions. Either you donate energy to fulfill others' needs or you give your energy just because of how the qualities of your energy are defined. Frequently, you give your energy away unconsciously through the features of your personality, although any aspect of your energy can be involved when you are giving energy to others.

If other people feel validated or accepted by you, you may be *giving* that energy to them. Or perhaps you give others energy through your generosity, support, love or care. Or if you are devoted or faithful, you may give *yourself* to others. And if you are happy or nice, you may just radiate your energy all over the place. To become aware of your avenues of engagement, you will want to focus on how you interact with other people.

Because the feelings that people seek must ultimately come from within themselves, feelings cannot be given to others. Feelings of security and safety have to come from within. Validation and acceptance have to come from within. You cannot give these feelings to another person. Therefore, if you notice that you are giving your energy away, you have an issue to heal.

To heal your giving, start by relaxing into and through whatever it is that you are giving. If you are supportive of others, feel your experience of *giving* support and relax through that feeling. If you are giving others the feeling of security and safety, heal your generosity by relaxing through the feeling of *giving* security and safety. When done successfully, you will feel the focus shifting from the other person to you. Instead of a flow of energy *moving out* from you, you will feel the energy *moving into* and through you.

Since every dysfunctional personality and energy quality developed as a way to get your needs met, **there is always a block to your own flow of energy underneath your giving**. Under every dysfunctional quality, there is either a feeling you seek or a feeling you wish to avoid. Perhaps you give because you have an issue about your own scarcity, inadequacy, incapability, or invalidation. You may have sympathy for someone else's blocks or maybe you get some validation for your energy contribution. No matter what your motivation, your block engages the other person's block. And while you respond by giving energy through a defense or a quality of the false self, you are also experiencing your own block and trying to get your needs met at the same time. It may be useful to look back at Figure 5 on page 220 to see how this looks. To heal the entire pattern and separate from the other person's issues, you have to ascertain your underlying issues and resolve them.

With healing, you evolve the qualities you bring to your interactions so they begin to reflect your healthy true Self. You heal the qualities through which you give your energy away and cultivate them as being part of you.

Remember, if you are trying to go through some quality like caring and you become stuck in it, it is probably not your feeling. It is someone else's idea of what caring is and you will need to *separate* from the definition because you cannot relax through or heal another person's energy.

Alternatively, **your energetic definitions may dictate that you *absorb* other people's energy in your relations.** In these interactions, you take on others' energy through the qualities of your personality and other aspects of your energy.

However, carrying other people's emotions does not feel good because their emotions and feelings just sit in your space and you cannot heal them. Therefore, the only solution is for everyone to heal his or her own feelings. All you can do is *separate* from other people's feelings and disengage from them through healing. This is the *only* way!

To heal your absorption of others' energy, start by relaxing into and through your contribution to the interaction. If you are accepting of others, feel your experience of being accepting and relax through that feeling. If you are absorbing others' energy through your caring, heal it by relaxing through your feeling of caring. When done successfully, you will feel a relaxation of your energy and a restoration of your energy flow. The focus will also shift from your engagement with the other person to you. Instead of feeling stuck, your energy will start to flow again.

Some people think that they have been giving help or assistance to others without any benefit to themselves. Their *altruistic* behavior appears to be giving energy or taking on others' issues without concern for themselves. It seems to be for the good of others at little or no cost to the contributors.

However, if you examine this behavior closely, you will discover several problems with this so-called altruism. First, it is impossible to give others energy or to take on their issues. You cannot provide for others, nor can you go through their issues. You may carry their burden for a time but your "service" cannot be prolonged forever. Thus, this "altruism" is not truly helpful, though it may *appear* to be useful to the participants based on their ideas of altruism.

Secondly, people's behavior must be examined to see if there is an incentive for their altruism. Do they get something out of their contribution? If there is any payoff for their actions, the behavior is not truly altruistic. This is true even if the reward is only from within themselves.

Are you being nice because "that's the way you are"? You may not have noticed the validation that you receive for behaving in that manner. Are you kind and generous with your time and energy? You have to look at the hidden return for being such a good person. Do you help people in need? If helping others makes you feel good inside, you are being reimbursed for your efforts. Or perhaps you received a tax deduction for your charitable contribution.

Because you cannot exchange energy on a permanent basis and because there is always an agenda behind energy exchanges, altruism does not exist in the way that people commonly imagine. Doing things to benefit others or for the good of the whole is not possible *unless you are being your true Self,* because genuine altruism does not involve Self-sacrifice. Only when you are being your true Self is there no agenda behind your actions and only then are your actions truly for the good of everyone. **Real altruism and charity do not involve any reward or energy exchange and can only occur when you are in the flow of your true Self.**

EXERCISE: In Defense of Altruism

If any resistance, anger, judgment or other defense arises while reading this section on altruism, there is an underlying feeling that has been triggered off and needs healing. What feeling resides under your defense?

EXERCISE: Attaining True Altruism

Many people have performed acts of kindness and thoughtfulness. Whether great or small, their actions often appear to be done simply out of the "goodness of their hearts."

Focus on an occasion when you offered a gift or did something for someone. Whether you were conscious of it or not, there was probably an underlying emotion compelling your behavior. Can you feel what that emotion was? Was it a need for validation, a quest for acceptance, or a desire for love? Was your generosity prompted by feelings of guilt or obligation? Were you just trying to avoid criticism? Were you acting on your competitive drive or your need to feel successful?

If you had an agenda and you heal your motives, you will operate more from your true Self and, therefore, experience genuine altruism.

＊　＊　＊

Sometimes you may get involved with people you do not like. When you do not like someone, you have an issue that requires healing. Either the other person triggers you off or you have become energetically engaged with them. In both cases, you are responding by defending yourself and are attempting to get away from your issues by not liking the other person. In addition, if you are energetically engaged, not liking that person is a defense against a block to block interaction, as illustrated in Figure 5 on page 220.

You may think that you do not accept, love, care about, or feel devoted to these people. However, your energy engages you with everyone whether you want to or not. Perhaps because of your definition of acceptance, you have already accepted them into your space and engaged with them. If engaging with someone does not feel good, you will have difficulty liking them.

Are there people about whom you do not care? Often this is just a defense, and underneath it, most people truly do care. You cannot help it. It is what you identify with. And you are caring with everyone, friend or foe, whether you want to like someone or not.

The people you do not care about are usually people you have already engaged with through your caring but then defended against by not caring. You have already engaged with the other person and you are trying to disengage. This form of not caring is just a façade or defense.

Perhaps your caring and cooperation engage you with someone's need in a false self to block connection, and you get angry with them, resist them, or withdraw from them to defend against your engagement. The goal of your defensive response is to disconnect or disengage from the other person. But instead, you have added a connection (defense to block) to the original false self to block connection; and the engagement will persist until you heal your dysfunctional energetic definition of caring or cooperation.

Once you heal your own issues, you will no longer engage with other people in dysfunctional ways, and they will not get into your space no matter what they have going on. You may even find yourself liking everyone because you will not be engaging with their issues, and you can see them as they really are—as simply human beings who have issues.

The personality traits with which you identify have developed with input from many sources. You have taken on other people's ideas and energy around appropriate ways to behave. You have taken responsibility for other people's issues and developed your attributes in response to their needs. You have had your own needs and sought to get them fulfilled by others. You have had your own unfulfilled needs and learned to give others what you desperately wanted for yourself. And, of course, you have ideas and ideals about what the different qualities of your personality should be like.

With healing, you can evolve yourself so that the various features of your personality are truly functional and healthy. Instead of engaging through dysfunctional exchanges that drain your energy, take you off your path, and drag you into a confusing muddle with uncertain resolution, you can engage in ways that honor and express your true Self. When you no longer engage with others to get away from feelings or to get your needs met, all of the qualities of your energy will look and function differently.

An energy exchange is not a necessary element of connecting with others, but you have to heal how you connect with others to avoid it. You can heal your helpfulness, compassion, and cooperation to stop interacting through unhealed emotions. As you continue along your path of healing, you will evolve the various attributes that you possess. When you get to a healthy level of a particular quality and you are truly owning it, it simply flows through you. Then you will start *being* the feeling and you will live the feeling.

With healing, you will discover how to be a true friend. If you are really trying to help me heal my issues, you will not engage with me *through* them. A caring friend will not take responsibility for my issues or take them on. As my friend, you will not try to fix me. Instead, you might remind me of my opportunity to heal and encourage me to heal my feelings.

With healing, your interactions will involve less of an exchange of unhealed energy and express more of the healthy engagement of healed beings. Instead of exchanging the energy of your issues and connecting through them, you can connect through healthier feelings on a true Self level, such as mutual interests, creativity, curiosity, playfulness, and cooperation. Your interactions will be based more and more on true Self security, success, love, worth, and kindness. Your connections will be inspired, imaginative, and expansive instead of being based on scarcity and limitations. *Fun*ctional interactions are truly *fun!*

In true Self to true Self connections, you connect and let go continuously. You connect from your path and *not* through blocks or issues (See Figure 6). There is a different kind of compelling nature to true Self to true Self connections: You experience the profound depth of being genuine with another person. And with nothing coming between you and the other person, there is an unparalleled closeness to the experience.

Figure 6: True Self Connections

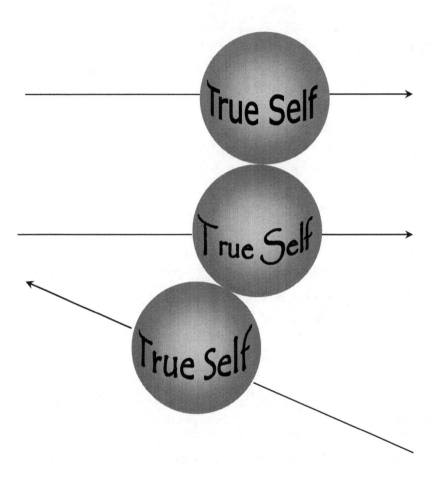

Figure 6: When you no longer connect through issues or dysfunction, you connect true Self to true Self. You touch the true Self of another and have a direct experience of that person without anything intervening.

Even when you are moving along a path together with another person, there is always the connecting and letting go. Nothing is holding you together or keeping you in that place. There is a free and easy feeling to the connection. You are with each other because you are in the flow of your true Self together.

An example of a Self to Self connection occurs when you go out into the woods or nature and connect with the natural world. You do not have to work at it. A connection already exists because you are a part of nature. You may have to reawaken your awareness of the connection, but the connection itself is already present. It is a part of you and, even if you are not conscious of it, all you have to do to feel your connection is to relax. When you are aware of this connection, you experience nature's never-ending beauty and the movement of the seasons within your Self. You also feel when nature is being harmed. This connection exists whether you pay attention to it or not, even in the midst of a city—although it may be more difficult to feel and sustain that connection in a city. This same feeling exists when you connect Self to Self with another person.

Every aspect of the world can function in healthier ways. New and wonderful possibilities result from the application of this healing process to creativity, communication, education, business, and health care. Healing creates an alternative experience of humanity and community.

Imagine an accomplished musician who is aligned with his or her true Self and the music that would emanate from the instrument that person is playing. Then imagine a group of such musicians playing together and the magic they would create as a result of their healthy energetic blending.

Visualize the performance of a talented athlete whose physical body expresses his or her true Self. Now visualize the performance of an athletic team whose players are synchronously attuned to their true Self.

Picture a government that is motivated by what fosters healing. Envision schools and businesses whose directors and staff are focused on healing, on being true to their true Self, and on facilitating the expression and evolution of the true Self in others. Imagine communities and businesses whose choices and decisions are based on what is healing. Now imagine growing up in such an environment.

Heal everything that keeps you from experiencing what is possible. If you heal everything that gets in the way of experiencing the possibilities you envision, you will create the experience you desire. And your engagements with the world and with others will be genuine.

EXERCISE: *Evolving Qualities of Engagement*

You can get a better idea of how you contribute to your engagements with others and heal those "gifts" at the same time with the following exercise. One at a time, say the following affirmations to yourself and *feel* them.

"I accept other people."
"I understand other people."
"I am devoted to others."
"Other people think that I am helpful."
"I care about other people."
"I love other people."
"Other people trust me."
"I cooperate with others."
"I nurture other people."
"I trust other people."
"I try to please other people."
"I am generous."
"I am supportive of others."
"Other people feel secure and comfortable around me."

What do you notice? If you feel an outflow of energy when you contemplate a statement, you are *giving* energy to others. If you feel an inflow of energy *from* other people when you contemplate a statement, you are *absorbing* energy from those people.

Relax into and through the specific quality of engagement. With relaxation, *your* energy will flow inward and through you. By healing each feeling, you raise the vibration of that quality and begin to heal how you use that quality to engage with others. As a result, you disengage from dysfunctional connections.

EXERCISE: Evolving Yourself

One way to evolve your personality is to heal every quality that you identify with. Refer to the description of yourself from the chapter titled "Energy" and heal each of the attributes on your list.

Every characteristic can be healed. Beliefs, employment, physical features, and personality traits can all be processed emotionally. What does it feel like to work at your job or hobby? What does it feel like to be male or female? Short or tall? Congenial or stubborn? A father, mother, son, or daughter?

The meaning of each quality will change with healing.

EXERCISE: Contrast Healing

Referring to the description of yourself, go through your list and practice feeling the *opposites* of what you wrote about yourself. If, for example, you described yourself as cooperative, practice feeling uncooperative. Then go back and forth between the two contrasting qualities and heal both of them. Many people discover that there is a healthier quality that exists somewhere between the two contrasting qualities that they are feeling. Through healing, you can evolve the energetic definitions of your personality traits.

Besides assisting in the development of more functional personal attributes, this exercise assists in releasing any attachment you may have to your false self and in strengthening your connection to your true Self.

✳ ✳ ✳

Throughout this book, many qualities are described from the perspective of the true Self. New energetic definitions for these qualities are presented, detailing how they might look and how they might be experienced once you move beyond the intention of exchanging energy with others. They are all based on the energetic understanding that you cannot heal other people by taking on their issues or giving them energy.

This perspective should be kept in mind when you read about the alternative definitions for these qualities, as they may look quite distasteful from the perspective of desiring energy exchanges with others. If you are triggered off by any of the descriptions, please use the opportunity to exercise your healing process.

Of course, many other possibilities exist for the energetic definitions of these qualities. I encourage you to come up with your own concepts of what is possible when these qualities are free of dysfunction and limiting definitions. And then do the healing to realize these possibilities.

Responding Appropriately

E veryone has learned to respond in specific ways to the situations they face. Unfortunately, many of those responses are not healthy or appropriate. For instance, many people are so used to being nice that even when other people's energy is directed at them in non-responsible ways, they still respond with niceness. This does not feel good to the person being nice nor does it stop the behavior of the other person. Instead, it provides evidence that the response is inappropriate.

What is the appropriate response to someone who does not have the intention to heal or who wants some energy from you? How would you respond to a situation in which somebody seeks you out with the intention of being a victim? What is the best way to deal with someone who wants to play a manipulative game with you? How would you handle an interaction in which the other person is trying engage with you through competition? What if someone is judging you or blasting away at you by directing their issues at you?

In the course of healing, you will learn to respond differently to these kinds of interactions. First and foremost, whenever you engage with another person in a way that does not feel good, you will want to perform your healing process. When faced with someone grabbing at your energy, dumping energy in your space, or directing his or her own issues at you, you are going to want to heal the way you engage with that person. If you have engaged through a quality of your energy that is dysfunctional, that quality requires healing. This may mean redefining "nice," for instance, because if you are getting beat up for being nice, your energetic definition of nice is not very functional and you are not being nice to yourself.

In addition, it is not appropriate to participate in energy exchanges. If someone seeks validation, it is not beneficial or benevolent to give them *your* energy. Or if someone is trying to avoid a feeling of scarcity, it will not help to take on their issue. The proper response to other people will not engage their issues and will not contribute to energy exchanges.

Along with healing your engagement issues and energy exchanges, you must learn to respond more appropriately to other people. In this regard, it is the intention behind your interactions—your own and other people's intention—that you will want to use as a guide to know what is most appropriate. Because intention is the real motivation behind everything, it defines the most appropriate response to all behavior and interactions. **Healthy responses to others must be based on the underlying intention of their words and behavior.**

With this in mind, there are only three options for interacting with other people:

- You can choose to ignore their intention and respond to their façade.
- You can respond strategically to the other person's intention.
- You can be genuine and respond from your true Self.

If you choose to ignore the real intention behind a person's behavior, you are participating in and contributing to the illusion that their intention does not matter and that their façade is real. Once you begin your healing process, you will soon realize that this is not a very good option. Engaging without regard for another person's intention creates undesirable vulnerability to their agenda and to energy exchanges. A genuine connection will not develop and you will diminish your energy by interacting through an unhealed emotional issue and exchanging energy inappropriately.

Alternatively, you may choose to respond strategically to other people, especially when they do not have the intention to heal. In this case, you acknowledge the underlying intention of the interaction, but respond based on whether being genuine will be more troublesome than being strategic.

Sometimes when you are responding strategically, you can be direct with the people with whom you are dealing, while at other times you may just heal yourself and move on. You may not always express your true feelings, especially if the other person has no intention of healing. Nonetheless, you will want to ascertain the appropriate response to every situation and take action based on your true feelings.

On a related topic, while it might seem like a virtue to always tell the truth, there are some significant consequences to take into account. If you are courageous and don't mind triggering off other people, getting energy thrown at you, and wrestling with other people's energy, then telling the truth is for you. It may seem like the ideal way to be in the world, but you have to be able to handle a lot on an energy level. Sometimes, withholding your truth may be the best strategy for dealing with someone who has no intention to heal, who has no desire to hear your truth, and who is just going to throw energy at you.

Of course, the ultimate level of social function is when you can just be your true Self and respond to everyone's intention in alignment with your Self. Perhaps this is the only way to be. However, while it is more mature to respond to other people's energy instead of their façade, it is not generally considered socially acceptable and may create numerous unpleasant interactions.

On the positive side, responding to people's intention is the only way to create the opportunity to connect genuinely. **Being genuine means that you respond to other people's intention with your real feelings.** You do not pretend that whatever is going on is not going on. You do not sugar coat your feelings to make them palatable. And you do not suppress your feelings or tread softly around other people's issues to avoid triggering them off. Being genuine is the fastest and most effective way to assist others in being aware of their motivation and in functioning on that level.

This in no way means that you can direct your own issues at others. And if you have engaged in any dysfunctional way, you have your own healing to accomplish. In addition, you may have to use your healing process to even be able to ascertain your true Self's truth. Nonetheless, you will always want to strive to respond to the intention of others, while being in alignment with your true Self.

Functioning on the level of intention takes a specific focus and tremendous self-control. This is mainly because it requires that you respond to the energy of intention rather than engage with people through a façade or other energy as is typically learned in "normal" social discourse. By focusing on and responding to the true energy of engagement, you will have a clear understanding of what is transpiring and your relations with others will be based on something that is genuine. And significantly, you will open the door to creating true Self to true Self connections with others.

EXERCISE: The Comfort of Being Your Self

You may need to do some healing to become comfortable with being genuine with other people. What issues arise around not engaging with other people's issues? Do you feel awkward, wrong, or offensive? What issues arise around being truthful with others? Are you being rude, uncaring, harsh, or mean? These feelings may require some healing to own that you are just trying to be true to your Self and to be genuine with others.

Are you comfortable with other people not liking you, being angry with you, having a negative impression of you, or having erroneous ideas about you? If not, heal the feelings that arise.

EXERCISE: *Inappropriate Responses*

Monitor your behavior and watch for situations in which you do *not* respond appropriately. Do your healing work.

EXERCISE: *Defending Your Intentions*

What issues arise for you when people start to respond to your intention? Do you defend yourself by shutting down, getting angry, or denying what others are saying?

EXERCISE: *Becoming More Genuine*

What does it feel like when you are trying to be genuine, but end up interacting with another person's façade? Can you feel the movement away from your Self when you interact with others in this way? Can you feel how much energy it takes to interact with another person's façade? Interacting with another person's façade and false self takes a lot of energy and is, therefore, tiring.

What do you feel when you interact with someone through the energy of your façade? Can you feel the lack of a true connection?

How does it feel when you are interacting with other people and are not being genuine, perhaps when you are using a strategy to deal with their lack of intention to heal? Do you notice a lack of connection and perhaps falseness?

How does it feel when you are being genuine with another person who is being genuine? Notice that it takes very little energy and there is a feeling of a real connection when you can interact with someone on the level of intention.

EXERCISE: *Giving Others What They Want*

There is a time and place for everything and sometimes, under the proper circumstances, it is appropriate to give people what they want. No, you do not want to give your own energy to other people. But, when someone is blasting you and all they want is some approval, sometimes the best strategy is to find a reason to give them that approval. If you can approve of them in a genuine way, give it to them! You can enjoy being your Self with others and help them run their energy at the same time.

In these cases, you simply notice what another person wants and find a genuine reason to give them that feeling. It is an easy way to maintain a pleasant interaction and to acknowledge what the other person wants at the same time. You are not giving them your energy. You are helping them to run their own energy. For instance, many people just want your validation. Can you think of something to say that is validating about the other person, even if they are acting inappropriately at the moment? If so, then you can be genuine and extend the validation that they want without compromising your Self. This takes a level of mastery in which you do not expect the other person to be totally functional or energetically aligned with healing. The other person will usually back off once they have gotten what they want.

Healing Your Relationships

Emotional healing is the only essential element for creating healthy development and movement. To experience progression in your life, there is no substitute for healing.

Since relationships are such a significant aspect of life, it is useful to focus on healing them to make them as healthy, fun, and fulfilling as possible. No matter what part of your energy participates in your relationships, you can evolve them and make them better.

By healing, you help your relationships become more about enjoying your Self in relation to other people—not about arguing over who is going to get their needs met today or battling over undesirable feelings. You can raise every relationship to a higher level, creating dynamic and joyful interactions, instead of taking them down to the lowest level where blocks diminish or destroy them.

After you have interacted with another person, you will want to become aware of whether there is any persistent energy residue from the interaction. Are you still focused on the other person? Can you not stop thinking about the other person? Are you arguing with that person in your mind? Do you want to avoid that person? Is your mind trying to grasp what happened? Did you get a positive feeling that you are trying to hold onto?

If you are still engaged, there is an unhealed interaction going on and you will want to set about performing your healing process to release the dysfunctional connection. Every interaction has four elements that you must consider:

1. Separating from the other person and his or her energy
2. Healing your own issue(s) by relaxing through it (them)
3. Giving yourself the feeling(s) that you wanted from the interaction
4. Healing the quality or qualities you contributed to the interaction

Not every interaction will involve all four of these elements. Nevertheless, you will want to look at all of them to develop your awareness of them and to make sure you are dealing with all of the energy that is involved in your interactions. The result will be that you reclaim your own energy, separate from the other person's energy, heal yourself, and proceed on your path.

Many engagements with others are based on trying to avoid a particular feeling. When you are trying to avoid a feeling, you must heal it by relaxing through the undesirable feeling. In the beginning of the development of your process, you may only be aware of your active feelings and, therefore, this will be the place to start healing.

Other interactions are initiated with the intention of getting a particular feeling from another person. Giving yourself the feelings you desire is a powerful way to further your development and disengage from other people's energy.

You can simply ask yourself, "What would it *feel* like if I got what I wanted from this interaction?" And relax into that feeling. Even though it is helpful to name the feeling you are looking for, it is not necessary. All that is necessary is that you *feel* whatever it is that you want.

EXERCISE: *Generating the Feelings You Want*

Make a list of everyone you have encountered recently and identify what you wanted from everyone on that list. Maybe you wanted someone to be sympathetic, to notice you, or to validate you. These are feelings that you want to have flowing through you so you become their source and connect with your true Self.

If you know there is a feeling that you want, you can learn to generate it for yourself. You can either imagine what it would be like to feel a certain way or remember a time when you felt that way and bring the feeling up in your consciousness. Focus on the feeling you want, relax into it, and let it flow through you. Totally relax and let the positive feeling flow. It is very much like the process for relaxing through and letting go of negative blocks.

Issues may arise around giving yourself what you want, such as feeling that if you give yourself what you want, you may lose your connection with a particular person. If this occurs, relax through the feeling of *loss* as well.

A client came into my office recently who could not give himself the love that he wanted because he did not feel worthy of it. He had to go through feeling *unworthy* and then give himself the feeling of *worthiness* before he could let himself have the *love* that he wanted.

❈ ❈ ❈

Some of the qualities that are attractive in other people are qualities that you do not know how to generate yourself. You are chasing feelings that you do not experience within yourself. Even in the event that the person to whom you are attracted has the desired feeling, the other person's energy can only be experienced temporarily. A truly permanent solution requires that you generate the feeling for yourself.

More frequently, other people do not have the qualities that you desire. Often people ascribe some meaning or value to something in them that is not really there. Why does a certain look mean confidence, for example? In truth, the confidence has just been projected onto that look and an illusion has been created.

Perhaps you look at someone and think, "Gee, they're sexy!" However, that might not be an accurate interpretation of the situation. Sometimes you are just noticing that the other person runs a lot of sexual energy, which does not necessarily make *them* sexy. And sometimes, when you have that reaction, it is *you* who feels sexy and the other person is just the trigger. If it is your own feeling, you need to own it. Otherwise, you may end up pursuing that feeling all over town!

In a similar vein, movie stars are often seen as heroes. They have acted something out and we are attracted to their act. They create an illusion that we, the viewers, accept and in which we participate. Not surprisingly, this is part of a larger cultural pattern that encourages us to spend time and energy developing our own look, façade, or act. We learn to create our own illusion, complete with the feelings that we desire and the people who support our illusion.

When you find yourself attracted to something, stop for a second and think, "What would it feel like if I had that?" Since the source of that feeling is not out in the world, you can generate it and own it for yourself. If you have a feeling that you enjoy when you see someone, relax through that feeling as well. Even the qualities that you attribute to your "heroes" are qualities that you will want to develop within yourself. Then you will be connecting with your own energy and no longer need to get those feelings from an outside source.

EXERCISE: *Healing Attraction*

If you find someone attractive, there is often a feeling you are looking for outside yourself that you do not own. Make a list of people you find attractive and ascertain what you find attractive about them such as their abilities, independence, openness, self-confidence, intelligence, or physical attributes. Then relax through each of those feelings. By practicing this exercise, you will learn to generate the feelings of everything you find attractive in others and discover those qualities within your Self.

❋　❋　❋

Next, you will want to evolve the qualities that you contribute to your interactions. If anything about an interaction does not feel good, the energetic definitions of the qualities you bring to that interaction need healing. Once you have mastered the earlier step of giving yourself what you want, this will become the most common way that you engage with others.

Becoming aware of how you engage in interactions may be a challenging step. Your participation in social discourse on an energy level has become so much a part of your way of life that it may be difficult to detect. You engage with others all the time and may not even notice it.

If you look at the people with whom you have interacted recently, you almost certainly engaged energetically with every one of them. With practice, your awareness of how you participate in your interactions will expand. Once you are aware of what you contribute to an interaction, you can heal it by relaxing through the feeling of that quality. **Relaxing through the feeling of a particular quality raises its vibration to a healthier level.** This will immediately improve your interactions with other people.

You can heal *trust* by truly feeling how you trust, how it engages others, and how it feels when you own it flowing through your Self. This dissolves any dysfunctional characteristics of the feeling while assisting with the development of its higher aspects.

Perhaps you are *loving* in your connections with others. This may mean that you do what others want, that you try to make people feel good, or that you are supportive of others. Unfortunately, you will probably be engaging in ways that do not feel good and that lack total enjoyment. If you notice that interacting through your love does not feel good, you can evolve it. To evolve love, feel your experience of love and relax through that feeling. This raises its vibrational quality, disengages your energy from the other people involved, and helps you separate from their needs. In addition, if you love as a way to connect with others, you will also want to relax through the feeling of *not connecting* and generate your own feeling of *connection*.

EXERCISE: Nurturing Your Self

Think of people you interact with in your life. Then identify how you engage with them, such as through understanding, caring, support, security, compassion, acceptance, cooperation, love, or loyalty. Heal yourself by relaxing through the feeling of what you contribute to every interaction.

❊　❊　❊

Now it's time to put it all together. Whenever you notice that an interaction requires healing, you can use the steps outlined on page 251 to guide you through your healing. Continue to cycle through the steps until you have reestablished the flow of your true Self. Once you have successfully healed an engagement, you will know that it is possible to be your true

Self in your relationships. You will experience the joy, freedom, and fun of being your Self.

By practicing these skills, the qualities of your interactions will become more and more fulfilling as you get to be more and more your true Self. There is no limit to how good you can feel, to how much love can flow through you, and to how much joy you can have. You can then bring these qualities into relationship with others, creating avenues of engagement that are truly expansive and exciting.

The intention to heal can be the guiding principle in your life. It is something you can apply to everything you do and especially to your relationships. With the intention to heal, you will create healthier, more satisfying relationships. By practicing your healing process every time a block comes up, you take care of yourself and open the door to new and wonderful ways to relate with other people. And by communicating with the intention to heal, your communication is going to facilitate healing as well.

Even when you have active issues, you do not have to engage with other people through those issues. With awareness and healing, you can have issues going on while you connect with people in other ways.

It takes courage to heal because, with every change, there is no guarantee that you will reconnect with the same people. Still, you will see people for who they truly are and the connections you make on a true Self level will be the real thing. And you will have a greater appreciation for people than ever before.

You can contrast the risk of not connecting with others with the price you pay for being in relationships now. Are you willing to compromise your Self to have a dysfunctional connection? Are you willing to shut down or stop doing what you really want to do to create or maintain a connection? And if you are not being your true Self, how can you expect relationships to be fulfilling or to truly work?

With healing, you are not going to be able to compromise your Self anymore. You are not going to be able to shut down. You are not going to be able to be anybody but your Self. And what a freeing experience that is!

Relationships provide wonderful opportunities for learning and healing. Ultimately, you can learn a different way of being in relationships: You can be your Self!

EXERCISE: Heal the Feeling of Not Connecting

If the idea of not connecting with others when you are being your true Self brings up issues for you, heal each issue to reduce the obstacles to being on the path of your true Self.

The Steps for Healing Dysfunctional Engagements

1. **Awareness** that a dysfunctional engagement has occurred.

2. **Focus** on the energy or feeling that you are aware of.

3. **Separate** from the trigger or foreign energy and refocus on your own issue.

4. **Intention:** determine the intention of your strategy
   a. Avoiding an issue: proceed to step 5a
   b. Wanting energy: proceed to step 5b
   c. Dysfunctional energetic definition: proceed to step 5c

5. **Heal** the issue
   a. *Relax* through your issue.
   b. *Relax* into the desired feeling.
   c. *Relax* through the dysfunctional quality.

6. **Movement:** Are you moving through the issue?
   No? If you are relaxing properly, you are dealing with foreign energy—return to step 3
   Yes? Continue through the feeling and proceed to step 7

7. **Let Go**
   Continue to relax through your issue until the entire pattern is released

8. **Resolution:** Is the engagement resolved?
   No? You have more issues to heal—return to step 2
   Yes? Your healing work is complete!

Heal First, Act Later

O nce people become aware of their feelings, they often want to take immediate action based on those feelings. Usually, however, **the appropriate time to take action is *not* when you have just become aware of your feelings.** Instead, you want to implement your healing process and move through your feelings to clearly ascertain what you really want to create on a true Self level. Otherwise, you will be responding based on your issues or in defense of those issues.

If you suddenly become aware that you gave up your Self for the security of a job, you want to heal your issues before running off and quitting your job. It will take healing to find security within your Self and to remember what truly expresses your Self before seeking new employment or working for your Self. And, with healing, you may realize that you are already doing what you really want to do and now you can do it for a deeper reason.

If you wake up one day and realize that you gave up your independence for the "love" of a relationship, it does not mean that you must demand your independence or leave the relationship. You need to go through your feelings and become the source of your love and independence. You do not have to compromise or lose your Self to be in a relationship. You can own your love and independence *and* be in a relationship. You can have love, independence, and a relationship all at the same time.

Until your issues are healed, you may not know what to do with your job or relationship; however, once you have healed, you will know what you really want to do.

It is possible that no action is required. With healing, you may realize that you are in the right situation and can be there with a healthier perspective.

On the other hand, if the reason you have taken a job is for security and you heal that issue, you may not want the job anymore. And if the reason you have connected with someone is that you did not want to be alone, once you heal, you may find that there is no connection with the other person and choose to move on. However, if you move on without healing the insecurity or aloneness, it is likely that your issues will create other connections and "opportunities" based on your needs and the motivation of getting those needs met outside your Self.

Some people seek immediate understanding when they are triggered off and confronted with an issue. They may spend considerable time and energy figuring out what is going on and what to do about it. However, it is very difficult to fully understand what is going on in a particular situation before you heal. Your issues distort your observations and your understanding and obscure your clarity about what action is appropriate to take.

In addition, trying to achieve understanding before you heal is a defensive attempt to gain control over an issue or feeling. Since the natural movement of a defense opposes the direction of healing, being defensive creates additional obstacles to clear perception and accurate understanding, while further impairing your ability to take the action you truly desire.

A woman came to her visit determined to figure out what was going on with her relationship. In spite of the presence of numerous issues, she thought that by understanding the dynamic involved with her boyfriend she would know how to proceed with either deepening her commitment or withdrawing from the relationship. Unfortunately, without healing, she was trying to decide based on her resistance to her issues. Without the intention to heal, she could not restore her clarity and centeredness, from which she could have made a good, healthy decision.

You will want to **exercise your healing skills every time you become aware of an issue and heal everything about it *before* taking any action.** You can master how the energy engages you. You can identify your role in the pattern and heal the pattern completely so you are free of the dysfunction. This is especially important when you find yourself defending or figuring out a problem. You will want to immediately stop defending and focus on the underlying feelings to start your healing process.

Once you heal your issues, your understanding of a particular situation will change and new possibilities for how to respond to that situation will become evident. At the very least, without the charge of your triggered issue, your actions will take more of the form of separating from another person's issues rather than defending or trying to disconnect. And, rather than engaging in an energy battle, your response will involve simply letting go.

Let's say you become aware that a relationship is emotionally abusive. Instead of just getting out of the relationship, you have the option of staying in it and learning about how it works. You need to understand how you engage with the abuse and, only by healing, will you be certain that you have left the dysfunctional pattern behind. To master your energy, you need to discover and heal what you are opening for—what you want—and what you are contributing to the interaction.

Patterns of abuse will not change just with the awareness that a relationship is abusive. You have to use your skills to heal your energy and claim your knowledge of abuse. Then you are in your power. It is not going to change anything by just thinking or saying that you are not going to let it in your space again. You have to heal it to actually *live* the knowledge and embody the power of your awareness. And if you just walk away from a relationship without healing the pattern of engagement, you are likely to repeat the pattern.

Of course, if the relationship is physically abusive or you have difficulty functioning or healing in the relationship, you will probably want to terminate it immediately. Nonetheless, you will still want to heal the pattern of engagement.

EXERCISE: Heal What You Do Not Enjoy

To heal the parts of your life that you do not enjoy, apply the skills that you have been developing. The more intense the interaction and the involvement with others, the more difficult it may be to stay focused on your issues and to heal them. Nevertheless, the more difficult the situation, the more important it is to maintain your focus and to heal.

No Regrets

Events from the past can keep you looking in the rearview mirror. When you focus on the past, you send your energy backwards to times and events that have already happened. This anchors your energy in the past and keeps your energy directed at those times in your life. The parts of your energy that are engaged in the past are literally frozen at those ages. Focusing on the past keeps you from being present in the here and now.

Truly, this is happening all the time when you act out blocks that you developed and programming that you learned when you were younger. However, it is particularly noticeable when you have a conscious focus on events and people from the past. Focusing on past events can hold everyone involved in those experiences captive. It is especially debilitating when you are holding onto regrets about those events.

Regret functions as a defense, saying in effect, "I would be feeling differently right now if something else had happened in the past." You may be trying to defend against a negative feeling in the present, such as loneliness, insecurity, invalidation, or loss. You may be stuck on a feeling from the past and simply unable to heal it. Or perhaps you have regret because you previously had a positive feeling, such as validation, love, or success, that you want to be experiencing now.

Regret is a lot like guilt in that it tells you what you should or should not have done. Unfortunately, both guilt and regret hinder the healing of your underlying feelings and impair the flow of your true Self.

While most people believe that past events cannot be changed, you can at least bring your energy into present time by healing your *experience* of those events. By applying your healing process to everything about your regret and the underlying emotions, you bring your focus back into the present, free up frozen energy, and let everyone who was involved go about their life.

When you heal what you have going on in the present, there will not be any issues to reflect on and regret in the future. By addressing issues as they arise, there is nothing to deal with later. Healing allows you to live without regret.

EXERCISE: Healing Regret

If there are past events that continue to draw your attention, you will want to heal them so that all of your energy is present right now. You can use your healing process with a focus on the past to accomplish the healing that you desire.

Start by thinking about the event or person and focus on the feelings that arise. Then separate from the event or person and perform the rest of the healing process that you have been practicing.

Back from the Future

I t is easy to project expectations, hopes, fears, and doubts into the future. This can be useful when you are interested in exploring possible outcomes and in creating future possibilities. It is a natural and healthy aspect of your experience to explore.

However, focusing on the future can also be detrimental. It may take you out of the present, which is often a defense to avoid what you feel now. It can detract from the focus that is required to be present and to create in the present. And if you project negative feelings into the future, you dissipate your energy and create possibilities that you may not really want to experience.

Even with positive expectations, you may be creating a future that is just a defense against what you are feeling now. You will want to heal any feelings that you are trying to avoid in the present. Then you will want to heal any feelings that you are projecting into the future so they are *not* defensive but, instead, reflect what you really want to create. Whatever feelings you want to experience in the future can be experienced right now. By feeling them and relaxing into them, you can generate the desired feelings in your present experience.

After doing your healing work, you may still want to create the same experience in the future. However, healing takes the dysfunction out of the energy. Then the future becomes an expression of your Self and not a defense against your feelings.

EXERCISE: Being Present

Think of something you would like to have happen in the future. Is it a defense that takes you away from a current feeling? If so, feel the feeling you want to avoid and heal it. Is it a positive expectation, hope, or desire for the future? If so, what would it feel like to experience its fulfillment? Relax through that feeling and give it to your Self now.

Do you have any negative expectations, fears, or doubts about the future? Relax through any negative feelings and dissolve them so that they no longer cloud your future.

Responsibility

Who is responsible for what you do, how you feel, and what you experience? Who is responsible for your physical body and for your being on Earth?

If someone or something else is responsible, events and problems will seem to happen to you. You will be at the mercy of the people and forces around you who appear to hold your power. Your ability to express your Self in the world will be impaired.

Believing that you are *not* responsible denies your authority, purpose, choices, and independence. You relinquish your power to heal and to create an alternate future.

On the other hand, choosing to take healthy responsibility restores your personal power and allows you to create what you want. You can change how you respond to the events that occur and the outcomes you experience. You can reclaim your ability to express your Self and further your journey along the path of your true Self.

What is healthy responsibility? Healthy responsibility ultimately means that you take responsibility for your issues and only your issues. Not taking responsibility for your issues leads to the challenges discussed above. However, taking responsibility for issues that are not your own impairs your ability to function and creates dysfunctional relationships.

How can you develop healthy responsibility? To achieve healthy responsibility, you must attempt to heal everything that arises in your life. Only through the application of your healing process will you be able to determine your responsibilities. **The**

practice of healing will clearly reveal what is and what is not your responsibility.

What are your responsibilities? **You are responsible for everything that you can heal,** which means that **you are responsible for your own energy and *only* your energy.** What you *cannot* heal is *not* your responsibility.

You are responsible for your issues and for your part in any engagement. The intention behind everything you think, say, and do is your responsibility as well.

You are responsible *for your part* in relationships that are not working, a job that is unfulfilling, and any disease or illness that you experience. You can resolve relationship, work, and health concerns by healing your issues, which includes healing how you engage with others, with work, with your body, and with the environment.

If there is something that is not to your liking, you can change your response to it. If someone is bothering you, it is your responsibility to get out of the way of that person's energy through healing. If someone else's energy is in your space, it is your responsibility to move it out of your space. If someone triggers you off, whatever was triggered off is your responsibility. If someone *intends* to trigger you off, the active issue is still your responsibility, but the intention of the other person is their responsibility.

You are even responsible for aspects of your energy that you are unaware of. Perhaps you blocked a part of your energy from your awareness as a defense so you would not know what you were doing. Or perhaps, like most people, you just haven't become aware of all of your energy. Nonetheless, you are responsible for everything in your energy whether you are conscious of it or not. Your energy *always* knows what it is doing.

Of course, it is equally important to identify those issues that are not your responsibility. There are several items to consider in this regard.

Often, people take responsibility for others and for things that are beyond the scope of their responsibility. This may be a defense so that they do not have to feel loss or failure, for instance. Or perhaps they take responsibility so that a particular task gets done. Or people may take responsibility so they have a connection, get approval, or avoid being alone. In these cases, they will have to heal their underlying emotions and evolve their definition of responsibility.

Commonly, people take too much responsibility when they have been taught that they are responsible for what goes on around them. It is easy to see how you might have learned to take responsibility for more than your own issues. People directed their issues at you continually, and it was natural to assume that what you were being handed was your responsibility. If someone keeps giving you something, after a while you will probably just take it, especially if pain is involved with not taking it on. Also, if everyone seems happier or backs off when you give them what they want, it often seems easier to take responsibility for fulfilling other people than to have them hounding you all the time for what they want.

While some of what occurs around you is the result of your energy, actions, and issues, much of what occurs is not your responsibility. And if you take responsibility for the latter, no healing will occur and the foreign energy will be retained in your space. Through healing, you will learn to recognize your responsibility. In this case, healing involves eliminating a dysfunctional pattern of engagement by evolving the energetic definition of responsibility.

Since you cannot go through someone else's feelings, other people's feelings are *not* your responsibility. Thus, **whoever has an active issue has something to heal**. Even if you trigger someone else off, whatever is triggered off in them is their issue. You cannot do anything to take away the other person's issue, you cannot help another person avoid his or her healing, and you cannot fix another person when he or she is triggered off. If you take responsibility for someone else's issue now, that will not help them heal today and it will not help them take responsibility tomorrow. And even if you shut down after triggering someone else off, they still have their feelings to go through.

Some people may think that I am saying they are to *blame* for their disease or difficult circumstances. Or that I am suggesting they *wanted* their difficulties. Or they will hear this as *judgment* and think they are bad or wrong for having something going on.

However, there is no judgment involved and no one is doing anything wrong. I am not blaming anything on anyone, judging anyone, or implying that the difficulty was wanted. If judgment or other feelings come up, relax through the feelings and be done with them.

I am simply stating the obvious—that there *is* something going on. And the sooner you take responsibility for it and start healing, the sooner you can move beyond it. Having active issues is not only universal, it is normal. The more you make it acceptable to have active issues, the easier the healing process becomes. Resistance to taking responsibility, such as justifying why something is happening in your life or blaming others for your predicaments, is a defense against the underlying issues and just delays the healing process.

Taking responsibility for you and your energy is a practical and functional application of the intention to heal that can free you from your dysfunction and propel you along the path of your true Self. By taking responsibility for what is happening to you, you claim the power to transform your experience. If there is something that is not working for you, you can heal and evolve your Self. The world does not have to change for you to create happiness. Only you have to change.

Teaching responsibility to others is a very complex task. It does *not* involve giving your children or students responsibility for other people or for other people's issues. And you cannot just hand your expectations and goals to your children or students, and expect them to take them on.

Between the school environment—in which people are given tasks that they would never do in a million years—and the home environment—where children are immersed in their parent's issues, desires, and expectations—it is no wonder that people lose touch with their true Self, forget what they truly want to do, and simply sleepwalk through life. If you are to teach responsibility, you will want to observe when the other person is not accepting their true responsibility and help them to heal the issue that is present.

The father of one of my clients was always taking responsibility for his daughter's life. This involved her monetary issues as well as her behavior. The father's façade was that he was helping her meet her challenges. However, the underlying reason for taking responsibility was that he was feeling lost and unsure of himself. Taking responsibility for his daughter gave him a feeling of being needed. This created a connection through the issue of responsibility, which was not fulfilling for either and which contributed to a subtle resentment between them. And, unfortunately, this impaired the development of her Self-responsibility, which led to her having difficulty creating what she wanted in her life.

To heal, the father went through his feeling unsure of himself and feeling lost. By generating feeling valued within himself, his healing process instantly released him from trying to take responsibility for his daughter.

The daughter learned to separate from her father's energy by healing the need for permission from others in order to do what she wanted. She found the source of permission within herself and reclaimed her responsibility for creating what she wanted. This ended the resentment and her blaming her father for what she could not have. The relationship improved dramatically as they interacted more as equals and without resentment.

The real challenge for parents is to assist their children in taking as much responsibility as is age-appropriate and to avoid moving into their children's space to get things done or to take control. The trick is to get people to go through their issues when they are looking outside themselves for what they need and when they are not taking responsibility for themselves.

EXERCISE: Taking Responsibility for Others

Notice situations in which you take responsibility for other people's feelings. Did you accept what they directed at you? Did you feel what they were feeling? Did they put out that you triggered them off and, therefore, it was your fault? Did you want to make them feel better? Did you take responsibility for their fulfillment?

You can heal these situations by relaxing through your feeling of responsibility. By evolving your definition of responsibility, you heal yourself and separate from those issues that are not your responsibility.

Home for the Holidays
How to Enjoy a Family Get Together

Everyone has issues with the other members of their family. While some of those issues are hidden, the origins of significant dysfunction can often be traced to family interactions during years of growing up. So, what could be better than visiting your family to create an opportunity for healing?

However, do *not* go home looking for that great, fulfilling connection—although it may turn out that way. And do *not* go home expecting to relax or vacation. Go home with your awareness on high alert to notice every emotion that comes up and to notice the energy of every interaction. Go home prepared to put your healing skills to the test and, by using your healing skills, to get the most out of your experience. In other words, go home to heal!

And you will be put to the test. Everyone has issues and very few people have managed to accomplish much healing. Thus, many of the issues that developed during your younger years are still going to be played out in present time. Since most people do not know how to go through their feelings, they will direct their feelings at others. And since most people do not know how to give themselves what they want, they will try to get their needs met outside themselves. This is how energy battles begin!

Often family issues are held in a state of denial. Family members may pretend that the issues do not exist, or worse, pretend that they are all your issues. Consequently, you will have an opportunity to develop your ability to validate your Self in the face of denial, as well as to hone your perceptual and healing skills. It is no small achievement to validate your Self and heal when others are in denial.

Consciously or unconsciously, family members know how to trigger each other's issues and get each other to shut down. They know how to get others to engage in their issues and dump their stuff in each other's space. And they know how to get what they want from other members of the family.

If you visit your family, you must be on research duty. The goal is to find out what dysfunctional patterns you still participate in and to heal them. These patterns are very deeply ingrained and, when healed, their transformation will have the most profound effects on your life. You will be able to live a life that reflects more of who you really are.

While you are doing your family research, you can still enjoy your family. In fact, you can practice having fun while using your healing process! You just have to remember that you are healing and do your best to keep up with the events as they occur. You cannot fall asleep and pretend that nothing is going on.

Love, Care, and Devotion

The fully evolved true Self is complete; it is fulfilled from *within*. But until it attains completion, the true Self seeks its fulfillment and is nourished by various energetic qualities. These qualities delineate the path of its growth and prosperity.

With healing, we find the source of these energetic nutrients within our Self. However, before we discover their source within, we hunger for them. Our cravings compel us to hunt for them and seek them out.

Love, care, and devotion are three qualities that many people pursue. We search everywhere until we find them. Sometimes we find them in our parents, siblings, teachers, peers, or pets. This lets us know that they exist and therefore encourages us, but it also makes it appear that they reside outside of our Self, so we often continue to look for them in all the wrong places.

Conversely, many people have no experience with these qualities. This either stokes their drive to find what they seek or else they get used to their emptiness and give up their search.

Many people grow up only experiencing *love* in relation to others. Love appears to be outside of them and to come from others. And without this love, there is often pain and emptiness.

At this level of understanding, love becomes a reason for relationships. People learn to connect with others through their need for love.

All kinds of feelings become confused with love, which becomes an energy to exchange, a commodity. And since we need to maintain a steady supply of this commodity, control is often used to manage this love.

Healing takes us in a different direction in our search for love. With healing, we discover that pain and emptiness are the result of a separation from our true Self. And as we heal, we connect with the source of love within us, our healed true Self.

We *become* love and love flows through us. Then we love all the time, not just when we are being treated in an agreeable manner and not just when we want to love. Our love does not change depending on the people around us or their behavior.

At that point, love is no longer a reason for a relationship or even a reason to interact with others. Instead, it becomes normal to have love flowing through us and flowing through our friendships and relationships. We are free to co-create with our love since it is already present and we no longer need it from others. We are loving because that is who we are.

When people come into this world, they need others to take *care* of them. Their body cannot function independently. "Help! Feed me, change me, clean me up. How does this body thing work?"

As people grow up, it sometimes seems difficult for them to take care of their body. For them, health *care* may become a way of having other people take care of their issues.

The need for care often extends to the emotional level as well. Few people seem to be able to take care of themselves emotionally. Caring begins to mean that people engage with and absorb each other's issues.

With this definition of care, we can easily engage with other people's pain. However, since pain is the result of a separation from the true Self, engaging with others' pain does nothing for their healing. This includes both physical pain, such as an upset stomach or a headache, and emotional pain, such as grief or loss. Even though other people may not have to feel their pain if we take it on, they are still separate from their true Self and their pain will reappear at some point in the future. Blocked feelings do not go anywhere unless there is healing. **Feeling others' pain is not caring—healthy caring is *not* painful.**

Once we have engaged with people through dysfunctional care, we cannot possibly assist them with their healing. In fact, we have deprived them of a catalyst for awareness and healing. Engaging with others through dysfunctional care also impedes the flow of our Self.

While people may *not* have received care when they were children—or may have received care that did not fulfill their needs—their search for care will not be complete until they find it within themselves. Healing takes people into and through their feelings of helplessness, powerlessness, and not feeling cared for. The very act of healing relates to the vibration of genuine care, leading them to their healed true Self care.

When we discover that engaging through other people's issues never leads to the resolution of those issues, we will understand that healthy, functional caring does not engage people in that way. We will know that we are not caring by going to the level of other people's issues and exchanging energy at that level. And we will know that we cannot care about others by taking on their issues.

If our care engages us in other people's issues, we will want to heal and evolve it. If it is being used as a defense, we will want to heal the underlying feelings that we are trying to avoid. If our care has a dysfunctional energetic definition, we will want to evolve it.

To many people, healthy care is going to look more like *not* caring than what they call caring. It means that we care so much about everyone involved that we keep our engagements through blocks and issues to a minimum. Instead, we function at the true Self's level of energy and engage with other people at that level as much as possible. Healthy caring means that we honor everyone's ability to move through his or her issues and to connect with the ultimate source of their fulfillment, their true Self. It means that we honor who someone really is rather than buy into the illusion of their false self. It means that we support their true Self in its health rather than their false self in its dysfunction. It means that rather than engage through the powerlessness of the false self, we engage through the *power to heal* that everyone possesses.

When we discover our true Self care, we will take care of ourselves and assert what we care about instead of waiting for someone else to do it for us. We will become caring people who can listen without taking on others' issues, without trying to fix anything, and without buying into or validating other people's beliefs.

If we base our health care system on this concept, healthy health care will present the option of learning how to heal ourselves. It will meet us where we are and guide us along the path of Self care, one step at a time, one issue at a time, *without engaging our issues.* It will teach us to take care of ourselves with our Self care.

With our healthy caring, we will care about everyone, no matter how they treat us and no matter how they conduct themselves. If people insist on engaging through their issues, we will care enough about them and our Self *not* to engage with them in that way. They will have the choice of either healing or finding someone else to engage with through their issues. By caring, we will support their healing while honoring their free will to choose whatever path they wish to follow.

When people come into the world, they often feel that they are on their own. If they are uncomfortable with this feeling, they may seek out the security of a dependable commitment; they may seek the *devotion* of other people to feel at ease in the world.

Some people become devoted to others or to institutions for the same reason. They need someone or something in which to believe. They are not comfortable or secure with themselves and do not experience ease or security in the world.

If people do not feel their place in the world, devotion can help them belong. If people feel lost, devotion can give them direction. If people do not sense their purpose, devotion can give their life meaning. If people feel overwhelmed, devotion can help them cope. And if people feel despair, devotion can give them hope.

For these people, devotion involves attachments, making commitments to others, and believing in other people. It often involves holding on to other people, holding others back, or leaning on others. It may entail shutting down or holding themselves back to be with other people. It may mean compromising themselves for another person, creating something for others that is not in alignment with their true Self, or being more true to another than they are to their true Self. And because of their devotion, they may have to put up with whatever energy other people direct their way.

With healthy devotion, we are true to our true Self and we create in alignment with our Self. By being devoted to our Self, everything we do expresses our devotion and is, therefore, devoted to everyone else's true Self as well. We cannot possibly be true to our Self and *not* be true to someone else's true Self. **Everything we create that is in alignment with our Self is in alignment with everyone else's true Self as well.**

True Self devotion means that who we truly are will not be compromised. We are determined to stay on our path and honor the true Self in everyone else as well. This does not mean that we always demand that we get our way, which is just a false self game. Instead, devotion involves a commitment and loyalty to our true Self and bringing that into relationship with others.

Once we are in the flow of true Self devotion, our devotion extends to everyone. It is no longer dependent on what other people do, on how they respond to us, or on whether or not other people are committed to us. We are our true Self and that is all we can be. And it is only because we are devoted to our Self that we can be devoted to others.

One of my clients complained that his family was beating him up energetically. His sister had been triggered off by something he had said, and now the whole family was piling on trying to make him feel wrong. We discovered that he was engaging with his family through his devotion to them. His energetic definition of devotion meant that he had to accept everything that was directed at him by those to whom he was devoted. Once he relaxed through how he was devoted to others, his energy shifted and he no longer accepted his family's energy into his space. They were still triggered off, but at least he no longer had to wrestle with their energy. He was still devoted to his family, but it was a much more functional devotion.

How do we know if we are experiencing healthy true Self love, care, and devotion? Our love, care, and devotion will not have an agenda behind them. We will not be stopping or altering our true Self's flow to express these qualities. And there will not be a payoff for our love, care, and devotion.

If we desire friendship, connection, or appreciation for our devotion, it is not fully evolved devotion. If we derive false self satisfaction and validation for our love and care, we are not experiencing the purity of our true Self. Only when we experience and express these qualities in the flow of our Self without any expected outcome are they traits of our healed true Self.

❀ ❀ ❀

In relationships, many of us have learned to fill in the gaps for others and create connections through needs. While it is not hard to recognize those who need and want love, giving love to them is never going to help. Love, care, and devotion are not qualities that we can give to others. And if we go out of our way to be loving, caring, or devoted to others, we lose our Self.

Healing allows us to interact with others at the highest level, the level of our healed true Self, and to verify that the source is within each of us. Certainly, we have some healing to do to recognize and evolve our true Self so that we do not simply indulge our false self in a new way. However, with healing, we can create connections in which we stay in the flow of who we are. Then we can connect through health, through wholeness. We can be our true Self in our relationships.

Of course, our relationships will change as a result of our healing. With healing, when people grab at our energy, we will choose not to connect through need and will simply get out of the way. People who are *not* functioning with true Self love may not like that we no longer give them "love" when they reach for our energy. However, even though they may not understand and may get upset, we will know that we cannot give them anything.

On the other hand, those people who are at the same level of love, care, and devotion will be the most comfortable people to be around; they will be the easiest people with whom to have personal and professional relationships.

There is a myth in the popular press that we can be more loving, caring, and devoted to others than we can be to ourselves. Unfortunately, what this is really about is developing a better façade, which is the opposite of healing. This "altruistic" myth relies upon, yet ignores, the validation that people get for trying to live in this way. It contributes to the false self improvement movement that is truly a step backwards in our development.

It is impossible to love, care about, or be more devoted to another than we are to ourselves. This is because all that is truly loving, caring, and devoted has to flow through us. This is the only way our energy can be loving or caring. If we are not loving to ourselves, we stop the flow of our Self-love and do not have any love to express. We cannot be more loving towards another and less loving towards ourselves.

Thus, one of the greatest gifts we can share is to be loving, caring, and devoted to ourselves. Then everything we do is imbued with these qualities, and we will always be the most loving, caring, and devoted to everyone. It cannot be any other way.

Furthermore, if we are not loving to others, we stop the flow of our love and, thereby, lose love. We cannot be more loving to ourselves than we are towards another person.

We can learn to be loving by simply connecting with and being in the flow of our Self-love. We will not be holding onto love or any other feeling because that stops the flow of that feeling. It will just flow through us and be a part of everything we say and do. And it will feel easy and comfortable to connect with others through that flow. As long as we remain committed to healing and to our true Self, we will not want to stop our flow or even be able to stop the flow of our Self-love.

Having love, care, and devotion flowing through us is what is normal. Being in the flow of love, care, and devotion is as natural as being alive. Aliveness is flowing through us and isn't something that we give to others. It is who we are. We are not acting alive; we *are* alive. And everything we do expresses our aliveness.

EXERCISE: Healing Dysfunctional Caring

To test your caring, try affirming the following: "I do *not* care about others." What does that bring up for you? Notice whether you defend against that statement. If, for instance, any resistance, anger or judgment arises, you will want to get to the feeling underneath your defense and heal it.

In spite of any resistance you might have, people often do a better job of separating from other people's issues when they allow themselves to *feel* that statement. Do you feel a healthy separation from other people when you let yourself feel "not caring"? If so, then you experience a healthier relationship with others when you do not "care" about them!

To completely heal your issues around caring, you have to heal how you engage with others through your caring. The purpose of working with "not caring" is to become aware of any aspect of your "caring" that is not functional. By experiencing the contrast between caring and not caring, you enhance your awareness of your energy so that you can heal it and create a healthier caring. As I discussed in "Avenues of Engagement," be *care*ful not to use "not caring" as a defense.

EXERCISE: Fostering the Feelings You Desire

Think of a beautiful place that you have visited. Close your eyes and imagine being there right now. Feel the beauty. Let go of the place itself and stay focused only on the feeling. Let the beauty take over and flow through you. Feel the beauty going deeper and deeper. Relax more and more. This is one way to recognize, develop, and own the beauty within you.

You may want to do this whenever you are in a special place or whenever you feel a special connection. Feel the feelings, relax into them, separate from the object or the person, and just let the feelings soak into you. Then you have the energy of the moment within you. You are the beauty.

Now think of people or pets with whom you have experienced love. Think of that person or pet and feel the love now. Focus on the love and relax into it. Separate from the person or pet, continuing to relax more and more into the love.

Think of occasions when you have given love, care, or devotion. Can you feel the giving of that energy to another? Relax through that feeling until it feels like it is more within your Self. Now you are *being* loving and caring instead of *giving* love and care.

You can do these exercises with any feeling that you wish to foster. By relaxing into each feeling, you deepen your experience of it. By doing these exercises, you are teaching your Self to generate and own your feelings.

You can spend hours going deeper and deeper with individual feelings and still there will be more to relax into and more to be felt. There is no limit to how much love and beauty you can experience!

Compassion

By applying our healing process to everything in our life, we gain understanding—understanding of energy, emotion, intention, purpose, and healing. **How we use our understanding in our dealings with others and with the world is our *compassion*.**

Compassion expresses our understanding that the true Self is the one *having* the experience. Because the genuine portion of a person's energy is the true Self and everything else is simply his or her experience, we want to remember the central importance of the Self and the role of its experience when we interact with others. While appreciating the value of everyone's experience, we know its place in the scheme of things and apply our understanding to everything we do.

With that understanding, we distinguish between people and their experiences and do not confuse another's experience for who they are. Thus, people are not victims, though they may experience victimization. People are not poor, though they may experience poverty. And people are not helpless, though they may experience helplessness. As compassionate people, we recognize and support other people's true Self rather than their experiences.

Since involvement in other people's issues only impedes their healing and obscures the way to their true Self, we understand that we are most helpful by separating from others' issues. Compassion assists us in separating from others' pain, loneliness, failure, and invalidation, while fostering love, connection, success, and validation. Being compassionate means being kind and devoted to the true Self rather than engaging through another person's issues. When we separate from other people's experiences, our compassion facilitates the movement of their true Self through its experience.

Significant features of our experience include our façade, false self, defenses, blocks, and foreign energy. While recognizing the value of experience, compassion does not cater to people's experience because that impairs the development, learning, healing, and expression of everyone involved. A compassionate person nurtures and cares about another person's true Self rather than their experience.

We do not have to feel what another has going on to be compassionate. We do not have to go through what other people are going through to understand them. And we do not need to engage with others' issues to validate them or their experiences. Instead, we are compassionate by simply being present with other people. When we separate from others and are present with them, they are free to have their own experience with real support for their true Self.

Compassion has no judgment. What people go through is not right or wrong and it is not good or bad. It is just an experience and an opportunity to heal.

Compassion has no blame and knows no victims. There is no choosing of sides and there is no one who is wronged. There is no reason to donate energy to another person's "cause" and no reason to contribute to their position or agenda.

Compassion expresses our understanding that all paths and all beings are equal. There are no greater and there are no lesser. There is no reason to exchange energy with others.

Compassion expresses our understanding that all beings have their own challenges to face. There is no burden to share.

There is nothing to fix. We are compassionate by respecting everyone's path and process.

Compassion expresses our understanding that people can heal whatever is going on for them and reconnect with their true Self. There are no victims and no chosen ones. There is only healing or not healing.

Compassion expresses our understanding that with every choice we make, we choose either healing or not healing. Compassion supports the path of healing while also accepting a person's option to choose not to heal.

With compassion, there is a simple embracing of the truth— that the true Self is having an experience and that it can move through it. Compassion expresses our understanding that the healed true Self is the truth. And by supporting the truth, compassion assists everyone with their healing.

Generosity

Generosity is often misconstrued as a donation to other people. It frequently consists of attempting to fulfill others' needs or giving people what they want.

Sometimes "generosity" involves trying to rectify apparent inequalities and inequities. In this case, someone who has more love, money, power, or status than someone else tries to correct that imbalance.

Often people are "generous" by trying to be more than they are. Who and what they are does not seem to be enough to meet others' needs, so they become something more to compensate for the "inadequacy" of just being themselves. They try to be more caring, loving, nurturing, and accepting to be better people.

And for many people, their own energy bypasses them in their giving to others. They do not get to use, enjoy, or benefit from their own energy. They do not experience for themselves what they are giving to others.

However, as we have previously discussed, we cannot be more generous with our time or any quality of our energy towards others than we are to ourselves. **The energy must flow through us, otherwise it is not genuine.**

Furthermore, if our generosity engages with other people's issues, we are simply providing a complementary contribution that creates an exchange or transfer of energy. Since engaging through issues and participating in energy exchanges or transfers is not functional, responding to others' needs in this way is not truly generous. Although it may assist people in managing their situation temporarily, it does not help them resolve the issues that created their needs in the first place. In addition, as I discussed in "The Energy of Engagement," when we respond to others' needs with complementary generosity, we have our own issue—such as invalidation or scarcity—behind our generosity that requires healing.

Because we cannot give our energy to anyone else, this form of generosity does not work. And if we donate energy to another person's life or cause out of guilt, to do "good," or because we feel sorry for others, we have our own agenda and issues. These require healing before the interaction has any possibility of being healthy.

Once we fully grasp that nothing can be given to others, a different understanding about generosity will emerge. With healing, we will realize that generosity is just another aspect of our own energy. Since **generosity is a basic quality of everyone's energy**, it requires healing to evolve it to a healthy level of function. Thus, just like with love, success, power, and every other quality that we possess, all of us have to find and develop the generosity that is within ourselves.

With healing, we will discover that healthy generosity has a completely different function and usage than what is usually considered as generosity. As we heal our issues and experience our true Self energy flowing through us, generosity begins to have more to do with the resolution of blocks to our *own* flow of energy. **The degree of generosity that we experience is directly related to how freely our true Self energy flows through us.** Then our generosity contributes directly to everything we create, ultimately helping us to create what we truly desire.

Thus, **being generous means that we have healed our connection with our true Self and that we no longer deny our Self.** This is all about feeling the flow of our true Self moving through us, giving us what we desire from *within.* It has nothing to do with pampering our false self by buying things for ourselves or trying to fulfill ourselves from *outside* our Self.

Once we have healed the blocks to connecting with our Self, everything that we do in the flow of our Self *expresses* our generosity. Then we are generous with everyone by being our Self and sharing who we are. Thus, for instance, if instead of using our energy to inspire others, we bring that energy through us and live an inspired life, we will automatically share our inspiration with everyone. We do not give energy away to others and we do not hold onto it. We do not feed our false self and we do not have to be anything other than our Self. When we see what can be created in the flow of who we are, that is what we do. But we still do not give our energy to others. Instead, we embody the qualities that we have mastered and then everything we do expresses those qualities.

If we seek fulfillment, rather than looking outside our Self for that feeling, we can be generous with ourselves by healing and finding fulfillment within. Then we will be generous with our fulfillment in relation to other people just by being in our true Self flow, and everything that we are involved in will express our fulfillment. By healing the blocks to connecting with our Self, we create a flow of energy in alignment with our Self and, thus, are generous. Then everyone who interacts with us will experience the fulfillment and generosity that we bring into the world.

And once we heal the blocks to true Self prosperity, everything that we participate in becomes an expression of that prosperity. Then and only then can we be generous with our wealth. Without the healing of our blocks, we are not truly prosperous or wealthy, and we cannot be generous.

Are there things that we give to others that we want for ourselves? Maybe we are very "caring" or "loving" to others because we want those qualities for ourselves and know that others want them as well. Even though we do not experience them for ourselves, we give our energy to others, perhaps hoping to get something in return. Besides the fact that what we are giving is not fully evolved true Self love or care, now is the time to cultivate those feelings within ourselves rather than hoping that someone else will give them to us. By practicing our generosity and generating what we want within ourselves, we become truly loving and caring with others.

Fulfillment, love, happiness, abundance, and prosperity have to flow through us if we are to experience them and live them. The more we bring their energy through us, the stronger they are going to be and the greater their value to others and ourselves. By bringing their energy through us, we encourage other people to create these qualities as well.

Stopping the flow of our true Self cannot possibly help anyone else. If we block the flow of our prosperity, we reduce our prosperity and our ability to be prosperous with others. How can we contribute to the prosperity of anyone else if its flow through us is impaired?

In addition, if our giving to others bypasses us, we will not even experience our own energy and we will not be creating for ourselves. At the same time, our giving will not resolve other people's blocks so we will not be helping anyone else create for themselves either.

Some people deny themselves prosperity and abundance believing that their having something limits what other people can have. However, giving ourselves what we want *facilitates* other people having what they want. By allowing abundance to flow through us, we participate and create an energy flow that supports other people in experiencing their abundance.

One of my clients had a deep, but hidden, joy within her that was clearly visible to me whenever I would work with her. However, she rarely experienced this joy due to the patterns she had developed. One of those patterns told her that it was inappropriate to feel joy when other people were in pain or feeling unhappy. Another pattern told her she was uncaring when she felt good while others felt bad. Yet another pattern told her that other people's reality should take precedence, such as when other people believed they were victims. Clearly, these patterns kept her from feeling her joy, but suppressing it did nothing for anyone around her.

Now, with healing, she maintains her joy, reminding others of what they can experience and, thereby, encouraging their healing. She does not flaunt her joy when others are not doing well with their challenges, but neither does she hide or block the flow of her joy. This is the most supportive thing she can do for everyone involved.

Healing and letting our energy come through us in its highest form helps everyone. Being generous and giving ourselves happiness, abundance, fulfillment, and love is the best thing we can possibly do for everyone.

Remember, true generosity does not involve pandering to our false self—it involves healing the blocks *within* to connect with our true Self and to elevate our true Self to its most healed, functional state. Once we connect with our Self and have its healthy energy flowing through us, we can express the fullness of who we are and be truly generous. Also, notice that even though having money can reflect prosperity, money itself does *not* have anything to do with genuine prosperity. **Genuine prosperity only relates to a flow of energy through us from our true Self.**

Since we stop the flow of our Self when our generosity engages us with other people's issues, genuine generosity can only occur when we are functioning from the level of our true Self. When others have needs, we cannot give them anything that will do more than briefly sedate and obscure their issues.

Of course, there is nothing wrong with helping people get through their time of need, but that involves problem management rather than healing. Even though management has a significant role to play in our life, it does not replace healing. Sending supplies, money, or other support to people and communities that have survived a disaster obviously helps them get back on their feet, which is a wonderful contribution to make. However, it does nothing to help people resolve the feelings of loss, grief, pain, trauma, or terror from the disaster itself. No matter what we do to cope with the aftermath of an event, the experience itself must be healed to be integrated and transcended.

While we may choose to give to those in need, being generous also allows us to see that everyone has generosity *within* themselves. **When someone has needs and the apparent inability to create for themselves, they are simply not experiencing their true Self generosity.** Only through healing will they discover and nurture that generosity.

When we are truly generous with others, we do not support their feelings of scarcity and powerlessness by engaging through their issues. We support them in resolving their issues and creating what they want for themselves. We can respond to other people's needs, but we do not engage through them. We engage with the generosity within others through our own generosity. Our generosity flows through us and out into the world.

Some readers may find this view of generosity challenging. It does imply a different way of participating with others and of being in the world. And it will take some healing to achieve. But healing creates the possibility of being genuine with others. And by being our Self, we can be genuinely giving instead of giving to be nice or caring and instead of impairing everyone's healing by trying to fix problems in dysfunctional ways.

If you fear that everyone will just be indulging themselves and not caring about anyone but themselves, you may want to heal that fear and the issues that are underneath it. While it is true that those who are simply indulging their false self are selfish, those who are living as their true Self are generous.

Healing is what allows true generosity to exist and the application of our healing principles demonstrates the generosity of being our Self. When our generosity moves inward and through us, then out into our life and the world, we will have attained the full expression of our true Self's generosity.

EXERCISE: Developing Genuine Generosity

If this discussion brings up a defense like anger, judgment, dislike, or repulsion, you will want to look underneath that defense to discover what issues require healing. By healing those issues, you will raise the vibration of your generosity. If you are triggered off, you have something going on, and only after you have healed it will you be able to ascertain the truth of your experience of generosity. Continue to process your issues until you are no longer triggered off and see if that leads you to a different understanding about the nature of generosity.

Examine the feelings behind every aspect of your life that is not working. Do you have feelings of scarcity, that things are unfair, or that there is never enough? Those are the feelings that require healing to experience true Self generosity.

What do you want for yourself? Prosperity, love, power, peace, or success? Then be generous and learn how to generate those qualities *within* your Self.

Sometimes, giving to others just validates their invalidation and perpetuates their sense of powerlessness. Before giving through your "generosity," you need to examine whether or not you have an agenda and whether or not you are truly assisting that person. If you think of times when you have been "generous" with others, what was your underlying energy? Did you think that they could not create for themselves? Did it give you a good feeling to create for them? Did you get recognition, validation, or other benefits from your "generosity"? These are the issues that require healing so that you can be generous with others without any agenda.

Can you really give people something that eventually they have to generate for themselves? How can you be in the flow of your Self and be generous without an agenda, without giving energy to others, and without engaging with other people's issues? Explore your generosity and find a way to be generous in a healthy way.

Learning

In general terms, learning refers to the energetic connections and associations that we make in relation to our experience. While our mind learns from experience, learning is much more than just a mental process. Our neurological connections develop directly as a result of our energetic connections. Specifically, our learning flows from how we engage with our experience along with how we interpret, integrate, and apply what we learn from our engagement.

This relates to all of the activities in which we participate, whether we are learning body balance and movement, social skills, scholastic studies, or true Self awareness. Our learning process is epitomized by how we master the integration of symbols, sounds, language, and meaning to be able to communicate effectively.

The most important issue to consider with regards to learning is how we engage with the process. **Ideally, we learn for ourselves, which means we have a direct engagement with our experience without other people's energy in our space.** Unfortunately, that rarely happens. Our learning and learning process developed with a great many other people in our space and we did not experience learning for ourselves. Thus, typically, our experience and our method of engaging with our experience are still mediated by other people's energy. Since real learning has to do with the connections that *we* make using *our own* energy, having other people's energy involved in the process is detrimental to genuine learning.

In relation to our thought process, real learning involves thinking for ourselves, without the influence of other people's energy in our space. We can be open to other people's thoughts and ideas, but their energy stays out.

On a related topic, we want to consider what constitutes real knowledge. True knowledge does not have anything to do with the regurgitation of facts or the recitation of other people's ideas. It does not entail thinking like our teachers and giving the "right" answers on tests. Nor does it involve the internalization of other people's beliefs.

Real knowledge relates to what we know for ourselves. It results from the removal of blocks that obstruct the flow of our own energy and, therefore, our own knowing. It involves the enhancement of our awareness and the healing and integration of our experiences. The resolution of energy blocks and issues allows our true Self energy to evolve and flow through us. By dissolving beliefs and limitations that prevent our healed true Self energy from flowing though us, we uncover the full potential of our perception, knowledge, and wisdom.

If we do not know something for ourselves, we may look to others to get information. We can usually find someone to engage with us, and then run their energy in our space to try to function with their "knowledge." But, **anytime we look outside for energy to run in our space, we are pursuing false knowledge.** False knowledge is the result of internalizing someone else's thoughts, beliefs, programming, or other energy, and functioning with that energy. An illusion of learning and progress will be present, but we will then be dependent on that outside resource. The illusion of knowledge will be sustained only as long as we have the other person's energy in our space.

At best, using someone else's energy obscures our own energy. At worst, we are running energy that is totally unrelated to our own energy and knowledge. As long as the foreign energy remains in our space, we will not be thinking or learning for ourselves. As a result, our perception and responses will not be in alignment with our true Self, and we will have to continue our development until we learn them for ourselves.

Typically, we engage with others *through* our issues. However, **if we engage with others through our issues, we will not be gathering true knowledge or experiencing real learning.** The communication of knowledge and true learning does not occur through a dysfunctional engagement. The invalidation that initially motivated us to look for knowledge outside ourselves is still present, and foreign energy is brought into our space *on our issues.* This impairs our healing and real learning.

Genuine learning can only occur through the healing of any issue that prompts our interactions. Once those issues are resolved, we will have direct access to our own knowledge. Since true learning involves the resolution of our invalidation so that we access our self-knowledge, we must eventually heal all of our issues and separate from all foreign energy to claim our knowingness.

If you have trouble using your own perception, you can heal the issues that make it difficult. Rather than look outside yourself for information, heal the obstacles to perceiving as well as to validating and trusting what you perceive. If you take on somebody else's perspective, you may be able to function in the world—and it might even be a valid perspective—but that does not help you with *your* perception and no real learning has been accomplished.

If you feel aimless, or lack goals and purpose, you may look to others for your sense of purpose. But you will not find your purpose or goals by looking in the world for them. You must look *within.* You must heal any feelings of aimlessness and purposelessness to connect with your true Self and its goals. The challenge is to heal the issues that keep you from knowing. You may have taken on others' suggestions at school about what you should do or about what others thought was good for you to do. You may have patterns and interests that you developed as ways of meeting other people's expectations or needs. Or perhaps you went into some line of work to make money and feel secure rather than engaging in what you really wanted to do. To reclaim your knowledge of your life's work, you will have to heal all of the relevant issues.

If you seek guidance for what to do with your life, you might be able to get a counselor to tell you what you are best suited for or where your aptitudes lie, but that may not engage your energy or your passion. You need to remember what excites you on a true Self level, what really stirs you to the core. Again, everything that gets in the way of connecting with your true Self and knowing for yourself will require healing.

This is not to say that you should not avail yourself of others' guidance, since many people can and will contribute to finding and following your path. Other people's perspectives can be invaluable to you as you pursue your growth and development, and sometimes others can see your true Self more clearly than you can. In any case, guidance should assist in the resolution of your issues so that *you* discern for yourself and truly learn, rather than just use someone else's energy or information to run your life. Even if you stumble upon your life's path, if you have other people's energy in your space, that path may not seem very meaningful to you. **Only when you connect with your true Self's purpose directly, will you feel the passion and power that reside there.**

This book is not meant to give you yet another person's thoughts to have coursing through your mind. The objective is to teach you the tools to resolve your issues so that you bring your own knowledge through you. If the perspective presented in this book helps you ascertain your truth—or if it rings true and, therefore, reminds you of your truth—then it has served its purpose.

EXERCISE: *Claiming Your Knowledge*

Look at the people you turn to for knowledge, information, and guidance. What are you looking for? Are you looking for help to find it within you or are you looking for something outside yourself? If you are looking for energy to use from outside, what motivates you to look for it there? Resolve every block that is present. Every feeling of judgment, invalidation, inability, distrust, incompetence, powerlessness, and aimlessness must be healed. Claim your Self-knowledge. Look within for your guidance and answers.

Validation

The quest for validation is a very challenging endeavor. It is abstract and cannot be conjured up or manipulated by the mind. It cannot come from a façade or from our false self. Genuine validation has nothing to do with ego gratification, comparing ourselves with others, or getting confirmation from outside ourselves.

True validation is not just a matter of *deciding* to validate ourselves or to accept ourselves. We cannot simply choose to feel secure with our thoughts or with ourselves. We cannot just conclude that we are right, that our thoughts are valid, or that everything we feel is true.

Genuine validation can only be achieved through healing. That is how we discover something real and true. Our façade and false self disappear, exposing the reality of our true Self. Beliefs and illusions melt away, revealing genuine knowledge. Issues and blocked feelings are resolved, eliminating distortion and bringing clarity to our perception. **After healing everything that can be healed, whatever remains is real.**

A great deal of healing is required to be able to discern and own our truth. Healing uncovers what is valid and provides a platform for taking meaningful action in the world. Real validation involves going through all of our invalidation, insecurity, judgment, and non-acceptance to ascertain what is real and to validate ourselves.

The ultimate achievement is true Self validation. True Self validation has to do with connecting with our Self and functioning from there. It involves relying on our Self for direction and guidance. And it has to do with operating with the awareness of our Self *on our own*.

Our culture tends to rely on external validation for the verification and acceptance of our perception, knowledge, and ideas. Often, we monitor the reactions of other people for feedback on our actions, opinions, and observations. Books and other resources are frequently used as references for our beliefs and perspectives.

But what if our experience lies outside the arena of accepted thought and belief? And what if our perception does not agree with other people's views?

Ultimately, we are on our own and we have to be able to validate our own knowledge and perception. This does not mean that we cannot explore ideas and learn from others by accessing sources of information and experience outside ourselves. And it does not mean that we are unwilling to consider other perspectives, understandings, and awareness. It only means that we have to validate what we obtain from outside ourselves for ourselves—and no one else can do that for us. We have to be able to take action in the world based on our own awareness and that takes genuine self-validation.

The belief system in which we participate is only one way to organize our experience. We allow it to impose its structure upon us, forcing its particular classification on our awareness and influencing our interpretation of experience.

Research is often used to validate or invalidate ideas, concepts, perception, and knowledge. However, if its methods and procedures are steeped in a belief system, its findings are affected by every belief through which its observations are made. Therefore, research can easily be distorted and may not be useful in proving or disproving our perception. For example, when people believed that the Earth was at the center of the solar system, it affected all of their observations and perpetuated the resulting perceptual distortion. Something *within* the perceptual structure of a belief system has limited relevance for something that is *outside* of that system.

Science can be used to explore, examine, and describe our experience. And while it has the potential to assist with the expansion of our awareness and knowledge, it is commonly used as an approach that tells us about its own structure and function. It is usually used to corroborate what is and what is not part of its system. When used in this way, higher truths and greater realities that operate beyond the universe of science have no place within its limited context. It will not be able to validate what does not fit within its structure.

It is quite an accomplishment to perceive and function outside of an accepted belief system. And, it is an even greater achievement to function *without* a belief system. When we embark on such a journey, we have to *validate* our perception and experience for ourselves.

Once we validate ourselves, we are no longer dependent on other people for our validation. Even though we can learn from others, we trust and validate ourselves. Being in touch with our truth, we do not need books, other people, or science to verify what is going on. We can stand in our own truth *on our own*.

Because we each have a unique path to navigate, all of us must learn to validate ourselves. We cannot rely on feedback from others to know what steps to take to evolve our own distinctive path. While we can always be open to other people's wisdom and perspectives, it comes down to validating ourselves to know the way.

Unlike with competition, in which only one or a very few people can feel good about themselves at one time, genuine validation is something that everyone can experience simultaneously. And validating ourselves in no way detracts from anyone's experience or keeps anyone else from validating themselves. In fact, validating ourselves facilitates other people's self-validation. By validating ourselves, we enhance the flow of validation into our life, making it a more likely option for others to experience. And by healing our invalidation, we discover a path to our Self and remember the truth: Everyone is valid. As a result, we assist others by validating them.

EXERCISE: *Validating Yourself*

Make a list of the ways you validate yourself. Then take some time with each of these ways, separate from the trigger, and relax into the feeling of validation. Relax more and more deeply in the feeling of validation until you are saturated with it. The more you feel valid without having to do anything, the less you will compete for it in the world and the easier it will be to feel genuine validation.

EXERCISE: *Challenging Your Validation*

We commonly create an environment and surround ourselves with people who support how we validate ourselves. Imagine being plucked out of your world and dropped into an unfamiliar environment, surrounded by people you do not know. Could you still validate yourself? Or would you strive to find a way to get validation in the new world? In an unusual environment, you might not find the same support and, without it, you might get to experience some of your hidden invalidation. You would discover whether you were actually validating yourself or whether you were using something outside yourself to validate you.

Teachers

We are often so wrapped up in our own issues and perspectives that it is difficult to perceive what we are doing and how we are creating our life. An external perspective can be helpful in assisting us in becoming aware of our Self and our patterns. People who are intimately involved in our life may be "too close" to us or too involved in our issues to assist with our awareness. Thus, a teacher can be incredibly useful in providing such a perspective.

All too frequently, however, people see our issues and react to them as if those issues are who we are. And while we are not our issues, it takes an unusual person to differentiate between our issues and who we truly are. **Good teachers can make the distinction between our issues and us, and guide us through our issues while reinforcing our identification with our true Self.**

In healthy connections, people *separate* from our issues and, thus, relate with us from a place of *clarity*. Separation is required for someone to be able to assist us on the path to our Self. This enables us to engage with them in a healthy manner.

If there is no separation, people interact with us *through* our issues and theirs. Engaging through issues can easily create confusion around whose issues are whose and impairs our ability to heal. Furthermore, when someone engages with us through an issue, he or she creates a dysfunctional engagement. Since true learning cannot occur by engaging through an issue, such an engagement compromises a teacher's ability to assist in our development. Whomever we engage with in this way does not have the clarity of functional teaching, and requires healing to be of benefit to our development.

One common way to engage with others through an issue is when we seek knowledge from others. If we open for knowledge based on our invalidation, it is common for other people to move into our space through that issue. This does not help us resolve our issue or connect with our own knowledge. Since good teachers will not engage through our dysfunction, they will assist us in enhancing our awareness and guide us in healing our invalidation. Because healthy function requires Self-knowledge and awareness, **good teachers assist us in seeking the source of knowledge within our Self**. They guide us to rely on our ability to function with our own knowing.

Other common dysfunctional patterns of engagement involve looking for care, acceptance, and love. If our motivation for engaging with others is to get someone to take care of us, good teachers will assist us in healing the issues that keep us from experiencing our Self-care, rather than engaging through our need for care. If we open for acceptance, they will assist us in healing the issues that prevent us from accepting our Self. If the intention behind our engagements is to get love, they will assist us in healing any blocks to our Self-love. **Good teachers will refrain from engaging through our issues, and keep our focus on healing the intention behind our interactions.**

Teachers, parents, friends, and even strangers have directed and will continue to direct their own issues, beliefs, values, and perceptions at us our whole life. Often, other people's personal goals, biases, judgments, and other energetic burdens are transferred to us as well. These obscure our path and complicate our healing.

Good teachers interact with us from a place of *neutrality*. There is no investment in an outcome. There is no imposition of the teacher's own personal goals. They keep their energy to themselves, teach *without judgment,* and *do not project* their energy or issues onto us. There is respect for our journey: the lessons we have to learn and the choices we face and make along the way. A good teacher can guide us through our lessons so that we truly learn.

We have been open to outside influences and looked outside ourselves to know about ourselves and to know how to act and be. It is easy to "give up space" to others and to take on their beliefs or way of thinking or being.

Good teachers teach without the need or desire for students to give up space to them. They also teach us *not* to open to others to know about ourselves.

Other people's views and beliefs have been absorbed and integrated so well that we often do not notice how habitually we use and rely upon them. And we are still largely operating from that place even though it may not seem that way. While we must be watchful not to just take on someone else's beliefs or knowledge, this does not mean that we cannot benefit from other people's awareness, understanding, and ideas. It only means that we do not want to use them if we cannot validate them for ourselves. If it is not part of our own truth, we must continue to search for that truth.

Good teachers assist us in trusting our own perception and thought process. They assist us in finding our own truth and in validating that truth.

Some teachers desire the validation, power, adulation, and control that students can give them. However, those who do *not* thrive off others' energy accomplish the highest quality teaching. They already know the energy source within themselves and live that knowledge. Thus, **good teachers can guide without feeding off the energy of their students.**

Because many paths traverse the realm of energy, it takes awareness and knowledge to recognize a path to the true Self. It takes what we have called the intention to heal. Ideally, we would have teachers who have such awareness and knowledge, and who have the skills to *guide* us along the path to our true Self—people who have embodied the intention to heal.

Good teachers can also assist us in mastering all of the above intricacies of healing, so our developing skills are not misused. In so doing, they teach us their *mastery of teaching.*

If, on the other hand, *you* have embodied the intention to heal, you are well on your way to learning on your own and teaching yourself.

Becoming Your Source

In terms of energetic evolution, you have two paths from which to choose. Either you look outside yourself to fulfill your energy needs or you turn inward to find the source of your fulfillment within.

The first path leads nowhere. If you are following this path, you move from one energy source to another, always looking for a new energy reserve. However, because of the transient nature of using other people's energy, your quest will never result in a consistent experience of fulfillment. And because it is not your own energy, it cannot even remotely emulate your true Self and genuine fulfillment.

Alternatively, by healing and looking within, you will discover the ultimate source of your energy, your true Self. From that discovery, you can then evolve further so you identify with your true Self as yourself. At that point, you will have truly become your source and you will be in a constant flow of genuine fulfillment.

If the source within is obstructed or distorted, you either have to look externally to get your needs met from other people and from the world, or you stop searching. Of course, neither of these options is satisfactory. If you give up your search, you will never experience your true Self or your fulfillment. But, if you go outside yourself to fill a need, you delay your healing and bring foreign energy into your space. Frequently, that foreign energy is itself distorted and limiting.

For example, perhaps you do not know how to generate what you are looking for for yourself. You search for wisdom, knowledge, capability, validation, acceptance, wholeness and love because you do not know that these qualities are the natural result of healing yourself and connecting with your true Self. However, even if you find some energy that seems suitable, it cannot possibly match your own energy or compensate for the loss of your Self.

Furthermore, if your source is *outside* you, the intention behind everything you think, say, and do will be to get your needs met from the outside. You will search for people to love you and care about you. You will spend a great deal of time and energy seeking the feelings of success and fulfillment in the world. Conversations with friends will carry your cravings for acceptance. In short, **when the source of your fulfillment is outside of you, you will try to get the world to flow *into* you.**

Every word will grab at other people when you want their love. Every action will try to engage other people when you want their validation.

If you feel insecure and connect with others to find security, that will be the energy behind every interaction. However, no matter where you are, no matter whom you are with, and no matter how much you try to control what goes on around you, the insecurity will always be present until you heal it. You will not trust yourself and, instead, will make something happen— perhaps with work or with a relationship—to try to create the feeling of security.

Alternatively, you can heal your energy blocks, discover the source within you, and become your source—your true Self. When you connect with the source within and heal, the inherent qualities of your evolved true Self become known to you and complete you. You find qualities like *validation, trust,* and *security* within you.

The flow of your true Self is *valid*. You do not need any external validation that you are doing what you are supposed to do, nor do you look for it. Validation is a part of you and being your Self validates you.

You *trust* that all you have to do is to be in the flow of your Self and that everything is unfolding as it is intended. This is not simply an act of blind faith. It means that you are connecting with the flow of your Self and experiencing the trust that is inherent in that flow. You trust your Self instead of placing your trust in other people's hands.

When you are in the flow of your true Self, you have its innate *support* and *security*. You experience your Self-security instead of looking for it from others or from the world. And anything that takes you out of the flow of your true Self diminishes your sense of support and security.

Once you become your source, it will be natural to be in the flow of your true Self. When you connect with the source within, the feelings that you seek will flow through you, nourishing you and sustaining you. And by monitoring that flow and staying in it, you will be able to sustain your connection with your Self.

While qualities that you heal and integrate will flow through you and your life, it is important to note that you cannot give this energy to another person in the way that you might expect. These qualities become a part of who you are and you express them, rather than give them, simply by being your Self. Thus, you can only be the source for yourself. You cannot be the source for anyone else. Everyone must eventually connect with the source within themselves to experience their own genuine fulfillment.

EXERCISE: Fun With Feelings

You can practice connecting with the source within by generating the feelings that you want to experience. Make a list of the feelings that you want from the people in your life and from the world. Then start with one of the feelings on your list and begin to generate that feeling. Either remember a time when you felt the feeling that you are looking for or imagine what it might be like to feel that way. Then all you have to do is relax into the feeling. Stay focused on the feeling itself, not anything associated with it, such as another person, an event, or the world. Continue to relax and let it flow through you. Practice with the same feelings during several meditations.

As you relax through each feeling, one of two things will happen: Either the feeling will continue to take you deeper and deeper to a profound level of the quality that you are meditating on, or the feeling will dissolve to be replaced by the truth of your true Self that lies beyond that quality. Either way, you are becoming your source!

❊ ❊ ❊

To fully experience and understand every quality of your Self, you require *contrast* to create awareness of your energy. If there were only one color, you would not have an experience or concept of color. To understand love, you require awareness of its presence and something to contrast it with, such as the absence of love, emptiness, or hate.

When you resolve the contrasting and what often appear to be conflicting qualities, you will discover that no conflict exists—the two qualities define the range along a continuum of an illusion and a higher truth lies beyond it. Beyond the illusion, you find the truth of your evolved Self.

Your true Self is not the negative or the positive emotions that you are feeling. Your true Self is the one *having* your experience. Therefore, you want to heal both the positive and the negative feelings. With positive feelings, you want to practice going through them so that you release any limitations to their flow. With negative feelings, you want to relax through them so that they dissolve. The goal of emotional healing is *not* to strive for, create, or hold onto positive feelings. **One goal of healing is to resolve both positive and negative feelings to find the truth of your Self beyond them.**

Beyond the illusion of isolation and connection, there is only connection. Beyond right and wrong, everything is all right. Beyond achieving and beyond winning and losing, there is only *being*. You may experience emptiness or loneliness or love or loss of love—but there is only love. You do not want to be attached to the positive or the negative. The feelings are not what you are looking for; you are seeking your Self. Let the feelings flow and feel your Self behind them.

An important element of becoming the source for yourself involves the evolution of the energetic definitions of the various qualities that you experience and give. You will want to look at the qualities that you use to engage others and raise the vibration of those qualities to their highest levels.

As you become the source, what you used to call *love* may begin to look like need, and a higher love will become possible and eventually experienced. It means that you live and love at the highest level. The energy that you experience and live is pure. The love that you are experiencing is unconditional; however, no energy is given away. It is totally loving to your Self and, therefore, it is totally loving to everyone else.

When you become the source, you take *responsibility* for your issues and energy, and you separate from what is not yours. Whoever has an active issue is responsible for the healing of that issue. If you are triggered off, that issue is your responsibility to heal. If you trigger me off, the triggered issue is my responsibility. If you *intend* to trigger me off, that intention is your responsibility as well.

Your responsibility is to *take care* of you. This does not mean that you must do everything *for* yourself but that you address what you have going on, not ignoring anything. It means that you respond to and fulfill your energy needs.

When you become the source, you become *independent*. This does *not* mean being alone or isolated. It means that you have a separate sense of identity while recognizing your deeper connection with everything. It means that you have a clear sense of Self and that you get to be your Self everywhere, no matter what you are doing. And you do not lose your Self, no matter what anyone else is doing. You get to be your Self *with* others!

Being the source of *devotion* means that you are true to your true Self and that you bring your Self into everything you do. By owning your devotion to your Self, you express devotion to the true Self in others at the same time.

When you become the source of *acceptance*, you can own your acceptance of everyone. It means that you accept that people are who they are, doing whatever they are doing, experiencing whatever they are experiencing. However, you do not accept or bring anyone else's opinions, beliefs, or other energy *into your space*—everyone lives their life in their own space. It means that you accept people where *they* are instead of accepting or rejecting them where *you* are; you accept me in *my* space rather than accepting or rejecting me based on whether or not you let me into *your* space.

Being the source of *compassion* does not mean going through other people's feelings or living their experiences with them. It means you understand that the true Self is who they are and that they can heal whatever is going on for them, no matter what they are going through. You do not have to live their experience to understand them or to understand what they are going through.

Being the source of *generosity* does not involve giving energy or anything else to others; it means that you have healed the blocks to *having* within you. Then and only then can you express the prosperity of who you are and give generously by being your Self.

Once you identify with your true Self and heal it, the flow of your Self truth will be all that you experience and feel. You will no longer search for your life purpose; you will know your Self. You will no longer reach for love; you will have found your Self. And when you are in the flow of your Self, you will express the love and the purpose that are you. You will express your inherent validation, responsibility, acceptance, generosity, and care. And while the energetic definitions of your true Self qualities probably differ from your socialized definitions, they are who you are. And you no longer have to be anything but your Self.

Once you become the source, you will live and function as your evolved true Self. You will connect with others as your Self and you will recognize the true Self in others. You will not require anyone to be anything but themselves and you will honor who they really are at the true Self level—capable, lovable, valid, healing.

Once you become the source, everything you think, say, and do will be filled with your compassion. Every activity will become an expression of your true Self love, validation, success, and fulfillment. You will no longer grab at the world. Instead, the source will flow through you and will be expressed in your life and in the world. **Once you connect with the source within, the world will flow *from* you.**

EXERCISE: *True Self Meditation*

By reading this book, doing the exercises, and processing the issues that have arisen, you have been developing a single process with which to accomplish the four objectives of healing: remembering your Self, evolving your Self, identifying with your Self, and bringing your Self more fully into your life. By healing whatever issues are present in the moment, you restore the flow of your Self moving through its experience and fulfill the goals of healing. Elegant!

As a complement to this process, I wanted to offer the following meditation. It is presented in two parts because the interlude between them is a natural place to rest, explore, or be creative.

Please practice the two parts of this exercise *together* since the first part is not complete without the second part. If you find that you want to practice the first part *without* the second part, you may want to see if there is some resistance to being present in the world or in your life.

Part I: Remembering Your Self and Identifying with Your Self

Sit in a quiet place and close your eyes. Say to yourself, "I am not the foreign energy that I am experiencing. I am the one having this experience." *Feel* a separation from the world around you. Separate from the people, sounds, and other foreign energy from your daily life.

Focus on your personality. Say to yourself, "I am not my personality. I am the one experiencing this personality." *Relax* through the experience of your personality. Continue to relax until your personality has dissolved.

Focus on your physical body. Say to yourself, "I am not my body. I am the one experiencing this body." *Relax* through the experience of your physical body. Continue to relax until your physical body feels like it has dissolved.

Notice the flow of your thoughts. Say to yourself, "I am not my thoughts. I am the one having these thoughts." *Feel* a separation from the mental portion of your experience.

Focus on your mind. Say to yourself, "I am not my mind. I am the one experiencing this mind." *Feel* a separation from your mind.

Focus on your emotions. Say to yourself, "I am not my emotions. I am the one having these emotions." *Relax* through the experience of your emotions. Continue to relax until your emotions have dissolved.

Now your true Self is all that remains. Enjoy the experience of who you really are.

Part II: Evolving Your Self and Bringing Your Self into Your Life

When you are ready to return, bring your Self back into your body, into this world, and into your experience. Say to yourself, "I am my true Self. I now express, experience, evolve, and enjoy my true Self through my body, mind, emotions, thoughts, and personality. I choose to be present in the world now."

As you come back into your body, be watchful for any issues that are waiting for you. *Relax* through any resistance and the underlying issues that you notice.

As you reenter the world, be alert for what takes you out of the flow of your Self and heal what arises. Be attentive with your relationships, your thoughts, and other aspects of your experience. Pay special attention to any foreign energy that you perceive and perform your separation process.

Live as the person you really are!

Integrity

Integrity means that all of your energy is in alignment. It means that your words, emotions, thoughts, will, intention, true Self, and all of the rest of your energy are harmonious and express the same energy. It means that you are living as the person you truly are.

When you start the process of healing, you will have many voices expressing many different intentions. You may say one thing that reflects what you want to feel while other parts of you are expressing contradictory feelings.

When there are many disparate parts within you, there is no power in what you say and do. Your energy cannot move easily in one direction and there is less of an ability to create what you want.

Some people try to align around ideals or beliefs about what they *should* feel and pretend that those principles are what they *do* feel. They blot out those feelings that disagree with their new beliefs. They identify with the parts of themselves that agree with their ideals.

However, integrity does not relate to any ideal or to any noble idea that you may have. It does not relate to any judgment about what is right or wrong. No part of you can be denied or ignored to attain integrity. Nor can you achieve integrity by forcing an alignment within yourself.

If you try to force such an alignment, you create a false sense of integrity. Since creating a false integrity is the opposite of healing, it will have to be undone to achieve the desired healing and the resulting genuine integrity.

To raise your level of integrity, you have to become aware of the various parts of your energy and heal them. All the different feelings and voices that you experience, including your ideals and beliefs, require healing to attain the highest level of integrity.

Healing enhances the voice of your true Self and diminishes the influence of those parts that take you away from your Self. Everything that you heal brings greater alignment and integrity within your energy. Only through healing will you discover your true nature and align your life to express that nature.

By asserting your determination and doing the work that is required, you can become aware of every aspect of your energy and heal it so that you function as a congruent whole. Only through healing will you be able to speak with one voice.

This alignment of your energy gives you power. The removal of obstructions that have previously restrained you enhances and releases that power.

With greater integrity, your energy facilitates an alignment with whatever it encounters. Much like a seed crystal in a supersaturated solution, your life aligns with your energy. You get to experience more of your true Self and more of what you want to create in your life.

As you achieve greater and greater integrity, there is more and more energy aligned behind your words and actions. And with sufficient integrity, a solitary act or the expression of a single word can change the world.

Freedom

Freedom offers a unique choice for how to live: You can travel along the path of your true Self and properly address anything that disrupts your journey. You can heal your limitations and express your true Self in everything you do.

It has nothing to do with avoiding the challenges you face or doing whatever you want. It has nothing to do with being alone or not participating in life. Instead, **freedom has everything to do with engaging fully with others and with life *as your Self.***

The intention to heal is of fundamental importance if you are to attain and sustain your freedom. Every issue that arises distorts and obstructs the flow of your Self. Every issue must be resolved through your healing. While the issues that arise delineate your path, it is their healing and integration that allows you to flow freely along its course.

Holding onto anything outside your Self stops its flow, creating pain and an immediate loss of freedom. Thus, *letting go* is not only a vital step in your emotional healing process, but its mastery is also essential for creating freedom.

Letting go requires that you no longer hold onto anyone or anything, and that you do not allow anyone or anything to hold onto you. *Letting go* allows everyone to remain true to their true Self and to continue on the path to freedom. The element of *letting go* is vital for creating the ultimate true Self connections that can only occur when everyone is free to follow their own unique path.

Every time you *stop* to engage with someone, you *stop* the flow of your true Self. Every dysfunctional engagement moves all of the participants off their path and creates a pause in their respective journey. To have freedom, it is necessary to master the avenues of engagement so that you interact with others *from* your path. By remaining on your path when you engage with others, you interact with them through the healthy and functional qualities of your true Self.

EXERCISE: Asserting Your Freedom

Make a list of everyone and everything that keeps you from being your Self or that prevents you from doing what you want to do. Heal all of the feelings around each of these issues. Assert your freedom!

Take note of everything that you allow to pull you off your path. Heal whatever issues are present and honor your Self by staying on your path.

❋ ❋ ❋

True freedom cannot be given because there is nothing that can be passed from one person to another. You must claim freedom through healing and the mastery of your Self. All you can do is master freedom for your Self and then, perhaps, guide others to find that path within themselves.

Nothing outside you can *take you off* the path of your Self. As long as you are willing to heal, you can remain true to your Self and maintain your freedom. Freedom cannot be taken away because no one can reach inside you to take what you own.

Nothing outside of your Self can *keep you on* your path. It is up to you to free your Self and keep your Self free. Since no law can affect what is within you, freedom cannot be legislated. Only you can liberate your Self.

You cannot sell anything from within your Self and, thus, freedom cannot be sold. You cannot own anything from outside your Self and, thus, freedom cannot be bought.

Freedom does not require protection from other people. There is no need for a barrier to keep people out, which would also prevent you from being your Self by keeping you trapped within. The power of freedom is that you can heal and be your Self no matter whom you are with and no matter where you are.

Freedom does not require isolation. If you isolate yourself from other people, you are also separate from your Self. By avoiding the world or other people, you are avoiding your healing and the path of your Self.

Freedom does not release you from responsibility. In fact, freedom requires that you take full responsibility for your Self. Only by taking responsibility for your Self and your issues will you be able to heal and claim your freedom.

If you give up freedom, you never had it in the first place. Once you own the flow of your Self and the freedom that is inherent in that flow, the loss of freedom is too painful to ignore and you will heal whatever obstructs that flow.

There is no need to fight for your freedom, for fighting engages you with other people through a lack of freedom. There is no more blood to spill and no more pain to suffer. Instead, you heal the battle for freedom within your Self and resolve your own experience of limitation.

With freedom, there is no anger when others attempt to control you or try to get their needs met through you. This is not because anger is wrong, because you have succeeded in suppressing your anger, or because you have decided that you will not be angry. You do not respond with anger because there is none. You are free from engaging in someone else's issues. You are invisible.

If you engage others through their loss of freedom, you lose your Self and you lose your freedom as well. Nothing is gained through the control of others. With freedom, you exercise your Self-control by healing whatever arises. You do not participate as either the captor or the captive. There is a letting go of control over what is outside your Self.

If you block the expression of your Self, you act out of fear and powerlessness. With freedom, you choose to express your true Self. You heal the powerlessness within and become wholly involved in life.

Everyone is free to be themselves. If that brings up issues for you, you maintain your freedom by healing those issues. If anything engages you in a way that does not feel good, you choose to heal those engagements.

No matter where you are or what your environment, you can heal everything that crops up. You are not your blocks or issues. The only way you lose your freedom is when you engage with the world or with another person through your blocks or issues.

You cannot fulfill another person's needs. By healing every way that people hook you into their life, you free yourself to be your Self and you free other people to be their true Self.

No one else can fulfill your needs. By healing every way that you hook others into your life, you free yourself to be your Self and you free other people to be their true Self.

The world cannot fulfill your needs, nor can you fulfill the world's needs. By healing every way that you participate in the world through dysfunction, you free yourself to be your Self and you free the world to be its Self.

Some people think they are free on weekends. Some think they would be free if they won the lottery or if they did not have any responsibilities. And some people believe that they will be free when their Earth life is over. However, the reality is that you are only free when you have accomplished healing.

Whatever you have healed is what you have freed. If you have not accomplished healing, you are not free.

This is just like what happens with other qualities of your energy. Are you going to wake up tomorrow with more love, validation, or success? These qualities only develop when you have done some healing to resolve your blocks and issues. The same thing is true with freedom. You do not suddenly wake up with more freedom unless you have accomplished your healing. **Wherever you go, whatever you do, you take it all with you—the healed and the unhealed issues, the freedom and the limitations.**

Freedom results from healing your dysfunctional patterns and issues; it is these patterns and issues that keep you imprisoned. Truly, nothing can prevent you from being your true Self. Healing provides an avenue to get you back on the path of your true Self and to keep you there. Eventually, you know who you are and you live and function with your true Self energy. Then you are *being* your Self. And being in the flow of your Self, you are free at last.

❋ ❋ ❋

Your true Self is the one *having* your experience. It is the part of your energy that is moving *through* life. Anything that takes you off your path separates you from your Self and causes the loss of your freedom. Anything in your experience with which you identify stops the flow of your Self and obstructs your Self-freedom.

Freedom does *not* mean that you do whatever you want, whenever you want to do it. **Freedom means that you do what you want in alignment with your true Self**. Anything that is in alignment with your true Self has the inherent quality of freedom associated with it. Freedom involves being on and staying on the path of the true Self and, of course, connecting with people, work, and life situations as your Self. When you are free of your attachments, you are free to be a healthy being and to participate fully in your life. Thus, being in the flow of your Self gives you the freedom to hold a job, maintain a schedule, and make plans and commitments without compromising your Self or your freedom.

Healing liberates you from everything that is not your true Self. You are not attached to your mind, body, thoughts, or beliefs. You are not attached to your issues or false self. You are not attached to anyone or anything. By releasing all attachments, you are left with what is real—your true Self.

As your true Self, you no longer give your energy to anyone, nor do you need anyone else's energy. You stop trying to be someone you're not. You do not need to be more than your Self, nor will you be less than your Self. You can just *be* your Self.

Having the freedom to be who you are, you let go of everyone, honoring their freedom to do whatever it is that they are doing and to follow the course of their life. You may not know exactly where everyone is going or how they are going to get there, but you respect everyone's freedom to follow their own path and to be true to whatever they wish.

To some of you, this view of freedom may appear to be cold, aloof, distant, and, perhaps, even undesirable. This will occur in the presence of feelings of isolation and insecurity that result from a separation from your true Self. Those feelings will arise if blocks and issues mediate your relations with others. Thus, the avoidance of these feelings may seem more appealing, though the healing of those issues is what is required to experience the joy and power of freedom.

Truly, freedom brings the warmth of your Self into everything you do. Self-freedom infuses every thought, word, and action with exceptional significance. Your interactions are filled with an affection that does not exist without freedom and without your Self. Everything else will seem empty and meaningless by comparison.

It may also appear that freedom has a price—that you have to lose something or give something up in exchange for your freedom. If those feelings arise, their healing will allow you to know the truth: With freedom, you gain your Self and a genuine relation with everything else—and nothing is lost.

Indeed, your most valuable connections are created *because* of your freedom. Your freedom allows you to relate with others in a real and healthy manner. It produces pure relations that are free of any sensation of isolation or insecurity. Nothing is holding you there, and the need for controlling other people is absent. Connections through freedom are rich with meaning and value as you bring your true Self into your life.

What could be more fulfilling and powerful than being your Self? And what could be deeper than being your Self and choosing to connect? Self-freedom creates the possibility of the most profound and intimate encounters with the world and with others. The depth and nature of these interactions are extraordinary because nothing intervenes between you and other people. You connect directly with other people and with the world. You experience the wholeness of life, the oneness of energy.

EXERCISE: The Path to Freedom

While most people spend their entire life trying to avoid negative feelings and chasing positive feelings, the path to freedom follows a different route: **The path to freedom is through the negative feelings.** By moving through negative feelings, you remember your Self and you experience your Self moving through your experience. To follow this route, you must move directly into your negative feelings and through them.

The most powerful accomplishment on this path is to learn to *enjoy* your negative feelings. When you have done this, you are truly free.

How can this be? When you enjoy feeling worthless or feeling like a nobody, those feelings no longer have any power over you. You will no longer have to avoid them or try to be somebody. You will then be free to be your Self.

Settle into a negative feeling and learn to enjoy it. You do not want to identify with the feeling, hold onto it, or get stuck in it. You want to completely diffuse it, changing it from something with negative implications to something that is neutral or even positive. When you enjoy and flow through feeling uncertain, insignificant, worthless, powerless, helpless, stupid, unwanted, unlovable, and uncared for, you will be free. Remember that if you become stuck in a feeling, it is likely to be someone else's issue and you will have to do your healing work to separate from it. When you are flowing through your own negative feeling, you will experience your true liberation.

After Words

Anything is possible and healing is what makes it so. It opens the door to your Self and to fulfillment. It allows you to make sense out of what is happening in the world and with your Self. It reveals the path to your Self and can guide you all the way home. Healing illuminates the path to freedom.

✽ ✽ ✽

I wish you well on your journey!
With all my love,
—Michael

Acknowledgments

B etty J. Moore has been my co-creative partner in the writing of this book and in the teaching of the principles of healing. Betty created the *Appendix,* all of the graphics, and several of the exercises for the book as well as the artwork that graces the cover. The outstanding creativity, enthusiasm, and devotion of my talented assistant have been invaluable. It has been fabulous to work with someone who is as dedicated to learning and healing as Betty is. Thanks for having so much fun with me on this adventure!

I am profoundly grateful for the involvement of my parents, Janet and David Winer, who reviewed the manuscript throughout its development and provided stimulating and incisive questions for consideration. They inspired the birth and development of many facets of this book. Thanks for everything!

Barbara Jakesz, M.D., contributed countless hours reviewing and editing my work. Thank you, Barbara, for your fine mind and mighty pen!

Dr. Carolyn Martin, PhD., also played a significant role in the evolution of this book. Her great ideas helped to make it more complete and more readable. Thank you, Carolyn!

The energy, commitment, encouragement, and passion of my other reviewers have been inspiring and greatly appreciated. Katharyn Duffy, Anne Maddeford, LeAnna Dolan, Diane Coughlin, Dr. Jeanne Young, D.C., and Sylvia DePue contributed their outstanding critiques, questions, and ideas.

And Beth Shaffer, Mason Dwinell, Katherine Lynch, and Erik Lynch offered valuable feedback during this endeavor. Their contributions assisted me in presenting my experience of healing in the truest manner.

I am grateful for every teacher I have had through the years, all of whom have helped me to find my Self and my way. In particular, Robert A. Monroe shared his understanding of life, healing, and human development. Kevin Ryerson encouraged me to write the books I always wanted to write. And Jacquelyne Ellis's insight and encouragement have been inspiring, fun, beneficial, and very much appreciated.

I also wish to acknowledge all the clients I have worked with during my years of being in practice. I am so grateful they have participated with me in discovering a way of healing. They have been great teachers and travelers to meet on the path to freedom.

Transition from Book I to Book II

I n this book, I use the terms *energy* and *true Self* as simplifications of much more complex concepts. By reducing the number of terms and concepts, I could focus on exploring the emotional basis for dysfunction and the development of an emotional process to effect healing.

While the use of these terms is valid from a certain perspective, a more comprehensive context is necessary to achieve greater understanding. In the second book of this series, *Light Medicine: Evolving Our Body, Our Life, and Our Planet*, we will begin to build that larger context.

What I call energy in this book will be explored as part of a larger concept called *Light*. And what I call the true Self in this book will be shown to include numerous aspects of Light.

Light is the most fundamental aspect of everything, with every aspect of our experience being an expression of Light. Energy is a special subset of Light that includes emotions, programming, intention, and thoughts as its most recognizable components. Energy creates a force within Light, affecting its expression. Thus, in Book I, energy is the most relevant concept to discuss, as we have been interested in evolving the force that we use to create our experience.

The term *true Self* is an excellent way to describe the part of our experience that is genuine. It is a way to distinguish what is real from what is an illusion; to recognize that there is something tangible and real underneath the illusion of our experience. But now that we have recognized the genuine part of our energy, in Book II we can explore its components more thoroughly. With the expansion of our conceptual framework, we can begin to move into a larger world and to develop the skills to thrive in that world.

Light Medicine:

Evolving Our Body, Our Life, and Our Planet

From the first book, *Healing: The Path to Freedom*, we learned how to heal our emotions and discovered the significance of the intention to heal. With these skills, we can now apply our healing process to every area of our life to find fulfillment and freedom within our Self.

In the second book, we will apply the principles of healing to issues involving our body. For many people, the physical body and its health are among their foremost concerns. Our discussion will expand on the perspective that Light and energy precede everything in physical form. We will gain greater insight and understanding about energy and about how our body expresses and responds to Light and energy.

Health issues will be explored from an energetic perspective. Disease, dysfunction, or suboptimal function develops when unhealed issues distort or obstruct the flow of our energy. In this book, you will see how our body adapts to energy and how we can use our emotional process to evolve through any health challenges that we face to heal our Self and our body. And since we *are* Light, the energetic realm is the place to focus to develop the vibrational qualities required for physical health, nourishment, and well-being.

Light Medicine will also explore physical body expression and potential. By working with Light and energy, we can access the unlimited and largely untapped potential that lies within us. Our body can evolve to express unprecedented possibilities. And we can bring our evolving true Self into our body and our life to experience anything we can imagine.

Appendix

As you practice your healing process, the following lists of emotions may help you identify or name the feelings with which you are working. Listed are many of the possible emotions that you may experience. Scan through the negative and positive emotions to find the feeling that most closely resonates with the energy you are feeling or want to feel.

When you try these emotions on for size, you may want to play with word tenses and subtle variations of the words to achieve the proper fit. As an example, the word *control* may seem to be your current emotional issue, but, as you relax into it, you may discover that *controlled* or *controlling* more precisely describes your feeling. Or perhaps you want to experience the feeling of *worth* but find that either *worthwhile* or *worthy* is more appropriate. Sometimes using a double negative may fit better than a positive emotion, such as using *not rejected* instead of *accepted*. Or, using a negated positive quality may fit better than a negative emotion, such as *not loved* instead of *isolated* or *rejected*.

There are, of course, many possibilities that are not on these lists that may match your feelings more accurately. Simply use them as tools to explore your emotions as you practice your healing process. Play at your learning and have fun discovering your Self!

I have also included a list of the exercises that were presented throughout this book. This should prove to be a handy reference for finding a particular exercise when you wish to explore it further.

Positive Emotions

calm	acceptance	affection
carefree	agreement	altruistic
comfortable	appreciation	care
content	approval	caring
freedom	belonging	charitable
grace	boundaries	concern
harmony	connection	considerate
in charge	cooperation	compassion
integrity	equality	close
know	fairness	devotion
knowing	flexible	faith
letting go	forgiveness	faithful
on top of things	good	gentle
one	honor	gratitude
oneness	justice	innocent
patience	open	kind
peace	openness	kindness
pleased	own	love
purity	permission	joy
satisfied	responsible	nurturing
truth	separate	sensitive
wisdom	surrender	sincere
	understanding	
	wanted	

Positive Emotions

attractive	abundance	assertive
appealing	achievement	bold
awe	balance	brave
beautiful	clever	capable
beauty	complete	confident
blissful	create	control
eager	creative	daring
encouraged	curious	determined
enthusiastic	express	fearless
excitement	fortunate	independent
existing	fulfill	intent
happy	fulfillment	on my onw
hope	generous	powerful
inspiration	perfection	proud
interest	prosperity	reassured
joy	purpose	safe
joyful	purposeful	secure
involvement	valid	stability
optimistic	validation	strong
passion	whole	support
passionate	wholeness	sure
play	worth	trust
playful	worthy	trusting
unlimited		will
vitality		

apprehensive	abandonment	ashamed
anxious	abuse...	bad
cautious	(emotional,	competitive
doubt	mental,	defeat
distrust	physical	embarrassed
expectation	sexual)	failure
fear (of...)	apathy	false
fearful	betrayal	grief
hesitant	displaced	inadequate
hurt	enslaved	inferior
ill	isolation	invalid
injured	mistreated	invalidation
insecure	misused	losing
intimidated	neglected	nobody
nervous	not cared about	not existing
panic	not cared for	nothing
shock	offended	right
terror	offensive	shame
threatened	rejected	stupid
tragedy	tortured	superior
uncertain	unaccepted	useless
unsafe	used	weak
worry	unwanted	worthy
	victim	worthless
	violated	
	vulnerable	

Negative Emotions

affliction

aimless

alone

depressed

disconnected

discouraged

dismay

empty

heartbroken

helpless

hopeless

lonely

loss

lost

meaningless

on my own

out of control

pain

purposeless

sad

uncertain

unfulfilled

unhappy

want

wanted

compromised

control

controlled

controlling

dishonest

dishonesty

immature

injustice

irresponsible

obligated

oppressed

pressured

responsible—
   for others

suppressed

troubled

uncaring

unfair

angry

annoyed

bitter

conceit

confused

defending

defensive

envious

frustration

guilt

impatient

irritated

jealous

judgment

resentment

resistance

passionless

scarcity

suspicious

ugly

vain

List of Exercises

For additional information or to contact us, please visit us at

www.michaelwiner.com

22319785R00214

Made in the USA
San Bernardino, CA
30 June 2015